How do you know who you are?

£2-50

How do you know who you are

Derek and Julia Parker

with 191 illustrations

Thames and Hudson

Designed by Lawrence Edwards

Printed in the United States of America by
R.R. Donnelley and Sons

TO TONE

Contents

1 *Finding out about you*

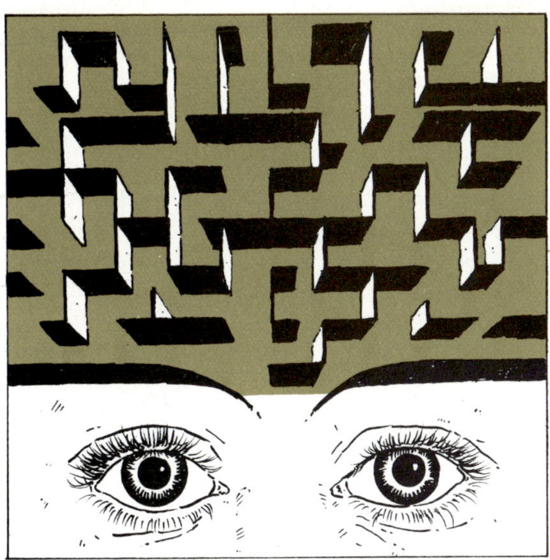

Why should you want to know more about yourself? And if you do, what method should you use? Few people today rely on phrenology, onychomancy lithomancy; many more are interested in biorhythms, astrology; still more in psychology. Know yourself. But how?

'EXPLORE THYSELF!' said Henry David Thoreau; and added, 'Herein are demanded the eye and the nerve.' The thirst for self-knowledge, a century after Thoreau's death, was to become voracious – millions of people began to read their horoscopes in the astrology magazines, attempted to discover their Intelligence Quotients; phrenologists carefully mapped the protuberances on their clients' heads in order to reveal their characters, palmists stared at the creases on their customers' hands, graphologists pored over their calligraphy. Many others strode confidently down the open road mapped by Freud, Jung, Adler and the other early psychologists and soon the whole landscape was networked with twisting byways as their followers pioneered new and sometimes devious lanes to self-knowledge.

The thirst for self-knowledge has by no means abated. In fact, it has become so insatiable that some people have found it suspect. André Gide suggested that too much staring into one's own mind retards one's development: 'A caterpillar who wanted to know itself well would never become a butterfly.' But it is still generally believed that the better we understand our own motives for the way in which we behave, the better we can forecast our own reactions and recognize their nature, the more nearly we can approach happiness – or at the least a certain phlegmatic acceptance of ourselves.

One of the main drawbacks of 'civilized' Western life in the twentieth century is that it tends to dull the senses. This is partly the result of having so many machines to do for us what in other ages we would have had to do for ourselves. Before we could sit rigid in front of a television set on whose screen actors live out fantasies for our pleasure, we used to read. Certainly this only meant that invisible, imaginary characters lived out their fantasies for our pleasure; but we took part in those fantasies by re-creating the characters in our minds. We had to add our imagination to the author's to bring them to life. We had also to *act*, if only by turning a page. Before pocket calculators placed arithmetic at our fingertips, we had to discover some kind of relationship with figures. Before motorized transport we had to make do with our own legs, or make contact with another living creature, the horse, in order to get from point A to point B. And we walked or rode along roads empty enough to enable us to look about without being knocked over or run down by heavy traffic.

This is not to grumble – or not unduly – about contemporary life and its quality. Few people, if they thought about it, would choose to live in any other age than the twentieth century. But it is none the less true that because so many things are done for us, and because we have to get out of the way while they are being done, we sometimes find that we make dull company for ourselves.

It is perhaps the feeling that we are in some way not so keenly involved in life, that we don't know ourselves as our ancestors seem instinctively to have known themselves, that has resulted in the formation of so many cults and movements aimed at 'self-discovery'. Sometimes, this has meant 'self-discovery' at the expense of the man or woman next door – an intense selfishness founded on the conviction that if we burrow deeply enough into ourselves, we will discover bottomless reservoirs of reassurance about the real value of life. More often than not, the waters prove to be only deep enough for a kind of irritating splashing, and we are left with damp feet and a sense of futility.

A vast amount of material has been published on every one of the theories

How should you explore your character? Not, it is certain, by falling for any of the crazier theories. Phrenology, which related the shape and size of the skull to the strength of the faculties, was soon discredited.

discussed in this book: on the way we use gestures to express our meaning and character, for example; on the body and the way in which its health or lack of health affects the mind; on human intelligence and how it may be measured, on human sexuality, the genetic process, psychology, astrology, graphology. Few people – perhaps nobody – will read the whole without suspecting that one or two chapters gulp too readily at the theories expressed in them. Readers who feel basically unsure of their own personalities may be ready to snap up any theory which promises an instant resolution of their doubts about themselves and swallow it whole. This would be a mistake.

It will rarely be the case, we believe, that any two readers will find the same chapters unrealistic. If you find the astrological section fascinating, you may not be very impressed by the IQ tests. If you work through the IQ tests and they seem to confirm your own idea of your quickness of mind, you may find the preceding psychological tests unconvincing. You may think it extremely unlikely that because you are a mesomorph you are therefore probably an extrovert, or that because you are a Quaker you are very possibly an introvert. It may seem lunatic to believe that because today is the day of the week on which you were born, you may therefore be more vulnerable to emotional upsets than you will be tomorrow.

In fact, we have omitted some wilder theories which seem now so thoroughly discredited, for one reason or another, that while amusing they are unlikely to be very helpful. There is little faith, these days, in phrenology – once so great a craze that Queen Victoria had the bumps on her children's heads meticulously catalogued. There is no chapter here on onychomancy (divination of character by reflections from the oiled fingernails of a young virgin) or lithomancy (divination by the sound made when two stones are struck together).

Not all the subjects discussed will appeal to all readers: the ones that make an unexpected appeal, if only an emotional appeal, may underline the foolishness of dismissing any theory until you have tested it to your own satisfaction; and our bibliography suggests sources for those who wish to take their testing further.

The subjects you do take seriously will probably be in an area in which you are taking some interest now. But suppose you decide that the people and organizations which believe in biorhythms may not be throwing away their money and time? If the discovery that you are driving on a highway on a 'triple critical' day makes you a touch more careful, it will be worthwhile – even if the theory has still to be conclusively tested. An astrological interpretation which warns that you may tend to lose your temper over small things can hardly exacerbate that temper; the knowledge that there is only a tiny genetic difference between you and a member of an apparently radically different race, surely cannot further alienate you.

Scattered throughout the book are a number of tests – questionnaires, the answers to which, when converted into 'scores', are interpreted to suggest whereabouts on a rough graph of modern psychological, physical and intellectual trends you may stand. The purpose of these tests is not to reveal yourself to yourself with the accuracy claimed by an astrologer writing a 6000-word analysis, or an analyst after many hours of conversation and discussion. But apart from being, it is hoped, amusing, they may suggest facts about yourself which you may not have suspected or realized.

This is where Thoreau's 'nerve' comes in: to see ourselves as others see us is not always easy or comfortable. If it were, it would probably not be worth doing. This book ventures on the road to self-knowledge. We hope that it may take you in the direction of any one of several systems by which you can attempt a discovery or rediscovery of the motives which make you act as you act; may persuade you to question your most vigorously held prejudices; may provoke you to question your ideas of the meaning of 'youth', 'love', 'health', 'intelligence' – 'life'.

Derek and Julia Parker

2 Putting on the style

First impressions may be misleading
or very revealing.
Do you manipulate other people
by constructing an image to present
to the world? Or hide behind one?
Men and women have done both
for five thousand years. . . .

VERY FEW PEOPLE can remember at all clearly what it was like to be a baby. But you can be sure that almost as soon as you could walk, you consciously or unconsciously began to present an image of yourself, to adopt a 'style'. For every moment when you behaved quite naturally, as yourself, there were other moments when you behaved as mommy or daddy would have wanted you to behave – and you, like all of us, were good at sensing how that was. Sometimes you will have calculated wrongly and have been accused of 'showing off'; but there is a sense in which 'putting on the style', tending an image which it is believed will result in getting the best reward most quickly, getting the best job, the best partner, the speediest attention in a restaurant, the loudest wolf-whistles, is something which every man and woman does throughout life. And it is, in that sense, 'showing off'.

The terms *image* and *style* should be defined, in the context in which we use them here. Your 'image' – and it is a term much over-used and devalued in our time – can be taken to mean the public idea of what you are 'like'. As in a political party, the image presented and the reality need not coincide more than is absolutely necessary. But it is quite possible for the biggest fraud, the man or woman whose manufactured image is totally at odds with reality, to have a personal *style*, for by that is usually meant merely the general characteristics of an individual and his way of life – his conscious choice of phrases, gestures, dress, behaviour, 'life-style'.

It is not always, or often, that the image we seek to present to the outside world precisely coincides with the reality of our private selves. How many young people really want to smoke, drink, take drugs – and how many do so because smoking, drinking, taking drugs is

'Is this me or is this you?', intoned the Sex Pistols, first of the 'punks'. Punk, as it emerged in the late 1970s, was one extreme manifestation of 'putting on the group style' – a human characteristic through thousands of years.

apparently a condition of belonging to a group? How many men in the 1930s would really like to have worn their hair long, if that had not then been considered at best slovenly and at worst effeminate? How many men during the seventeenth century wept openly, because that was the fashion; how many during the twentieth century have wept only in secret, because 'men don't cry'?

Some of you will claim that you adopt no image, that the style *is* the man. But the man (or woman) who has been content to be what he really is, is rare. It is a truism that the most successful actor harbours a secret desire to be a great pastry-cook; the first-rate accountant to be a marvellous surgeon. The same instinct seems to prompt us to disguise our personality behind a façade, as though we fear the truth is a dangerous weapon likely to be used against us. In the rarefied air of big business this may be true, just as it may be in an insecure personal relationship – a weakness shown will be a weakness used. But the truth is more probably to do with a craving for acceptance, admiration, love; we must prove that we are like those we wish to make our friends – for whatever reason we want to resemble them.

You can be sure that your choice of an image is not random. The decision to go on wearing the fashion of twenty years ago, or to grow a moustache in the latest style, to follow slavishly the dictates of the fashion magazines or even to strike out grotesquely along lines of your own, may be made for any one of a number of reasons. But it will certainly be a *decision*, even if it has been unconsciously arrived at.

For most of us, our everyday appearance – and to some extent our behaviour, our 'manners' (another aspect of style) – is based more or less rigidly on current fashion. If a restaurant owner decides not to admit men unless they are wearing ties, it is because he believes that it is the current fashion that 'respectable' men do not go out in the evening without one; that the majority of his customers are, or are expected to be regarded as, 'respectable', that the nonconformists must either be encouraged to adopt the style of the majority, or leave.

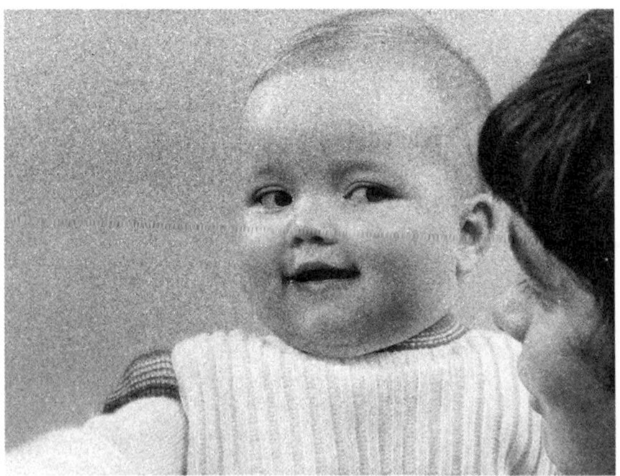

At a very early age you showed the ability to juggle, apparently consciously, with your parents' affections.

The disadvantage of a rigid conformity to fashion is that in a world which steadily grows smaller, the speed of travel far outruns the speed with which national customs change. Taboos of religion, politics, social structure, no less than of sex or gender, have a tangible local effect on appearance and behaviour. These taboos vary wildly not only from country to country, but also from class to class within countries. There is not much sign of a weakening of the barrier between, for instance, East and West – between the totally veiled Arab woman and her sister in a monokini on a beach in southern France, or between the white Anglo-Saxon Protestant in the American Middle West and his brother in Iran. We should ask ourselves whether we conform much more rigidly to national or local customs than to our own idea of ourselves as examples of a particular style of living. Yet businessmen of the Arabian countries, in which alcohol is prohibited by religious custom, are not invariably averse to it when travelling abroad, or even necessarily in the privacy of their own homes. Indeed, it is said that there is something of a social cachet in possessing a well-stocked drinks cabinet. This is no doubt as much to do with the cultivation of a 'Westernized' image as to any liking for alcohol. And within their own society there are men and women who may be regarded as having a radical life-style, with or without alcohol, and others who will be thought of as conservative.

Most of us conform to the style set by our own generation; which means that the style adopted in dress, behaviour, language, life in general, can only be partly our own. For the most part we are the slaves of fashion – and as much the slaves of a majority fashion as of a minority fashion. You may be one of the group of highly fashion-conscious women which waits upon the dictates of the Paris fashion houses, or of some small, exclusive, way-out designer; more probably you will be among the majority of people who dress as they think the class or peer group to whom they belong 'should' dress. In the business sections of most major Western cities, for instance, even today the white-shirted, dark-suited middle-class man presents the image of respectability, dependability, with conformity as a god and with a distinct aversion to being 'noticed' except as a 'good man' in whatever organization he may work.

But do not suppose, if you are one of those who has adopted the opposite style, the 'uniform' of the ill-kempt, that you are displaying your individuality! In fact, you are announcing that you are a member of a society with rules only a little less stringent than those of the 'respectable' world you seek to reject.

It takes courage to step out of line. It may be foolish to be the slave of fashion, but it is safer than to be one of the leaders. Away from one's environment, it is a little easier to experiment. The English or American girl who ventures to join the topless European girls on a Continental beach may feel perfectly at ease – until a conventional stranger of her own nationality appears, when she will become confused and uneasy.

Even the leaders of fashion are on a rein, for fashion is subservient, it appears, to public events – to the sweep of history; perhaps most notably to public morality. Puritanism, especially as regards dress, has always been a major feature in the development of fashion and thus of personal style. In different societies it takes different forms; sometimes fashion – perhaps in particular women's fashion – ignores or positively combats the complaints of the puritan elements in society (often embodied in the religious establishment). Sometimes, and often it seems gratuitously, a fashion will emerge which seems so deliberately offensive to the puritan conscience that we can only believe that it originated with an individual whose psyche was sufficiently strong to enable him not only to get away with murder, but to encourage others to be murderous.

Take, for instance, the codpiece – perhaps the most overtly outrageous of all male fashions. This was originally simply a metal case designed to protect the male genitals in battle, and later became a leather pouch worn with normal dress for much the same reason. But in the sixteenth century it was to become an eye-catching fashion accessory – padded, shaped and embroidered with jewels and beads, decorated with ribbon and often in colours contrasting with the colour of the breeches, making it even more ostentatious.

The history of the period offers no real reason for this sudden emphasis on the male genitals. It is quite possible that the fashion developed as a result of the personal preference of a small group of men whose predilection was for such an emphasis. Male fashions have often been concerned with a display of sexuality, at least in time of peace – as though lacking the aphrodisiac weapon of success in arms, men need to intimate that they are sexually potent in order to attract women when the latter are in the majority in a society suffering the effects of a war. In wartime, sexual energy has other outlets. Just as the American football player will be carefully guarded from women in order to conserve his energy for the game, so the army doses the tea of its soldiers with preparations to reduce their sexual energy.

The sixteenth-century man with a codpiece almost obscenely mimicking the erect penis cannot have been unconscious of its suggestive nature. Such an overt display has never happened again in male fashion and when there have been signs of it the reaction has been furious – as when the great dancer

In ancient Crete women bared their breasts; thousands of years later, Yves St Laurent's model employed an erotic chiffon drape. Men have often been equally extreme in the search for style, especially in the short-lived fashion for the codpiece.

Nijinsky was dismissed from the Imperial Ballet at St Petersburg in 1911 because he omitted to wear the trunks which male dancers normally wore over their more revealing tights.

Many of the protests with which rock singers were greeted in the 1950s stemmed not so much from dislike of their music as from the sexuality of their gestures and the tightness of their trousers, displaying the genitals too freely. Rumour has always had it that many of them padded themselves – that Elvis Presley had an iron bar sewn into his

skin-tight jeans, that Mick Jagger produced a similar effect by padding his trousers with a pocket handkerchief. With his own zany humour, Elton John replied by wearing a cod-piece which emitted a flash of light when a certain chord was played. To what extent this kind of gesture existed or exists outside the world of pop music is an open question, though advertisements commonly appear in popular newspapers for padded briefs 'to enhance that masculine shape'.

These are more an open joke than a serious fashion; nor is there any evidence that women pay much attention to the genital area in clothing. Fashion designers in serious business still concentrate on a social rather than a sexual image. They are more concerned to create, say, a suit designed to disguise a paunch than one which emphasizes the buttocks (listed in surveys as that part of the male anatomy most likely to attract the attention of the opposite sex). For those whose paunches are recalcitrant, an attempt was made in 1978 to convince men that women found a plump waistline sexy: a shirt was advertised in England and America cut to fit 'the bulge' – an attempt at image-making which seemed doomed to failure from the start.

With women designers it is a very different story. Doubtless many of them may be completely oblivious of any overt plan to capture the attention of the male. But the intention to 'decorate' a woman when dressing her is in contrast to the intention for the most part simply to 'cover' the body of the man; and attention to the female breast as a major area of erotic attraction is undeniable.

Over the centuries breasts have been raised, flattened, displayed (discreetly or otherwise) and concealed in a cycle which relates to no very obvious outside influence. In Greece the *strophium* (an early equivalent of the brassiere) supported completely naked breasts, while at other periods of history they have been totally concealed. Even today, when almost every female visitor to the French Riviera persuades herself to eschew the top half of her bathing costume, the topless evening dress (briefly introduced in the 1960s) has been sold only to be worn in private or semi-private.

At times when the most 'daring' fashions have been available, it has only been a minority of women who have worn them in public. This has partly been because there has always been a puritan argument against too great an exposure of the body or too great an erotic emphasis on it. The Abbé Boileau was not alone in arguing that 'the sight of a beautiful bosom is as dangerous as a basilisk'; and the Mayor of New York City, three hundred years later, averting his eyes from a girl in a topless bathing dress, confirmed the opinion of a number of sedate citizens when he observed that 'there is nothing of artistic or cultural value in this sort of thing'.

You will not be unusual if it has been inhibition which has prevented you from adopting a style – in dress or behaviour – running against the accepted social practice. Yet it is doubtful whether this is because of a *natural* caution about what you wear. As the early psychiatrist Céline Renooz wrote in 1897, 'In the actual life of the young girl there is a moment when by a secret atavism she feels the pride of her sex, the intuition of her moral superiority, and cannot understand why she must hide its cause.' The moment a social inhibition is eased, most women will take advantage of any freedom they are offered. Comparatively recently it was only the publicity-seeking starlet who would 'accidentally' lose the top of her bikini at the Cannes Film Festival. But within a few years topless sunbathing had become commonplace on the Continent and now the clamour for official naturist beaches grows annually.

Yet naturism has nothing much to do with fashion and not a great deal to do with any abstract conviction that it is especially healthy. It has to do with the advertisement of a natural sensuality which, whatever the Naturist Associations may claim, is the source of nudism; healthy it may be, natural it may be – but it is also the means of projection of a sexual image which even the most shapeless, elderly or downright unprepossessing of us shares, though we may not permit it to influence the image we *choose* to project. Inside every satyr is an Adonis waiting for release. Whether we allow him to act depends on the strength of our libido.

Exposure of the body, or the titillation which results from covering up or revealing any part of it, relates to the basic human being beneath the image. If you burn your bra, and exhibit your breasts beneath a see-through blouse, you may be asserting your individuality. The fact that the rejection of the brassiere was an early symbol of the women's movement underlines the way in which clothing can become a mark of the restriction of personality; some women saw the bra as the garment most associated with man's idea of what women – or rather, 'woman' – should be: a carefully presented, glamorous *package* rather than a human being. But there may be more complex reasons than this, or than the fact that you are just a happily sensual creature released by some alchemy from the inhibitions of your less carefree sisters. You may be a woman whose marriage has broken up, who is saying as clearly as possible without actually articulating, 'I am lonely – I need love and affection; this is what I have to offer.' Or you may be advertising the fact that your companion (who may or may not be embarrassed by your dress) does not understand your needs, is rejecting or ignoring you. 'He isn't taking any notice of me – but, after all, aren't I attractive?'

Every woman (to some extent, every man) has to come to decisions about dress; personality and psychological background control these decisions much more than physique. '*Dare* I wear that?' is a question perhaps too infrequently asked by the 'girl' of forty, or the man whose figure is not necessarily best set off by knee-length shorts and tee-shirt. Freed sufficiently from inhibition, both may say 'to hell with it' and wear what they like; and the genuinely carefree can usually get away with any costume. More commonly, we decide either for reticence because our desire to be thought 'sensible' or 'under control' is greater than our desire to project our personality through now somewhat worn physical attributes, or for revelation because our sexual drive, or our estimation of our physical attractiveness, outweighs reticence. Confidence in our image of ourselves is sometimes too strong for caution.

Men have less possibility of attracting a partner by overt display than women: the codpiece adventure was short-lived and the buttocks have rarely been a focal point of fashion (though in the fifteenth century there were heavy fines for those men who wore tunics short enough to show their buttocks – if they were not of that social class where such display was permitted). The shirt worn open to the navel is of questionable value as a sexual signal and, while the limited success of women's magazines featuring male nudes may indicate that women do enjoy considering men's bodies at leisure, no designer of men's clothes has yet succeeded in capitalizing on the fact in any very obvious way.

One of the chief areas of the male body which has been used to project an image has been the head – through the length and style of the hair and beard. What are your reasons for choosing to wear your hair long or short? Have you thought what it *really* signifies?

Hair has been associated with strength from the earliest recorded times: the legend of Delilah sapping Samson's strength by cutting off his hair is a powerful one and embraces the link between the hair and sexual potency which is equally strong. *Vir pilosus, seu fortis, seu libidinosus* – 'the hairy man is either strong or lusty' – the Romans claimed. (They did not refer, incidentally, to body hair, for this is dissimilarly distributed among the races, the Mongoloid and Negroid races – many of whom are magnificent warriors and have in addition a reputation for sexual insatiability – having very little.)

The theory is nonsense. And it might be assumed that in the 1970s, except among relatively small enclaves, fashion in hair length is unimportant: that, as with clothes, both men and women in Western societies can create their own image. But clearly there is still a strong magical undertow. Both Bjorn Borg and Ilie Nastase made a point of not shaving while they were playing tennis at Wimbledon in 1978. 'For luck', they said; but in fact at the dictation of some potent instinct. And it seems to be a fact that few men in the second half of the twentieth century have survived puberty without a battle with their elders about the length of their hair, especially during the 1950s when many pop heroes were beginning to wear it long.

The conformists – in particular perhaps the men who had served in the Second World War and could not reconcile long hair with any of the values they had fought to preserve (and maybe they were right) – were among the most violent objectors. Since most of them were parents and since their wives were mothers who (as has probably always been the case) were likely to be worried or frightened by the emerging sexuality of their sons, there were many family battles. Long-haired youths were described as 'hippies' or 'students' – equally pejorative terms.

The most common adjective used to describe long hair or beards in the young has been 'dirty', a word commonly used by middle-class parents to describe youthful sexual activity. The common association between hair and male potency is extremely ancient, but is now taken as a matter of course, and stated overtly by anthropologists such as Professor Edmund Leach, who has gone as far as to associate the head with the phallus, the hair with semen, and – it follows – the cutting of the hair with castration; hence, long hair displays an unrestrained sexuality, short hair a restricted sexuality and close-shaven heads, celibacy.

It seems that a youth can *choose* to announce an emotional commitment by the length of his hair, without a word being spoken, just as the man who between the wars wore his hair short chose to suppress some aspects of his personality, and as those in the armed services had these aspects suppressed by the same means and by a uniform which reduced man to a cipher. (Whether he is conscious of it or not, the officer who invites a soldier to 'get his hair cut' is recognizing in the growth of that hair the beginning of the emergence of a distinct individualistic personality.)

The strong conformity which dominated most Western men between, say, 1914 and 1945 resulted in the general feeling that the natural state of men's hair was short; it should be insignificant, kept under strict control – like his sexuality. While the 'short back and sides' was the general rule, the rest of the hair was very often smothered with oil or grease, 'to keep it in place' – a phrase not without sexual significance.

As for beards: have you stopped to think why you choose to wear one, or why you remain clean-shaven? Is it more than habit? The beard is now less a mark of eccentricity than it was during the first half of the century, when small boys followed bearded men to bait them with cries of 'Beaver!' Before the turn of the century, a handsome full set had been a matter for congratulation. The nineteenth-century paterfamilias seemed incomplete without his whiskers; the authority he personified is rooted deep in history, for the beard has been traditionally

adidas

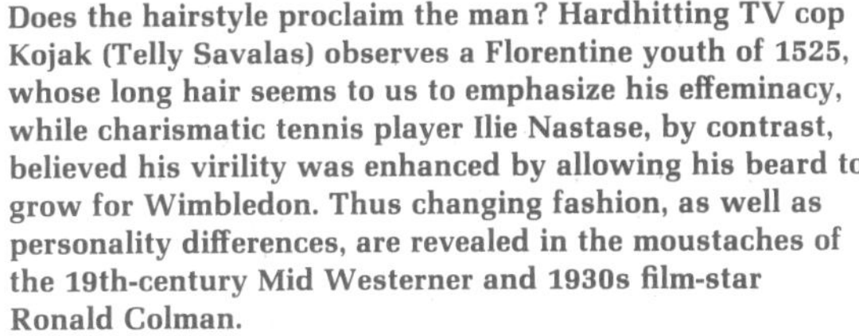

Does the hairstyle proclaim the man? Hardhitting TV cop Kojak (Telly Savalas) observes a Florentine youth of 1525, whose long hair seems to us to emphasize his effeminacy, while charismatic tennis player Ilie Nastase, by contrast, believed his virility was enhanced by allowing his beard to grow for Wimbledon. Thus changing fashion, as well as personality differences, are revealed in the moustaches of the 19th-century Mid Westerner and 1930s film-star Ronald Colman.

the sign of authority, of domination, of wisdom, or of leadership. For centuries Christ, clean-shaven in the earliest representations, was depicted wearing a beard; if he is regarded as the leader of a cult, it may certainly be said that the beard operated as a cult signal. If the upper classes were bearded, the slaves (in the ancient world) were clean-shaven, and vice versa. There were also practical reasons for the fashion: Alexander the Great ordered his soldiers to shave so that the Persians could not grasp their beards in hand-to-hand combat – and set a fashion which lasted a thousand years. On the other hand, soldiers in the Crimean campaign were encouraged to grow beards to keep their faces warm during the bitter cold.

The beard, like the hair of the head, is strongly linked by tradition with sexual potency and in our own time has been strongly affected by the young as a signal of independence or nonconformity. There is, in fact, some evidence suggesting a physical connection between the beard and sexual activity: at least one scientist has claimed to detect a stronger growth of beard in men having regular sexual intercourse than in those abstaining.

As a compromise between the naked chin and the full commitment of beard and moustache, the moustache alone has never been entirely out of fashion during the present century. Certainly it has attracted mischievous comment and occasionally styles have been ludicrous (the heavy moustaches of stage villains at the beginning of the century, for example); but it has proved sexually attractive and some film-stars have successfully exploited the moustache and made a

'Make-up', says the dictionary, is all to do with enhancing your appearance – but not, it seems, without reference to changing styles. For many of us, ignoring the fashion rules is too dangerous, but we should still be aware of the limitations of fashion: the wearing of sunglasses indoors is only the modern equivalent of an old device – the use of mask or fan.

cult of a particular style – the 'Ronald Colman', for instance. The 'Che Guevara', initially worn as an imitative political gesture, was for some time a lugubrious high fashion.

You will not be alone if you have secret worries about baldness. The constant harping, however *sotto voce*, on the connection between the hair and sexual potency is probably the most powerful reason why modern man has such a horror of baldness (despite the advent of Yul Brynner, and later Kojak). Even today, the success of hair-weaving establishments and firms making hair-pieces (the word 'wig' now has an air of shame about it) shows that enlightenment has not demolished the old myth.

And the connection between hair and virility *is* a myth: over-production of male hormones (androgens) is one of the major contributors to baldness, so you may well lose your hair because you are over- rather than under-sexed. (Hippocrates pointed out that 'eunuchs do not go bald'.) Women seem never to have been taken in by the myth: it has never been true that baldness has been unattractive to them. (Indeed, sexual attraction is extremely difficult to analyse: H. G. Wells was physically unattractive but captivated a string of mistresses; asked why she had fallen into bed with this short, squeaky-voiced, plain man, all one of them could find to say was that his skin smelled of honey.)

The loss of hair is an even greater shock to a woman than to a man; there was never any question that the British National Health Service would not provide free wigs for women, recognizing the loss of their hair as being almost in the same league as the loss of a limb. The shaving of the heads of women collaborators in France in 1944 was not only a visual signal, but a deep-rooted psychological degradation.

There have been some periods in history when man's hair has very obviously been a focus of fashion and a major weapon in the projection of personality and image; and other times when it has virtually been ignored. Women's hair, on the contrary, has always been of paramount importance to her as a sexual weapon. St Paul knew how potent its attraction was: 'If a woman has long hair, it is a glory to her', he wrote; and it was insisted that the hair should be covered in church, lest it might distract the male worshippers. Robert Burton, in *The Anatomy of Melancholy* (1621), summed up the attraction succinctly: 'In a word, the hairs are Cupid's nets, to catch all comers, a brushy wood in which Cupid builds his nest, and under whose shadow all loves a thousand several ways sport themselves.'

The giving of a lock of hair to a lover has always been one of the strongest signals of attraction. Byron possessed a box-full of them, each wrapped in a separate screw of paper and initialled; one Spanish girl cut off a whole, heavy hank of her hair and sent it to him – a gift of her very self.

Why the blonde, rather than the brunette or the red-head (the latter of course had a reputation of her own for fieriness), should be regarded by Western men as most attractive, sexually most desirable, is obscure. The first overt sign of this was perhaps seen in Renaissance Italy, where women went to a great deal of trouble to bleach their hair as brightly as possible – wearing, for instance, hats with enormous brims (protecting their faces, which remained pale) but no crowns,

bringing their hair up to lie around the top of the brim, catching the sun as much as possible. Most Italian women being naturally dark, those pale-faced blondes no doubt stood out in a crowd of sunburned beauties – but was there any other reason? There seems always to have been an association between blonde hair and purity – ironical, in view of the screen activities of the Hollywood blondes, notably Jean Harlow and Marilyn Monroe, who projected images of innocence but scarcely of purity. But the fact that a woman was pure did not mean she could not ensnare a man. And the blonde has an unfortunate reputation as a liar and deceiver, possibly because her hair colour was by far the easiest to achieve by dyeing, even in the earliest days of that art.

The most prominent of recent blonde fashions was probably the one initiated by Jean Harlow, the sensational 'platinum blonde'. Her hair varied violently in colour, gradually darkening as her short career progressed; she even dyed her pubic hair blonde – but this, it was explained, was because she wore no underclothes beneath her close-fitting virginal white dresses! After the death of Monroe, the Hollywood blonde seemed to vanish, and bleached hair now has a 'yesterday' look, the brassy image old fashioned and unsought.

The red-head is still popular, especially in Italy and Greece, and red hair has swung into and out of fashion for many hundreds of years. Dye for red hair was not especially difficult to make: the glorious red-gold hair of Titian's Venetian women, when not natural, came from a mixture of soda, alum and black sulphur. Other red-heads were 'natural' – Queen Elizabeth I was a red-head when she was a girl, and this set a fashion for most of her time. Nell Gwynn, Charles II's ravishing mistress, was a red-head, as her splendid portrait by Lely shows.

At other times in history, the red-head has been positively oppressed. The tradition that Judas was red-headed was perhaps one of the reasons for this. Jean-Baptiste Thiers, in his *Histoire des Perruques*, wrote: 'Red-heads should wear wigs to hide the colour of their hair, of which everybody stands in horror because Judas, it is said, was red-haired.' And Rosalind, speaking of Orlando in *As You Like It*, points out that 'his very hair is of the dissembling colour' – Judas-red. In some of the witch trials of the sixteenth and seventeenth centuries young women were put to the test and the torture solely because of their red hair. But the prejudice is not only Christian: Brahmins were once forbidden to marry red-headed women.

The styling of women's hair, or the length of it, may not recently have been such a factor for psychological discussion as that of men's, but its importance to women themselves can scarcely be questioned – and in choosing a style, amending or altering it, you can make as definite and pronounced a statement about the kind of woman you wish to be, as any man can.

Body hair is another matter. Surely no woman has ever cultivated facial hair as a desirable characteristic? It has never been a factor, for instance, in homosexual signalling, as perhaps it might have been; indeed, the woman with an incipient moustache has always been acutely embarrassed by such a strongly marked 'masculine' appendage. It probably does signify too great a proportion of male hormones in her make-up; but no more. The depilation of under-arm hair and to a lesser extent of legs has been common in the Western world for centuries, although recently some members of the women's movement (presumably because some women see depilation as something desired or required by men, and therefore an image of female subjugation) have neglected it. The shaving or shaping of pubic hair is necessarily a private gesture, no doubt often overtly sexual, the result of the request or demand of a partner.

If the dictates of fashion seem as important as, or perhaps more important than, advancing any personal image you may have of yourself, this probably only means that you prefer to be seen as belonging to a 'superior' group leading or pioneering a new style which sets you 'ahead' of your contemporaries, rather than advancing your own individual image. So you will instruct your hairdresser to copy, with only the slightest modification, the latest style set by a fashion model, a film-star, a member of 'society', either ignoring or firmly putting aside the fact that it may not altogether suit your own style and personality. A wiser woman will recognize, alone with her mirror, that the style does not work for her.

Similarly, trends in make-up which arise for often very obscure reasons and vanish or change under the pressure of newer, as obscure fashions, lay down rules which the majority of women follow. It is interesting that the phrase, 'I must put my face on,' is still a common one. More than structuring the hair, perhaps even more than in dressing, when you make up your face (or ostentatiously fail to do so) you are choosing the mask by which you advertise the self you claim to be.

While both men and women have no doubt always used make-up as a disguise as well as an enhancement, it is in our own time, with the multiplication of available creams and colourings, eye-shadows and lipsticks and liners, that it has been possible to build a new character upon your face with all the skill formerly the property of the actor or actress.

Only a few women would now claim that 'painting' is wicked – as the Puritans used to. The Quakers made the point that painting the face, like writing a novel, was lying; and in using cosmetics to make yourself appear younger or more beautiful that is precisely what you are doing. The vast increase in the sale of male cosmetics in recent years shows that women no longer have a monopoly in the field. It may be argued that the farthest men go in the direction of make-up is in the application of a little after-shave – but they do this not only because their image is enhanced in some mysterious way: the emphasis of television commercials and advertisements suggests that if you pat on some after-shave or splash yourself with 'body lotion' you take on some of the attributes of the racing driver, pop-star or ultra-masculine boxer hired to show off the product.

So far the application of make-up to a man's face has been restrained. The careful shaving of the beard is one thing; the application of a little coloured cream to disguise a beard-shadow is quite another – despite the awful example of Richard M. Nixon, whose masculine objection to the application of make-up is always said to have lost him his television contest with John Kennedy in 1960. Kennedy, properly made-up, looked like everyone's idea of the all-American boy, while Nixon – with his strong black beard-line – looked like everyone's idea of a film villain. The political arguments lost out to the basic imagery; and Kennedy's majority was tiny enough to make it quite possible that make-up decided the election.

How long will it be before male pride finally capitulates to the advertisers? At present even the entirely sensible argument that man's skin is at least as sensitive as woman's, and as susceptible to the ravages of time, has not defeated the deep-rooted idea that make-up is 'sissy'. How long before male cologne sells as

'And he wears . . . Zendiq for men.' After-shave still demands the hard sell if it is not to be associated with effeminacy.

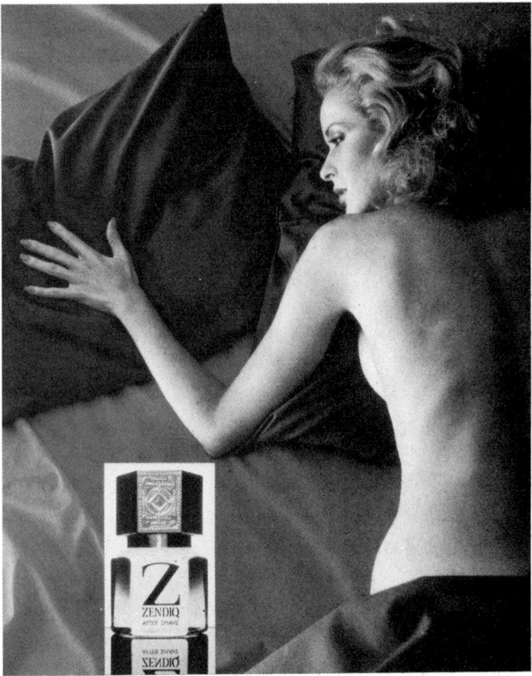

well as after-shave (the distinction is surely in name alone)?

The origin of perfumes may have been as much in hygiene as in luxury. Just as judges carried nose-gays of sweet-smelling flowers to ward off the germs of the plague, so perfume was used (like spices to disguise bad meat) to camouflage the smell of the unwashed human body at a time when an annual bath was considered quite sufficient.

We are told by some observers that we now wash too much and use too much deodorant – so that some perfume manufacturers have busily produced perfumes based upon the musky smell of the human body, believed to be aphrodisiac. The elimination of all natural odour from the body is unnatural (which is not to say it is mistaken, or even anti-aphrodisiac). But so many perfumes are now available that it is as easy to choose the smell you wish to give off as to choose the shade your hair or lips should be. It seems that, while women use perfume much more readily than men, it is women who are chiefly attracted by it. Paolo Mantegazza, in his *Physiology of Love* (1889), pointed out that when a woman smells the scent of her favourite flowers, 'she will close her eyes, breathe deeply, and, if very sensitive, tremble all over, presenting an intimate picture which otherwise she never shows, except perhaps to her lover.'

While wholeheartedly assuming, without much proof, that a woman's perfume is aphrodisiac to men, the perfume manufacturers have not so far succeeded in making a persuasive connection between colognes and perfumes for men and a thoroughly heterosexual masculinity: they have certainly done their best, by naming their products with extrovert outdoor brand-names – as though it were important to convince the woman in the case that her man, while wearing perfume, was nevertheless 'all man'. One of the problems is that perfumes tend by nature to be 'sweet' and that it is difficult to produce a

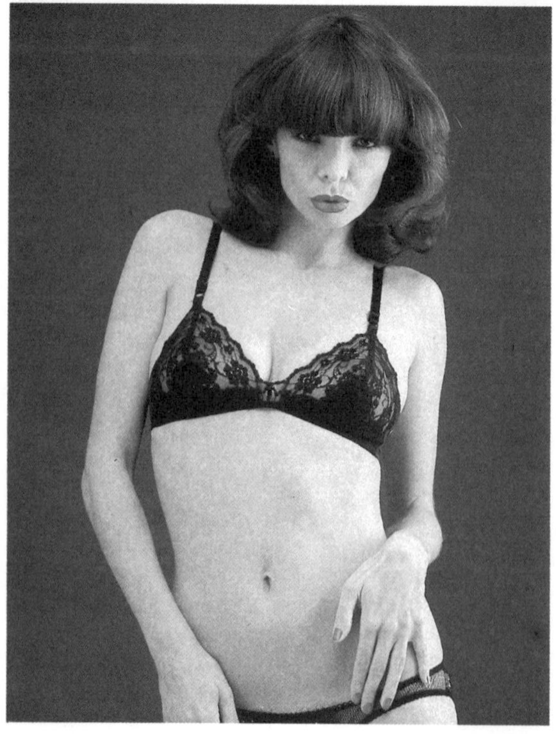

Schoolma'am or sex symbol? The same woman may present different aspects of her character to different people. How much control do *you* have over *your* image?

masculine, strongly assertive perfume which does not at the same time seem slightly effeminate.

The connection between an odour and a certain life- or personality-style is obviously very suggestive. Odour can be immensely nostalgic – if you wear a new perfume on a first visit to a city, for instance, a whiff of that perfume years later will call up that very place. This nostalgia is why perfume has always been so popular as a gift from one lover to another. But there is the obvious difficulty that it is extremely rare that you can predict what any one person's reaction to an odour is going to be. Ideally, no doubt, everyone should have a personal, individual smell; originally, perhaps, everyone had – but it has been washed and deodorized away. As things are, you must choose for yourself and, wishing to be individual, you must simply – as when choosing clothes – join a more or less large group.

In the relatively recent past – before, say, the steam age and the introduction of the railways – fashion in faces as in clothes and manners developed and changed fairly slowly. As communications speeded up, so the styles began to whirl and, with the age of film, the effect became positively kaleidoscopic. In the early years of the cinema studio make-up was heavy and this had its effect on street make-up.

The reason for the enormous influence of the cinema on make-up (as on dress, speech, behaviour) is obvious; more than the novel or the illustrated paper, the film puts before us alternative images of ourselves. The woman who saw Jean Harlow or Joan Crawford as her ideal naturally studied her every characterization, her total image, with the greatest care, as though to look like her was to become her. Men, only a little less openly, did the same – when Clark Gable removed his shirt in an early movie to reveal that he wore nothing underneath, underwear manufacturers took an impressive cut in profits. Capitalizing on the stars' extraordinary influence, Hollywood forced many of them to play the same sort of character in a long series of films, reinforcing the image which, it was fancied, the customers required of them.

The cultivation of a style is to a very large extent a conformist trend. The degree to which you modify the current fashion to suit your own idea of yourself is a mark of individuality – which is why the eccentric in fashion is always at once a centre of ridicule and of often grudging admiration. A Zandra Rhodes makes clothes that only a very few women have the courage or necessary flair to wear successfully in public; but the force of her conviction is such that it is in the end indisputable; the woman who commissions a dress from her is announcing not only that she is a radical in fashion, but an individual not content to dress herself in clothing that is a reflection of what 'everyone else' is wearing. She is the rich counterpart of the impoverished student who searches the secondhand shops for some outrageous piece of nineteenth-century tat and converts it to her own use. In fact, in recent years (and for the first time in the history of fashion) styles have tended to originate at the lower end of the social scale, with glamorous tears and tatters in 'up-market' dresses based on the consciously old and worn clothes of the student, glamorous because of their association with the young and 'trendy'.

The style and length of hair, the use of make-up, the general tone of your dress make general statements about your personality or image which are obvious and often extravagant. The accessories which surround you in everyday life underline various aspects of your character, sometimes unconsciously, sometimes to definite purpose. The wearing of sun-glasses is a case in point: they may be used to hide behind, to project an image of mystery, or for any other purpose unconnected with the protection of the eyes. It is a commonplace that certain pieces of jewellery, certain ways of wearing a handkerchief, certain tattoos, have specific sexual meanings in certain *milieux*. Once more, your personal image is used for the dual purpose of saying something about yourself and announcing your membership of a peer group.

The symbol of a certain style must be carefully used, however; you can betray yourself. If you walk about with an ostentatiously expensive camera dangling about your neck, you may believe yourself to be the counterfeit of a fashionable photographer; in fact, the camera is bawling 'tourist!', while the professional photographer carries a beat-up old Pentax in a battered leather case. A curious reverse snobbery now exists, too; at a time of relative prosperity, the fashionable, the rich, can afford to appear in ancient jeans. A secretary or personal assistant, on the other hand, may be expected to be immaculately dressed. The man or woman too urgently occupied in display of beautiful clothing or accessories is suspect.

The whole scene is very difficult to survey. If you wear an extremely expensive Gucci belt on very old clothes you may be saying any one of a number of things: 'I may not look wealthy, but see this!'; or, 'Though I choose not to emphasize the fact, I have staggeringly good taste'; or, 'I have unexpected depths of discrimination.' The belt is the equivalent of a quizzical lift of the eyebrow and interpretation is complex.

Jewellery is often rather carefully worn. Only the wedding ring seems a constant and this has been known to be used as a 'prop', an effect. Rings or pendants or brooches are now chosen to suit an occasion and sometimes designed as a visual 'double-take' – a solid nugget of gold may be roughly formed to look like a piece of junk jewellery, while big enough to be impressive if the truth is suspected about it. On the whole, however, the expensive piece of jewellery tends to be the more original, though it is not inordinately expensive to commission an individual design from a student. By commissioning or choosing a piece in a classical, modern, elaborate or simple style, you may certainly say something about your personality.

A piece of jewellery may be used as a signal that you belong to a certain group: a man's ring may bear a Masonic symbol, for instance, or a woman's pendant may take the form of her Zodiac glyph. Sometimes an open invitation seems to be issued, as with some of the pieces designed for and advertised in such magazines as *Playboy* or *Playgirl* – a simple screw made in gold was one of the most basic. But these are more badges of the 'with-it' than invitations to a direct sexual approach.

In a sense, if you wear any kind of 'badge', you may seem to be gesturing some people away and beckoning to others. A club or old school tie may have the same effect, which is perhaps why these are worn on the whole only by the more conformist element of society – people who consciously or unconsciously fear or mistrust those not likely to chime with their own view of life and its social strata. All social groups send out this kind of group signal – the flower children, the hippies, the punks, had or have their 'uniforms'. The safety pin worn through the ear is a mark of service in a peer group just as deliberate as the black shirt was for the Fascists in the 1930s or for that matter as the regimental badges of the soldier have always been.

A uniform, however informal, while in one way an announcement of some kind of commitment to a particular group of people, is in another way a disguise. One of the mysterious aspects of 'style' is that it is all too rarely individual – and when it is so, it tends to appear merely eccentric. The accountant who – with his conventional dark suit, white shirt and club tie – wears a chunky Zodiac bracelet or grows his hair to shoulder-length, seems to be giving too much of his personality away, to be taking time out to be obviously shocking: he is shouting, 'Look at me! – I'm *different*!' It is a cry most groups and societies resent; the outsider within a political party, a religious or artistic group, is more resented than any attacker from without.

This has, to a greater or lesser degree, been true of the man or woman who has invaded another 'class' of society than the one in which he or she was born. In most European countries, and in America, during the years between, say, 1880 and 1939, it was perhaps more unforgivable for someone of the 'lower class' to attempt to ingratiate himself with the 'upper class' than the other way around; within the past decade, the position has been reversed, and it is now perhaps more difficult for someone born into a privileged section of

The actor who discovered what it was to be middle class.

society to be totally at ease in a 'working-class' *milieu*.

But even such terms as 'lower class', 'upper class', 'working class' now sound offensive to most people, who wish to believe that there is no difference between the pauper and the prince. Of course, in human terms, there is not; in social terms, however, a vast gulf does still exist and it is difficult for anyone to throw off the instinctive phrases or gestures which label them. The same applies to the extremely touchy area of race: when Dick Cavett, the American television host, interviewing Mohammed Ali, asked him how it felt for a black man to have one grandparent who was '*pure* white', he was asking for trouble, and got it.

The snail's-pace at which different degrees of social differentiation are disappearing is quickly revealed in the behaviour of men and women of different social backgrounds in each other's company – even the relative freemasonry of the pop culture only operates within fairly restricted boundaries. One easy test is the smile. In a recent experiment at a large railway terminus in London, an actor dressed either as a middle-class traveller or as a working man in overalls, asked directions of other men using the station. When dressed in an office suit, he received a smile from those dressed like him, but not from those who appeared less affluent; when he was dressed as a workman, he was smiled at neither by those dressed like him, nor by the affluent.

Until fairly recently, a person's accent has, in some areas of work, had a vital part to play in chances of promotion; Ernie Bevin, the butcher's boy who became Foreign Minister of the British Labour Government after the Second World War, and Harry Truman, the haberdasher's assistant with a flat Mid West American accent, who became the US President, were both pilloried for accents which seemed not to match their pretensions to high office. The cruelty of mocking a man for his way of speech is to be found in all social strata; and comedians have always used regional accents as 'props' for humour, so much so that certain accents can raise a laugh simply by association. So some people have had, at a very early age, to make the uncomfortable decision to change their accent and manner of speech, in order (as they believe, and often rightly) to 'get on'.

While in general most people are happy to feel part of a certain section of society – conservative or radical in politics, puritan or rake in sex, introvert or extrovert in social behaviour – they will also like to feel free to adjust their image, appearance, behaviour within that group, according to circumstance or environment. You may be conservative enough to possess only one tie, or a suit which in material and cut has been copied from the previous one, which in turn was a replica of the one before it (there are tailors who specialize in making precise copies of old suits sent them for the purpose). More likely,

Nell Gwynn, 'pretty, witty Nell'. By dying at 35, soon after her lover Charles II, she froze her attractive image for ever. In *Sunset Boulevard*, Gloria Swanson (opposite) showed how a popular film-star crumbled when her image was no longer able to sustain her. All of us need to know how to play the right part – true to ourselves and to the times in which we live.

however, you will change your appearance slightly to suit the time of the day or week, or the company you are in. You will change into informal, or more formal, dress for the evening; you will wear rather more relaxed clothes at the weekend, or when on holiday. And in the same way, your behaviour, your speech, your gestures, your whole image may change.

Without consciously thinking about it, almost everybody has within one broad life-style a number of different images which fit given situations and which can succeed each other with startling ease. At breakfast, you may appear ill-kempt and sleepy, answering in monosyllables, eating noisily and ignoring everything except the morning paper or radio chat show. Shaved and suited, you may be hail-fellow-well-met in the commuters' train, joining the regular poker game with enthusiasm, ready to exchange vigorous comments about the Miss World Contest on TV, or the nude on page three of your popular newspaper.

Offhand to your secretary, or overattentive if you are trying to seduce her, you will be ultra-smart and attentive, efficiency personified, when called into conference with the boss. The neat tie and shirt-collar will be loosened in the gregarious atmosphere of the lunchtime bar. If an hour's golf can be played in the afternoon the sportsman image will smoothly take over, the rhythm of conversation becoming easier and freer.

Back at home, the negligent husband will become the admired, successful businessman when mother comes to call (though she, on the other hand, will easily see the slovenly habits of the small boy in the man who throws his newspaper on the floor, or has carelessly left his fingernails untrimmed). To the teenage son or daughter, might you not seem a pillar of dull respectable complacency when you invite them to turn the transistor down or get on with school work? Do you present to your husband, when he comes home, the sharp, bright image you present to the world at the PTA coffee morning or the church committee? Are you honestly the same man or woman to a lover or a mistress as to a wife or a husband?

Questioned, you might grudgingly admit all this. But you would probably claim that you were not particularly trying to present a particular image to a particular person; and you might be right. Most of our reactions in everyday life are automatic and trite. But that is not to say we are not conscious, and highly conscious, of our appearance, even if upbringing and environment, social habit, the attitude of a partner or of close friends and, above all, of our own personality and psyche still inhibit most of us from 'giving ourselves away' by wholly externalizing the image we have of ourselves. We choose to present an image which may be more extrovert, more introvert, than we feel to be truly the case. The Gay movements which have brought homosexuals out into society, for instance, have forced some men and women who regard themselves not especially as either 'gay' or 'straight' to be ostentatiously one or the other; thus today people who (like the vast majority of us) are neither wholly male nor wholly female in personality have felt it necessary to display a prejudice.

Everyday life is to some extent a form of theatre: home theatre, street theatre, office theatre, bedroom theatre. Like actors, we tend to play a multitude of roles, some more fully than others. The secret of presenting an image successfully is perhaps to recognize our limitations as role-players – in theatre terms, not to mis-cast ourselves, to get a sense of the scene which we are about to play and to regard ourselves critically as we approach it. Is the costume right for the part? Are we, physically, making promises we cannot fulfil? Will we attract too much attention – or too little attention – or the right sort of attention? Image-making is important in many areas of life; in others it is pleasant but unimportant; in yet others, mere fun. Certainly, it is a game and is usually played to rules – sometimes general rules, sometimes highly localized rules which may vary from office to office, home to home, party to party. Discovering the rules, and playing the game according to them, may be vital, interesting, or just amusing; but it is an activity which you cannot ignore.

3 Playing a role

The actor plays at being

you – or you – or you.

Perhaps instinctively, perhaps using

a system such as 'the Method'.

Is 'acting' also something you do

every day – something you need to do?

WE ARE ALL, in one way or another, actors, changing our performance subtly from day to day, hour to hour, according to the person we are with or the situation we are in. The difference between the ordinary man and woman trying to impress a prospective employer, get to know a new friend, or talk a bank manager into granting an overdraft, and an actor playing the role of someone in similar circumstances, is that the actor spends a great deal more time in preparation. A man about to lie to his wife may have some idea of a rough script, but little more than that.

It pays to observe other people whom you suspect of 'putting on a front' in the way a drama critic observes a theatrical performance – watch the eyes, the gestures, the general attitude (the next chapter gives some hints on what to look for). But it also pays to observe your own behaviour and to control it. Much of life is, after all, a lie – if only at the level of admiring the other woman's hat or the other man's golf swing, when the truth is that both are infinitely inferior to your own.

Actors have various ways of controlling and 'pacing' their performances and there is no truly international language of acting. The nearest, and it is one which any layman can put to use, is the system devised in Russia half a century ago by the great theatre director Constantin Stanislavsky – the system which became known in the West, particularly at the Actors' Studio in New York, as 'the Method'. It provides a useful set of tools for measuring behaviour, movement, speech – so that it is possible to plan a scene, on or off the stage, in great detail; and also to observe your own behaviour.

Stanislavsky taught his actors many ideals which hold in everyday life. An actor should, he said, above all believe in himself – that he has something to give to the people around him. Success, material or spiritual, begins *inside* a person: achievement begins with, 'I desire'; and goes on to, 'I *can*'. He believed too in emotional drive; that great emphasis should be laid on the strength and quality of a person's feelings. With the necessary drive, you can channel your thinking abilities to the greatest effect. A strong emotional drive will get you somewhere; thinking alone will not.

Much of Stanislavsky's theory is devoted to enabling an actor or actress to see himself more clearly and his hints also hold good off the stage. Everyone has a certain measure of feeling, thought and will-power, for instance, of which one will probably be dominant. Everyone has a certain emotional range; is in general either high-key (extrovert) or low-key (introvert), the first rather unobservant, talking too much, always giving out; the second rather lazy, content to absorb other people's ideas and theories, always taking in.

You should, he suggested, examine your five senses: do you use them all thoroughly and positively? How is your sense memory? Do you remember smells and tastes vividly? How self-contained are you? Can you be happily alone within the largest crowd? How easy is it to destroy a bad habit – give up smoking, drinking, whatever? – or induce a good new one?

Stanislavsky devised certain exercises to reveal and loosen up the personalities of his students. Two students will talk to each other simultaneously, each trying to engage the other's attention by what he or she is saying, in the chosen subject; this exercise hones the edge of a very useful weapon – how to hold the attention of the person to whom you are speaking. The 'eye-contact' exercise, in which a speaker attempts to catch and briefly to hold the eye of every member of the audience to which he is speaking, is useful in much the same way; many people talking to even a small group tend to address the table, or a

In public Hitler played to perfection the role of kindly uncle to the youth of Germany.

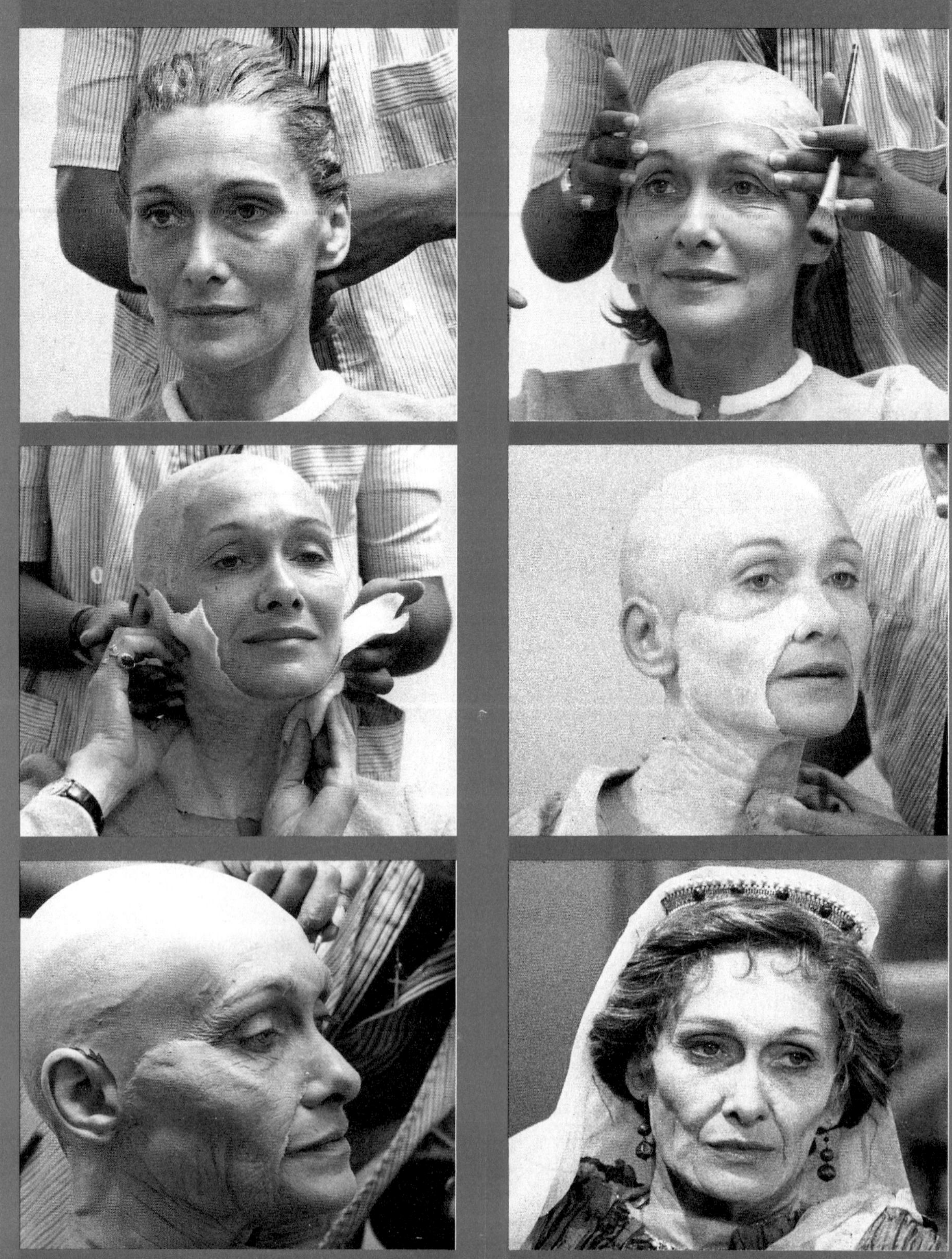

wall. A student will be asked to express himself in gibberish – meaningless sounds which nevertheless have to convey an idea, a state of mind. This is a quite spectacularly successful exercise for releasing tension and inhibition. There is also the simple exercise of finding a hidden object (often, symbolically, a key); as in everyday life, lack of tension is again one of the answers – the more 'worked up' and tense you become, the less likely you are to find the lost object.

Apart from such exercises, Stanislavsky also devised a scale on which speech and behaviour can be measured – a scale which runs from 0 (in effect, complete stillness – death) to 10 (hysteria). On this scale, the ordinary daily metabolic rate lies between $3\frac{1}{2}$ and $7\frac{1}{2}$. At 1, you are asleep, with the subconscious alone active. Up to about 4 on the scale, there is an introverted energy at work, receiving impressions, while from 5 upwards, an extrovert energy takes over, expressing ideas and emotions. At 4, you are still detached, in a state perhaps of 'public solitude'; at 6 you have become alert and alive, at 7 emotionally involved, from 8 upwards highly keyed, with energy dominant rather than controlled, and in fact tending altogether to lose control.

More than 7 hours of make-up preparations help to turn Sian Phillips into the Empress Livia in TV's *I Claudius*. Stanislavsky (below), on the other hand, used a direct analysis of human behaviour, movement and speech to help actors in playing a role.

Using this scale, you can chart a scene in a play or a scene in real life. Arguing with the bank manager, you may start at 6, but as he shows mistrust or antagonism, you may gradually lose control of your arguments, mounting to 7 or even 8 on the scale; then, as he begins his lecture, sliding rapidly down to 3, where, while apparently taking in his argument, you can rearrange your own before making a new assault. . . .

While it may be impracticable and undesirable to try to plot out every scene in your life as though you were an extra from a soap opera, it is often illuminating to remember an important interview or argument or meeting afterwards, 'plot' it as though you were a theatre producer and see where energy has been wasted or the wrong attitude taken, absorbing the lessons learned.

This is not to deny that in most areas of life 'natural' behaviour (whatever this may mean for the individual, and however strange it may seem to others!) is on the whole healthier than any attempt to force yourself to take on the colour of the social behaviour around you, or to 'over-act' or 'over-react' as though you were cast in a part foreign to your personality.

A few extroverts will always find it agreeable and perhaps profitable to climb to the very end of any available limb, to make capital out of being ostentatiously 'different' in speech and behaviour. Today, in urban Western society, they are usually tolerated; in that sense, a changing attitude to general behaviour has kept pace with the more tolerant attitude to sexual morality.

Though the 'over-reactors' might be less happy if they overheard the comments made after they left the party, the new tolerance certainly makes life easier for men or women who have to enter a society different to their own: they can admit to uneasiness and in the end are safer than people who pretend to an ease they do not feel. This applies in which-

Ignore time, place and your own personality at your peril. Louis XIV was effectively represented as unifier of French Christendom, but (opposite) majesty can be flattered (Napoleon as nude classical hero) or scorned (the plump, defeated general *en route* for St Helena).

ever direction they travel: the socialite who tries to be 'one of the boys' in the factory is walking on ground as tricky as that trodden by the 'working man' who finds himself at a Presidential dinner. The French President Giscard d'Estaing, making a determined effort to be democratic, found that inviting himself to a meal with an 'ordinary' French family merely exposed himself to ridicule; he soon discontinued the practice.

In the end, of course, what is in question is whether it is desirable or necessary under any circumstances to take on a personality other than your own. The danger of sudden revelation is never far away and the fall is then entirely in proportion to the care taken in disguise. 'To thine own self be true' is a good motto; and it embraces a willingness to be honest in relationships with other people.

4 *Recognizing the signals*

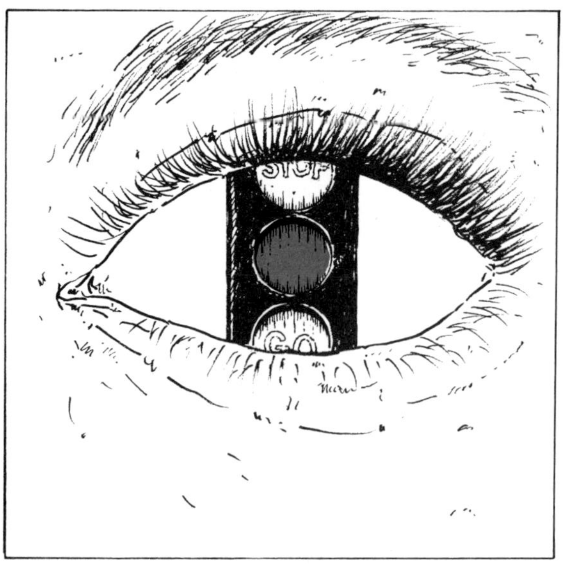

A gesture of friendship in New York might be an insult in Riyadh. Other gestures seem truly international. How do you learn gesture, expression? What signals dislike, aggression, sexual attraction? Can you consciously learn the language of gesture?

THE VARIOUS GESTURES we make with our bodies – not only with our hands, but with our heads, arms, legs, our eyebrows and mouths, our whole bodies in fact – are so much a part of our personalities that it is all but impossible to discover how we learn them or when we first use them. Some of them seem to be an integral part of the human personality; and we tend to feel that a large number of them are international – a kind of *lingua franca* of the human animal.

But this is not the case. It might be thought, for instance, that two of the simplest gestures – the nod for 'yes' and the shake of the head for 'no' – are universal. While a nod means 'yes' in most Western countries, the Japanese signal 'yes' by bringing both hands up to the chest and then gracefully down again. The Ethiopians throw their heads back and raise their eyebrows. The Dyaks from Borneo also raise the eyebrows for 'yes' (and contract them in a 'worry' gesture for 'no'). The Maoris thrust their heads and chins upward for 'yes'; the Sicilians make the same gesture for 'no'. A Bengali may swing his head freely from shoulder to shoulder for 'yes', while a Moslem may turn his head backwards upon one shoulder. And so it goes.

These gestures are part of a culture and have been learned by observation. Are there any truly inherent gestures? – gestures which are as natural as opening the eyes to see or the mouth to speak? As Darwin pointed out, there are some: very young children blush with shame, their faces go red with anger, they laugh and cry with pleasure or passion. These are physiological 'gestures' of the body, like a puppy wagging its tail when it is pleased or a cat when it is displeased. The human smile is perhaps partly in this category.

The smile on a baby's face is more often than not first seen in sleep, but within two weeks there seems to be a conscious smile. A week later there will be what seems to be a really 'giving' smile and at nine weeks old – when the child is able to focus on and recognize people and objects – the smile has become almost a weapon, used to give pleasure to adults and therefore more often than not to produce some kind of reward in the form of food or additional attention and play. The smile seems to be a particularly human function – unlike laughter. Several animals more or less reproduce the physiological signs of laughter as a signal of enjoyment or happiness. Any dog owner will have had the experience of seeing a dog's face contort in what seems to be a laughter pattern, mouth open, tongue slightly protruding and lips pulled back in a distinct caricature of the human face during a positive guffaw. But animals do not appear to smile.

Humans being the devious creatures they are, the smile does not always signify warmth, pleasure or welcome. It sometimes signals reassurance or agreement when reassurance or agreement are expected: as when we smile at the bad joke of an employer, or at a guest who has outstayed his welcome. Some people are better at disguising the false smile than others; but the tell-tale stretching of the mouth muscles too often reveals it – the word 'cheese', much favoured by photographers, produces a very reasonable facsimile of the false smile.

The development of 'laughter lines' about the mouth and eyes reveals how often we send out that particular signal. It is quite remarkably difficult to talk for any length of time to anybody without smiling, even if the person concerned is an enemy. For the smile is not simply an expression of warmth – you can,

The language of gesture: despair, nobility, fear, protectiveness, farewell, anger, triumph . . . all in Poussin's *Rape of the Sabine Women.*

and do, smile sarcastically, ironically, pityingly. . . .

The sycophantic smile is especially interesting. Even someone who does not think of himself as a sycophant will almost certainly smile more often at those more influential than himself – at people older, or richer, or socially 'superior'; in some cases, where a man may simply wish to be liked, he will be a compulsive smiler, sending out the signal quite indiscriminately, so that it is almost meaningless (and frequently, ironically, is recognized as such).

Just as the baby seems to cultivate a smile, at first, to attract the warmth and love of its mother, so very soon it learns that a smile can placate her for minor offences; and this lesson remains with us – the apologetic smile is very common; so common that it is often taken for an excuse ('There's nothing to laugh at!', the boss will say to the office boy).

Even with so simple a gesture there can be misunderstandings: in the West, a man or woman smiling in greeting will often at the same time nod and raise the eyebrows slightly. But in the Far East this may be construed as an indecent invitation and lead to considerable misapprehension.

With other gestures – particularly of the hands – this difficulty is emphasized. In some cases the different use of gesture is extremely subtle. David Efron in 1941 published a study of gestures used by Jewish and Italian immigrants living in New York City, showing an immensely complicated system – and a variety in the use to which gestures were put. The Jews tended, traditionally, to illustrate with their hands the *structure* of their talk, while the Italians used their gestures to illustrate and reinforce the arguments or facts they were speaking *about*.

Apart from different intentions in the use of gestures, the gestures themselves often have different – sometimes radically different –

In *Chironomia* (1806) Gilbert Austin illustrated a multitude of gestures useful to the orator.

Winston Churchill popularized the V for Victory sign, but the factory workers (opposite, top) seem fully aware of its ambiguous nature. Palm outwards it signifies triumph (above, the cast of *Hair*) and, though Mao Tse-tung uses it in this way, Prime Minister Margaret Thatcher seems to confuse it with a common obscene gesture. A 16th-century French relief (top), which may employ a form of sign language, confirms that gestures are by no means universal in meaning.

meanings. Take, for instance, the gesture for something minute or perfect: most commonly, this will be a bringing together of the thumb and index finger of the hand so that they almost, but not quite, touch – the other fingers drawn away so that what the thumb and finger make, to all intents and purposes, is a letter *O*.

This gesture, in the West, can also convey the message that all is well. But in some countries (France is one), the gesture can be a negative one, meaning that something is worthless. To a Japanese man, it can represent a coin and is a sign for money. In Malta, it is a male homosexual insult; in Greece, a simple obscene gesture made to either sex, rather like the inverted V-sign in some Western countries.

Many gestures of this sort are immeasurably old. The thumb-and-finger gesture just described has been common in Greece for many centuries and is found in ancient art. Within the last fifty years or so, however, as international travel has become more common, there has been some confusion as national gestures have been misunderstood, adopted, changed, adapted – so that now it is often extremely difficult to tell just what is meant by any particular gesture and it is unwise to be too readily excited by any signal, whatever its apparent meaning!

Nevertheless, in Western countries the obscene gesture is usually fairly unmistakable, in context. Gestures made by men in admiration of women almost invariably relate to copulation, either by an imitation of the male erection (the raising of the right arm, fist clenched, the left hand clutching the muscle, for instance), or of some sexual caress, as when the hands make the gesture of smoothing down the shape of the female body, or of caressing the breasts or buttocks. Going still further, a finger may be rapidly moved in and out of the clenched fingers of the opposite hand, or the tongue rapidly moved in and out of the open mouth (as in some Mediterranean countries). The raised middle finger, used in, for example, the United States, is an obvious phallic gesture.

The inverted V-sign can be used in a 'complimentary' sense, when the hand is at a low angle, as though the fingers were 'goosing' a woman; on the other hand, the women who are actually complimented by seeing this gesture directed towards them are few. The gesture, usually a vigorous one, is much more often insulting and its origin is almost impossible to conjecture. The common impression seems to be that it is associated with masturbation, and therefore – when directed by one man at another – with an unsubtle insult to the virility of the man at whom it is made. Since one of the common Mediterranean copulatory gestures is the so-called 'fig' gesture, in which the thumb is placed between the first and second fingers, the V-sign may make the comment that the man at whom it is made lacks virility in the sense of being deprived of a useful penis. The 'fig' sign itself may be ambiguous; it is sometimes to be found as a good-luck amulet and in Tunisia and (inexplicably) in Holland it can be read as a complimentary sexual invitation.

There are a few gestures which remain truly international and are rarely misunderstood. Any traveller stranded in a foreign country without a knowledge of the language should be able to convey the fact that he is hungry, tired, has a stomach-ache or a headache. In cases where there might be misunderstanding – rubbing the belly may mean either pleasure after a good meal, hunger, or pain – the facial expression or an additional gesture (mimicking the conveyance of food to the mouth, for instance) should resolve any problem.

The development of man's facial muscles is so complex that it is possible to use the mask of the face almost as freely as a piece of paper on which an artist draws. And in most human cultures the face adopts roughly the same contortion in expressing man's chief emotions – sorrow, pain, joy. A combination of expression and gesture can be used in a hundred different ways and some combination will usually get the right message across. There are many different manual gestures to illustrate idiocy or lack of thought; but combine any one of them with a vacant expression, a half-open mouth and dropped jaw, and the message will be conveyed.

The facial muscles are so expressive and the meanings conveyed by the various elements of the face so subtle, that it needs considerable practice to read accurately the messages being sent out by the faces of people around us. The next most mobile signallers are, of course, our hands. These send out two sets of signals: conscious signals, as in the various gestures we make to each other, and unconscious signals, as when we are relaxed. But one set of gestures shades almost imperceptibly into the other: in conversation, for instance, our hands are constantly in motion – at one moment we may be making a conscious gesture to illustrate a remark, describe a situation or a person; at another, our hands may be moving apparently without our direction, but are still very much a part of our conversation, the statement we are making, or perhaps the statement we are *not* making.

The almost infinite variety of movements made by the hands during a simple conversation can be revealing. The whole hand will gesture, each separate finger will participate, the wrists will turn, one hand will react to the other, the hands will open and close, the fists clench and unclench. . . .

In general, the more forceful the argument, the higher the emotion, the more crude and powerful the gesture. The use of the hands made by a politician at the most emotional or important moments of a speech is an obvious example: two-handed, two-armed gestures, the pounding of the table or podium with the fists, the shaking of the fist in the air . . . these are usually carefully calculated; Mr Khrushchev, on one celebrated occasion at the UN, did not *unconsciously* remove his shoe to pound the table with it.

The use of the fist is one of the most universal of all gestures, always with the implication of force behind it; normally clenched to strike, the fist always stands for power or a desire for power, domination or the desire to dominate. Only a little less powerful is the open-handed gesture with the fingers slightly bent, as though about to seize the arm or even the throat of an opponent.

Almost as potentially violent is the quick movement of the open, flat hand, as in a vertical karate blow. An argument will be forced home by a double-handed gesture, with the palms at right angles to the body, the thumbs pulled away from the fingers and the hands and upper arms moved in short, emphatic gestures to the rhythm of speech. But the hands are also commonly used in the same attitude – palms open, fingers together and thumbs slightly apart, though less tensely held – to signify calm (hands towards the persons to whom you are speaking) or innocence (hands facing upward).

The first contact between two strangers, the handshake, is consciously or unconsciously extremely important and impressive: the degree of pressure in the hand shaken, the firmness or slackness of the grip, the very feeling of the skin, moisture or dryness, convey an impression which may turn out, later, to be mistaken, but is none the less important.

The 'firm' handshake has in Western cultures – and perhaps especially in America – always been regarded as desirable among men, a sign perhaps of strength and 'manli-

Black Power at the 1968 Olympics. The association of the fist with force and domination is the basis for one of the least ambiguous of gestures.

ness'. But there are a number of reasons why this is not necessarily true. Some people – politicians, for instance – have to shake hands so many times during a tour or campaign that to invite a really firm grip would be madness. Surgeons, tennis players, pianists, similarly might be expected to avoid too much muscular strain. Women, until recently, tended to prefer a rather limp grip – though career women often employ the firm, 'male' handshake.

Something can nevertheless be inferred from the manner in which the hand is taken: the man who turns his hand so that it is on top of the one he is shaking often proves to be a domineering character, or at least someone who likes his own way; a particularly 'limp' or tentative handshake may indicate introversion, shyness, even reclusiveness.

There are gestures accompanying the handshake. Shaking hands with someone you are especially pleased to see (or to whom you wish to give that impression), you may place the left hand over the others in a gesture of additional warmth. This, perhaps the most restrained of the additional gestures, can be seen in film of heads of state greeting each other. Where still greater warmth is felt the left hand may be placed on the right arm of the person being greeted, or even thrown round the shoulder, though that approaches the kiss or hug ceremonially given in Eastern countries at formal occasions.

Public contact between people of the same sex has until recently been confined to such gestures – and, in the West, has not even been so warm. Tourists experienced a shock, as little as twenty-five years ago, to see young men walking hand in hand in the streets of North Africa or the Middle East. In Italy and the Mediterranean countries in general, men have often walked arm in arm or with arms about each other's shoulders (more frequently than have women). But this is still uncommon in England and America, except with homosexuals.

The full embrace has only relatively recently been seen in public between male and female; one observer noticed it for the first time in the streets of London on Armistice Day, 1918. Between males it is only regularly seen on the sportsfield and then usually only in connection with football. No doubt expressing pleasure in accomplishment, it is a gesture obviously meant to encourage the cheers of supporters: the footballers who embrace each other with such passion on scoring a goal might react badly to the suggestion that they would embrace as ecstatically under any other circumstances.

Gesture, expression, the position of the body can all be usefully studied without loss of individuality. Humphrey Bogart's approach to Lauren Bacall in *To Have and Have Not* **is no less effective for being stylized; and the 19th-century artist, Hayes King, provides apt expression for** *Jealousy and Flirtation* **(opposite).**

The behaviour of lovers in public has, in the West, become more exhibitionist during the past twenty years. While lovers walked hand in hand or arm in arm, there were strong inhibitions about kissing in public until relatively recent years (the 'polite' social kiss of greeting excepted). Lying together in an embrace has only been common in public parks or beaches since the Second World

War – and even recently has been prohibited by local by-laws in many places. Now embracing and fairly enthusiastic petting take place in public places as and when the weather permits; the participants are no longer offering the kind of gesture made by the early twentieth-century couple who appeared in public arm in arm: a gesture which asserted that they were 'walking out', or advertising a permanent liaison.

If in some cases contact is welcomed, it is carefully shunned or at least carefully regulated in others. We guard the space which surrounds us with perhaps unconscious but invariable care, against too close an approach by strangers, or even – in the selfconscious West – by friends. Standing near other people – in a queue, at a sportsfield – or sitting with strangers on a park bench, in a waiting-room, at a concert, we take care that a space is maintained between us and our neighbours. So keen is our sense of privacy that the regularity of the spacing between people in line is almost amusing. So strong is our consciousness of the privacy of our own air-bubble that a stranger who punctures it is sending us the most offensive signals; a stranger who, relaxing on a beach, touches the toe of the desirable blonde nearby with his own toe risks almost as much as if he went up and embraced her; similarly the 'familiarity' of placing a hand on the arm of a stranger when, say, directing him in the street, is interpreted as a questionable social act.

But it is not only physical contact which is avoided with a stranger. Sitting in a railway carriage, or in a waiting-room, strangers keep their eyes off each other; or, if caught looking too closely at someone, become embarrassed and apologetic. A glance at the other people in the room, even a smile, may be permissible. But anyone who catches the eye of a stranger and holds it with his own risks being accused of bad manners, if not worse. The old children's game of staring someone out is a test of psychological muscle quite as overt as a trial of physical strength. The punishing stare of the Army NCO at the raw recruit, or of any 'superior' to an 'inferior', is another example of the power to subdue. In crowds, even when likeminded people are together for a common purpose, physical proximity does not permit free eye-contact.

So we protect our individuality, as though prolonged eye-contact with another person might in some way drain some essential part of us away (much as primitives believed that, in taking a photograph, a camera stole part of the soul). There are occasions when this becomes quite difficult to organize. In a general conversation, we do not spend all our time avoiding the eyes of our companion; but neither do we stare constantly into them. We glance at his or her face from time to time, but then lower our eyes to our drink, or glance towards other people; or, if we are concentrating hard on what is being said, we may stare intently but blankly at some nearby object – but certainly not into the eyes of our conversational partner. Sometimes we can be almost maniacally careful about this – ironically, for instance, when we are talking to a stranger whom we find sexually attractive. Some men may stare openly, believing that is the way to conquest; but most of us will be especially careful not to do so, for fear of giving offence, and will consciously look away more often than we otherwise would – similarly, with someone who is especially irritating or annoying us, unless we want to provoke an open confrontation.

If by the end of the evening we manage to 'corner' the person we find attractive, and provided that all goes well, we may begin to make stronger eye-contact. It is at this point that our eyes may make their own decision to 'tell' him or her about our admiration, by the simple means of increasing the size of the pupils – as when we look towards the dark – which has the effect, with any luck, of making us more attractive, since the size of the pupils is a proven element of sexual attraction (shown two photographs of the same girl, whose pupils are in one case dilated, men will invariably choose that photograph as the more attractive).

The first physical touch with a stranger is often made 'accidentally', as though we were touching an inanimate object – but then, especially if there is a strong sensual attraction, we will make a more intimate move under the guise of being helpful or specially attentive. Handing a drink, the fingers will touch rather more obviously than they need; a man will help a woman to her feet from a chair, or guide her to one, although she patently needs no help. There may be a distinct difference between the welcoming kiss on the cheek when guests arrive and the farewell kiss when they leave – there certainly will be a difference if host and guest have established a strong rapport during the course of the evening: both hands may be placed on the arms of the guest as he or she is bidden goodnight, for instance. The first and perhaps strongest of the protective barriers has been broken.

The barriers we erect by guarding the space around us, by evading the eyes of another person or moving away from a touch, can be strengthened by more overt signals, perhaps the most obvious of which is the folding of the arms. Folded arms may be comfortable and we may delude ourselves that this is a simple way of disposing of the arms while standing or sitting in an easy position; but in fact we very rarely fold our arms when we are alone – more often than not they do form a protective barrier warning people to keep their distance, or perhaps reassuring us when we are under siege by another person. Keeping our coat buttoned up makes another barrier; the businessman uses his desk in the same way.

In a group of men, the one with folded arms often has his mind on dominating his colleagues; two or three men all with folded arms will usually be engaged in heated, or at least determined, argument. The hands will also be tell-tales: they may be relaxed, just lying against the side or on the upper arm; on the other hand they may be positively gripping the arms, or even be clenched. This is an obvious mark of tension; the man or woman feels even more besieged or under pressure than the folded arms suggest.

The crossing of the legs is a more difficult signal to interpret. Many people do cross their legs just for comfort, when they are alone and completely relaxed. Even then, however, the leg crossed and re-crossed – so that the foot twists around the lower leg it crosses – is probably a sign of tension (as standing with crossed legs may be). It has been suggested that, in argument, crossed legs can be a sign of intractability – that only when legs are uncrossed will agreement be in sight. As with crossed arms, the individual who keeps his legs crossed will be the final man to be convinced. It should be mentioned that in North America men cross their legs by placing the ankle of one leg upon the knee of the other, while in Europe the whole leg is crossed. The latter stance is in some cases regarded in the US as effeminate when used by men, though women wearing slacks often use the 'ankle-cross' position.

Attempting to 'use' a reading of gestures and stances in order to win an argument, choose a moment to press a case, or dominate other people, has its dangers. There are considerable areas of doubt in the interpretation of the signals. Watching a stranger to see how he reacts to you, for instance, you might see that he makes a large number of left-handed gestures. Certainly some observers have suggested that left-handed gestures are a sign of suspicion. But what if the stranger is left-handed? It has been argued that failure to make good eye-contact is a sign of mistrust; but judging between evasion and simple politeness is difficult. Open suspicion may be easier to spot: a knitting of eyebrows may, for instance, be a sign – or there may even be an instinctive turning of the body to one side. It may be that a crossing of the legs away from the person to whom you are talking is another sign.

Gestures made towards the face, and particularly to the mouth and nose, have been emphasized as signs of suspicion, evasion and sometimes of outright lying. The bringing up of a hand to cover the mouth when you have told a lie seems almost too obvious to be likely; but several researchers have recorded that people who have for one reason or another been lying (even telling 'white lies' – complimenting a bad cook, perhaps, on the excellence of a dish at dinner) have immediately afterwards rubbed, or touched, or made a gesture to their nose. At least two American researchers equate the 'nose-rubbing' with downright disagreement with what is being said. Others propose that it merely suggests doubt – doubt as to the propriety of the question asked, doubt as to how to answer it, doubt as to how the questioner will receive the answer . . . there are again many intangibles. In any event, when you are asked to weigh a question, or at other times during the course of an argument, it is likely that your hands will be brought to your face – to touch not only the nose (either with a forefinger, or with finger and thumb) but the eye, eyebrows, chin or ear. All these gestures are, incidentally, very different from the more vigorous gesture of actually scratching.

A release of tension can be signalled by a gesture of some kind, or by a general relaxation – the unfolding of the arms, the unbuttoning or removal of the coat, the uncrossing of the legs; a businessman convinced of the friendliness of a competitor may move out from behind his desk, or at least lean back in his chair in a position more like that of someone watching television than attending to business. At a party, it is fairly easy to spot the guests who are at home in the house of their hosts: the 'strangers' will simply be more 'buttoned-up', and the phrase will be literally true.

A great deal of attention has inevitably been directed towards the unconscious sexual signals we send out – such signals as the enlargement of the pupils of the eyes – and to observing reactions to them. There are very few overt signals of sexual attraction and those are so crude as to be unattractive. In adolescence, for instance, boys will suddenly become extremely truculent in their behaviour towards girls; they may sprawl about in an open-legged slouching posture, which in the earliest human tribes would have amounted to a primal sexual display of the crudest kind and today seems to promise rape rather than courtship. The girls, on the other hand, will be offensively giggly in return, will be at once openly provocative and openly dismissive.

In a more polite context, there are other equally unmistakable signs of attraction, however. Few women will have much difficulty in recognizing the signals sent out by a man who is attracted by her; perhaps centuries of polite injunction not to display specific interest in men have made it easier for women to conceal their own sexual signals. But it is reasonable to expect that one person attracted to another will look at her rather more often than is usual, will be attentive in more than a merely polite way, may make excuses to touch her when strictly speaking he may not need to – cupping her hands in his own when lighting a cigarette, touching her fingers when handing her a glass. There may be other signs; there will certainly be no crossing of arms or buttoning of coats. On the contrary, the man will probably sit forward in his chair, leaning towards the woman, perhaps propping his chin on a hand so that he can look more steadily at her. He will tend to allow her to 'lead' the conversation, and even when he disagrees will do so rather carefully. The liberated woman may find this kind of attention actually distasteful, but as yet man seems to have been unable to evolve a set of behaviour patterns to replace it.

The position of the legs: public manifestation of private preoccupations. We need first to become conscious of physical signals; it is then that interpretation may begin.

The history of social behaviour is outside the scope of this chapter; within recent centuries touch as a means of courtship has been out of the question, beyond the polite offering of a gentleman's arm to a lady to help her to descend from a carriage. To be seen walking arm in arm (except when escorting a lady in to dinner, or on some such formal occasion) was to make a commitment – to do more was to invite vulgar comment. The one time when a man and a woman could touch each other and not offend the rules of polite behaviour was at the dance – and this was no more than to offer an arm, until the invention of the waltz, against which no less vigorous a lover than Lord Byron inveighed:

From where the garb just leaves the bosom free,
That spot where hearts were once supposed to be,
Round all the confines of the yielded waist
The strangest hand may wander undisplaced;
The lady's in return may grasp as much
As princely paunches offer to her touch . . .

After 1812 familiarity on the dance floor became more and more acceptable. Sometimes, as in the tango, it became openly sexual and in the end an excuse for embraces close enough for almost anyone's satisfaction. With a loosening of morals, which made private encounters possible, public behaviour became more distant: on the dance floor men and women separated until they might dance an entire number without touching each other at all – although their movements might be more sensual than would have been permitted in public at any other age.

Many – perhaps most – people have neither the conviction nor the inclination to look out for, or calculate, the signals; they rely on instinct to carry them through. Often, of course, this is successful – just as we send out signals unconsciously, so we receive them unconsciously and interpret them in the same way. It can, however, be useful, as well as entertaining, to watch other people especially closely. Interpretation is often difficult, particularly with professional men and women, part of whose stock-in-trade is putting other people at their ease. A doctor's bedside manner, probably 'learned' through years of experience, embodies a number of tricks employed to relax patients: just the right amount of eye-contact and, since the sense of touch is professionally important, the most carefully paced approach in that respect.

Other professional visitors – say clergymen – will also gauge their manner carefully, in one case sitting back at ease in a chair to demonstrate 'openness' and friendliness in a home where reassurance is needed, in another sitting upright and behaving more formally. A lawyer with clients will very rarely 'unbutton'; the same is true of someone, who – however friendly a householder may be – will find it difficult to relax in a house which he 'serves' by, say, delivering food. Offered a cup of coffee, he will rarely be persuaded to sit down and will probably stand near a door, as though to mark the fact that his stay will be short.

But for the most part we are unconscious of our gestures, the way we stand, sit, walk and constantly betray our feelings. (It may be that life would be unbearably complicated if we *were* always conscious of them!) Occasionally, we may become aware: listening with increasing desperation to a bore from whom we are longing to make an escape, we may realize that we are spending much more time than usual staring fixedly at some object behind him, failing to make the usual amount of eye-contact – the result often being that we begin to stare more fixedly at the bore's face. But, more than likely, our body has already taken its own defensive action: our arms are crossed, or we have folded them and are leaning on a table; if we are sitting, we have crossed our legs and turned slightly away from the bore; if we are standing, we may have swung away towards other people in the room, or even begun to back away – with the result, it may be, that the bore has unconsciously begun to follow.

The extent to which the body signals intention almost before the mind conceives it, is surprising. A teacher or lecturer addressing a class, or a politician addressing an audience, will often begin quite suddenly to make more or less violent movements – sometimes simply broadening his gestures, sometimes actually beginning to move about the platform – before he has consciously realized that his argument is not gripping his audience. He will have read, without consciously appreciating it, the signals sent out by the slumped bodies of the audience, the leaning of heads on shoulders, the resting of chins on hands. . . .

It is easy enough to use such signals: giving a television interview, the very body of the interviewer reflects the attention of the audience. He has interviewed so many people that if he can be made to sit forward in his chair, ostentatiously paying attention, the same effect may usually be expected on the other side of the cameras. But the practised television performer, interviewer or interviewee, will have learned to disguise as best he may his own attitude. He will, for instance, have something in his hands – cigarette, drink, clipboard – to muffle the signals they might otherwise send out, of boredom or impatience or disbelief. He will be careful not to move away from his subject.

The 'moving-away' gesture is one of the strongest unconscious movements we make. We will begin to edge away from someone we dislike, someone doing something of which we disapprove, or even saying something with which we disagree. A man whose wife is spending much time choosing an item of clothing in a store will move away from her – not because there is anything more interesting to see elsewhere, but as a 'hurry-up' signal.

There are verbal 'moving-away' gestures. The over-used word 'Well . . .' is commonly used to signal that a conversation is about to end and one of the participants wants to move off; and it is often followed by a partner breaking in with a new subject, a new comment, as though physically shutting a door a guest has opened in order to make an escape.

If verbal signals fail, the body will begin to go into action. Crossed legs will be uncrossed, arms may be placed on the sides of a chair as though to help one up (whereupon the host may take up a similar attitude, as though in an attempt to persuade both himself and his guest that it is merely a more comfortable posture for conversation.) On his feet, a departing guest may have to do a sort of square-dance with the host in order to reach the door – as though the host were a chess-piece moved to obstruct a pawn intent on becoming a queen. This kind of game is so common that the host who does not play it runs the risk of being considered inhospitable.

On the other hand if he is eager to see his guests go, *his* body will start telling them so. He will begin to tidy small things near him – ashtrays, matches, coasters. In an 'interview' he may simply get to his feet and move towards the door in the most obvious indication that the dialogue is over. The interviewee who does not take that kind of hint runs the risk of suggesting that he is slow and uncooperative. Indeed, in professional life, the recognition of a 'dismissal' gesture is absolutely crucial to a good relationship with an employer – the man who continues to talk through a half-open door, while the boss toys with his executive game, or with a pencil, is playing with fire.

The 'reading' of gestures and body postures is a complex and doubtful skill. Some gestures are no doubt prompted by the psyche, some seem to be 'natural' in the sense that almost any human being will to some extent use them; others have been acquired through environment; some are the result of a particular culture and may have been forced on the person concerned by that culture.

Sometimes the body seems almost cruelly to be caricaturing the person who inhabits it. A homosexual man may be caricatured by his body as limp-wristed and having effeminate gestures. This may give the wrong impression of the man himself; but it is rooted in the physiological difference between the male and female bodies, which produce recognizably 'male' or 'female' signals. The characteristic tucking-in of the upper arms of a woman, for instance, means that a man who holds his upper arms against his sides and gestures outward with his forearms is, consciously or unconsciously, making a typically female 'signal'. Equally, the very 'physical' man may tend to be clumsy when trying to do fine work with his hands, or the 'mannish' woman may make 'mannish' movements.

Such natural styles of movement or gesture are difficult, or even dangerous, to suppress. The most obvious example of attempts to suppress natural facility in the body occurred for centuries in the West, when left-handedness was regarded as anti-social, unnatural or at worst diabolical. There is a sense in which this attitude was quasi-religious: and it stuck until modern times. Robert Hertz, a distinguished biologist and psychologist, as late as 1909 argued that 'society and the whole universe have a side which is sacred, noble and precious, and another which is profane and common: a male side, strong and active, and another, female, weak and passive; or, in two words, a right side and a left side.' In fact, within the first year of life, babies show almost total ambiguity as to the hand which they find it easier to use; gradually, one or the other preference will assert itself, only to be rejected. Not until the child is four will it usually begin employing the right hand predominantly – though one child in ten will find it easier to use the left.

Society's suspicion of the left-handed is deeply engrained – even to be found in some languages (the Latin *sinister* means left-handed; the Italian *mancino* may mean dishonest; the Spanish *zurdo* derives from the word meaning 'the wrong way'; and the French *gauche* is commonly anglicized as meaning 'clumsy'). Most European and American children were until recently bullied into writing with the right hand, though this sometimes seemed to have serious effects on their psychological equilibrium, resulting in stammering and other inhibitions. Some countries, notably in the Eastern bloc in Europe, still have it as a general rule that children 'should' write with the right hand – for what reason, other than uniformity, it is difficult to grasp.

The body is naturally predisposed to the right or left. Those of us who are right-handed are in general orientated towards the right; our right hands are controlled by the left hemisphere of the brain and in most cases this is the dominant hemisphere, controlling speech but also ensuring that, for instance, if we stand for a long period of time, we tend to put our weight more readily on the right leg, that in folding our arms, we place the right one on top, or even that we are right-eyed (pointing a finger at a distant object, we line it up naturally with the right rather than the left eye).

In left-handed people, about sixty per cent have their speech controlled by the left hemisphere of the brain; the rest rely either on the right hemisphere or on both. If there is brain damage to one hemisphere, the other can in time learn to take over, but this is much easier for right-handed than left-handed people; and it seems to be true that there is some difference between the kind of intelligence possessed by right-handed and left-handed people – the left-handed seem to be quicker and more adept in the use of language, while the right-handed are better at controlling their body-movements.

It is now at last more generally recognized that attempts to force a left-handed child to use his right hand are misguided. Yet parents still try to force children into behaviour patterns which are, for them, unnatural. Sometimes there are dramatically unhappy results, as when a mother may dress a very young boy in girlish clothes (perhaps because she deeply wanted a girl), having a traumatic effect on his sexual development.

It is difficult to draw any conclusion from any gesture and always unwise to be dogmatic. It is not easy to learn how to interpret human signals; and they should in any case be observed coolly and from a distance. The very act of listening to someone talking, for instance, distracts attention from the gestures they use. Similarly, it is difficult to observe and analyze your own gestures: like water in the mouth, they have always been there and tend to seem meaningless to yourself.

Other people are best observed when they are in communication with each other, but when you are not yourself involved. Discussion programmes on television are invaluable, provided the programme does not too much involve your own emotions or intellect. Acquiring consciousness of gestures is largely a matter of practice; they must be 'read' in the context of what is being said, of the relationship between the speakers, their generation, their nationality, their sex. . . . The language of gesture *is* a language and must be learned as consciously as you learn a foreign tongue. The rewards in terms both of personal advantage and of entertainment, are considerable.

5 A machine for living in

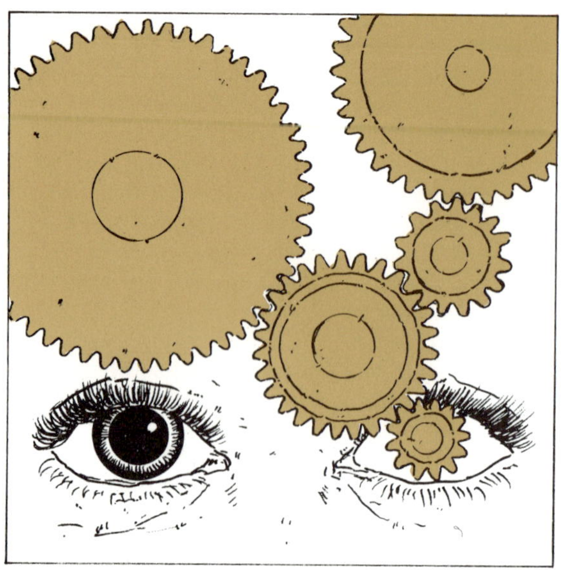

How does 'the good life' kill?

Cholesterol, nicotine, alcohol?

Need we live a life of dull food,

constant exercise, to survive?

Does it all add up to fat, unhealthy,

unappealing; slim, active, attractive?

THE OLD IDEA of 'a healthy mind in a healthy body' took some hard knocks during the quarter of a century immediately following the Second World War. The relaxation of restrictions made an easy or luxurious life immensely attractive to a generation whose childhood had, in most of Europe and later in America, been ruled by wartime conditions. The rule of a cold bath first thing in the morning, followed by a day in which hard work was punctuated by hard exercise on a rigorous diet, did not commend itself.

But within the past decade or so, as the diseases of 'the good life' – heart ailments brought about by lack of exercise and overeating, bronchitis and lung cancer as a result of smoking, liver complaints exacerbated by drinking – have begun to be recognized, people have turned back to the idea that an active and healthy body does contribute to the activity and health of the mind and to the general prolongation of an enjoyable life. 'The good life' in fact depends a great deal on the efficiency of the soft machine in which we live. If you feel, most of the time, sluggish and over-weight, simply out of condition, concentration and quickness of mind become just that bit more difficult. Apart from this, the healthy body usually lives longer and is a great deal more attractive and acceptable both to ourselves and to others.

Of course, this is more complicated than it sounds. For one thing, just as some manmade machines are inherently badly designed, or are merely as efficient as their weakest component, so some human bodies have inborn faults which cannot be corrected. Napoleon was born into a small body with a tendency to plumpness, one of Byron's feet was mal-

Properly controlled dieting can achieve miracles: Linda and John Jenkins were British 'Slimmers of the Year' in 1978.

formed, Nelson's frame was frail and almost effeminate. The spirits which inhabited their bodies 'took over' and compensated to such an extent that the men transcended their physical defects and – perhaps in part because they felt they must show that their imperfect bodies did not matter – rose to greater heights than most physically perfect contemporaries.

Others whose bodies were attacked by illness have also demonstrated the power of mind over material: President Roosevelt was crippled by poliomyelitis, but forced himself not only to be an efficient politician, but to campaign with the strength of ten men, standing for long periods to deliver fighting speeches. President Kennedy later overcame in the same way a less disabling but troublesome back injury. Almost every man and woman with a physical disability does seem to be able to transcend it in some way. Unfortunately, the opposite is not true: those born with good, sound, 'normal' bodies do not hesitate to abuse them.

Care of the body must begin in childhood: European men and women in their forties now have far more healthy teeth than either older or younger people, simply because of the wartime conditions which denied them the great quantities of sugar children otherwise eat. But the children of the 1980s are better protected from infectious diseases, because of the vastly increased incidence of vaccination or immunization – against the diphtheria and polio, measles and tetanus, tuberculosis and smallpox which killed or maimed so many of their forbears.

The provision of school meals provides, or should provide, a healthy and balanced diet, even within the often small budgets allowed by education authorities. Compulsory games may not be insisted upon at all schools, but a certain amount of exercise is nevertheless important. So is setting a good example: children whose parents do not smoke or over-eat, do not take much sugar, drink only in moderation, are less likely to die of cancer or heart attacks, or become alcoholics, than those who see their parents over-indulging.

Jogging: you are never too young, but – if you are very unfit – you may be too old to begin. Perhaps your sex is the decisive factor: twice as many men as women have heart attacks at the age of 45.

Early manhood and womanhood are the most active physical years, but this fact produces its own dangers. The young people who consistently take hard exercise in the late teens and early twenties should realize that it is dangerous to stop exercise completely when they are no longer young. Muscle then turns to fat; a hardworking set of muscles can become slack and turbid, a positive disadvantage. In middle age, too, comes the temptation to over-eat – the business lunch followed by dinner at home; simply too much food. The statistics, however they are qualified, are frightening: one in every three deaths among people over thirty-five could be postponed by a change of diet – in particular by cutting down on consumption of fats and meat, which provoke heart disease and certain cancers.

A look at the international incidence of heart disease tells its own story: it is most common in Western countries – the US, Australia, Finland, New Zealand and Canada, with England and Wales only a little behind Scotland in the league table. On the other hand, Bulgaria, Greece, Italy, Poland, Portugal, Sweden, France, Rumania and Taiwan have a much lower incidence of heart disease, and Japan is at the very bottom of the list.

There is obviously some reason why Japanese women have only a quarter the chance of getting breast cancer that English women have, and one-sixth that of Californian women. Other cancers are also far less prevalent than in the West. The reason is not a racial one: Japanese women living in California are almost as prone to the disease as Westerners. Many cancer specialists now believe that a rice and fish diet is healthier for mankind and womankind than a meat and fat diet. British women have one of the highest incidences of breast cancer in the world: 12,000 women may die of it each year. And Britain is among the countries which eats most meat, fat and sugar.

The case against fats must be regarded as proven. But just as we have the choice of not smoking, we also have the chance of not over-eating.

Are *you* too fat? It is difficult to decide this simply by weighing yourself. Although tables of weight/height relationships are published, not everyone conforms to them. A man of 5′ 10″ 'should' weigh about 140 pounds; but he may weigh as little as 112 or as much as 154, and still be perfectly healthy. So how do you judge?

Well, for a start, do you *feel* over-weight? Is it an effort to get up from a low chair, do you feel generally slow and sluggish? Look at yourself naked in a full-length mirror. Do you *look* fat? Are there folds of fat at the waist, the belly, the hips? When you take a pinch of flesh between finger and thumb at the back of your upper arm, is it more than an inch thick? If so, you are probably too fat. The same applies to the same test made just below the shoulder-blades – if you are a man. If you are a woman, things are a little more complicated: women carry, and should carry, rather more fat than men – a normal man has about ten or twenty per cent of his body-weight in fat; a woman about twenty-five per cent. One test is to look at yourself in a mirror and ask yourself quite frankly if you would like to be in bed with you!

An active life with a proper amount of exercise is one way of helping to control your weight. But the only real answer to a radical weight problem is a properly conceived and balanced diet. There are various dietary theories, different ways of working out just how many calories you need every day if you are of a certain height and build, a certain age, live a certain kind of life. . . . Plan that diet, probably with advice from an expert; and stick to it. There is no short cut.

Exercise is a slow way to slim (and it must be remembered that when you expend energy on exercise, you need more fuel – so a circular argument is involved). But you will feel better for taking regular exercise and it firms up and helps to maintain a good figure. This, apart from anything else, cannot be a disadvantage to a good, active sex life, which many doctors say is an excellent way of taking exercise. Many a man and woman who have 'let go' inside a plump and self-satisfied marriage have been shaken into slimming by taking a lover!

But there are other advantages of regular exercise. It keeps the circulation and the respiratory system in good order; it strengthens the heart and lungs, and increases muscular strength (which among other things makes it less likely that you will get back trouble); it also helps you to relax – it is almost impossible to take vigorous exercise of any kind and worry at the same time!

You are never too old to start taking exercise (though of course if you are elderly or unfit you should take great care at the beginning, and perhaps obtain the advice of a doctor before starting). There are many kinds of exercise: jogging has become something of a cult and is undoubtedly good for you – and probably less boring than going through the same set of 'physical jerks' every day. The problem of boredom should not be underestimated when thinking about ways of taking exercise: using a gym with good equipment eases this. Tables have been worked out which show the relative value of different sports and activities, in improving general endurance, muscular strength and mobility.

For general strength, for instance, basketball, boxing, speed cycling, mountain climbing, rowing, running, sculling, skin diving and skiing are rated high, with more 'ordinary' activities such as climbing stairs, dancing, hiking, jogging and digging in the garden a little way behind. Boxing, canoeing, digging, kayaking, rowing, sawing wood, sculling, weight-lifting and wrestling are good for building up muscular strength, while climbing stairs, fencing, squash are especially good for maintaining mobility. A few activities serve all three purposes well: among these swimming is by far the best and for anyone who lives by the sea or a river, or within reach of a swimming pool, it can hardly be too strongly recommended. Squash, tennis, cross-country skiing, playing football also provide excellent general exercise.

Too much can never be said about the dangers of smoking: fortunately this is becoming not only a dangerous but also an extremely unpopular anti-social habit; it is possible that its gradual disappearance will accelerate over the next few years. Alcoholism remains a major danger. As with smoking, non-drinkers underestimate the difficulty of controlling the appetite for drink once it has been thoroughly acquired, though 'healthy' drinking is far less harmful than the lightest smoking habit.

It is no use pretending that the healthiest body does not suffer some effects of age. But care for your diet and reasonable exercise can delay these effects and do much to keep you active and fit well into the seventies and eighties and longer. It is also important to remain active mentally, socially and sexually (see chapter 9).

Nothing can replace the value of properly servicing the body throughout your life. It is quite remarkably resilient and difficult to put out of order, provided the machinery is properly maintained and cared for. And this is one of the areas of life in which you can choose the category in which to place yourself: fat, unhealthy and unattractive; slim, active and happy.

Dance teacher Margaret Morris at 80. Opposite: health, it is officially suggested, can improve your sex life.

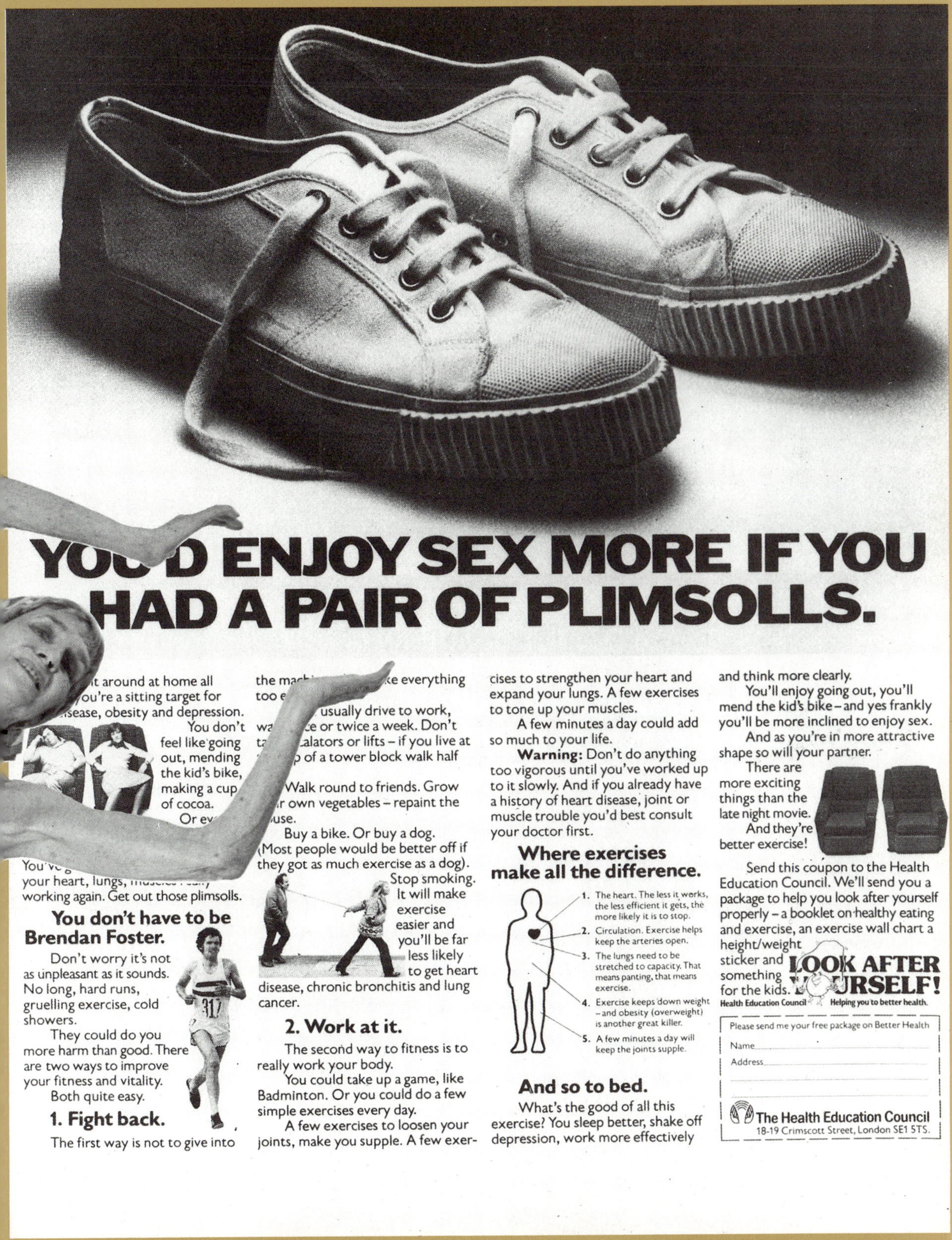

YOU'D ENJOY SEX MORE IF YOU HAD A PAIR OF PLIMSOLLS.

it around at home all ou're a sitting target for sease, obesity and depression.

You don't feel like going out, mending the kid's bike, making a cup of cocoa.

Or ev

You've your heart, lungs, working again. Get out those plimsolls.

You don't have to be Brendan Foster.

Don't worry it's not as unpleasant as it sounds. No long, hard runs, gruelling exercise, cold showers.

They could do you more harm than good. There are two ways to improve your fitness and vitality.

Both quite easy.

1. Fight back.

The first way is not to give into the mac ke everything too e

usually drive to work, wa ce or twice a week. Don't t alators or lifts – if you live at p of a tower block walk half

Walk round to friends. Grow r own vegetables – repaint the use.

Buy a bike. Or buy a dog. (Most people would be better off if they got as much exercise as a dog).

Stop smoking. It will make exercise easier and you'll be far less likely to get heart disease, chronic bronchitis and lung cancer.

2. Work at it.

The second way to fitness is to really work your body.

You could take up a game, like Badminton. Or you could do a few simple exercises every day.

A few exercises to loosen your joints, make you supple. A few exercises to strengthen your heart and expand your lungs. A few exercises to tone up your muscles.

A few minutes a day could add so much to your life.

Warning: Don't do anything too vigorous until you've worked up to it slowly. And if you already have a history of heart disease, joint or muscle trouble you'd best consult your doctor first.

Where exercises make all the difference.

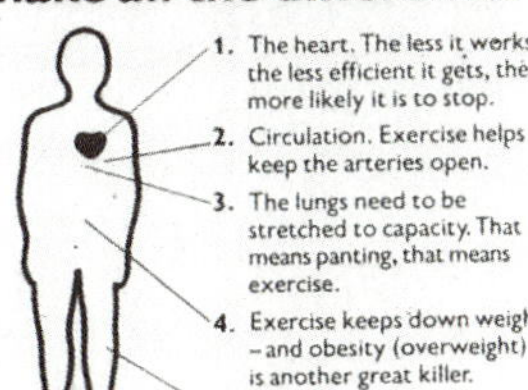

And so to bed.

What's the good of all this exercise? You sleep better, shake off depression, work more effectively and think more clearly.

You'll enjoy going out, you'll mend the kid's bike – and yes frankly you'll be more inclined to enjoy sex.

And as you're in more attractive shape so will your partner.

There are more exciting things than the late night movie.

And they're better exercise!

Send this coupon to the Health Education Council. We'll send you a package to help you look after yourself properly – a booklet on healthy eating and exercise, an exercise wall chart a height/weight sticker and something for the kids.

LOOK AFTER YOURSELF!
Health Education Council — Helping you to better health.

Please send me your free package on Better Health

Name

Address

The Health Education Council
18-19 Crimscott Street, London SE1 5TS.

6 *How healthy are you?*

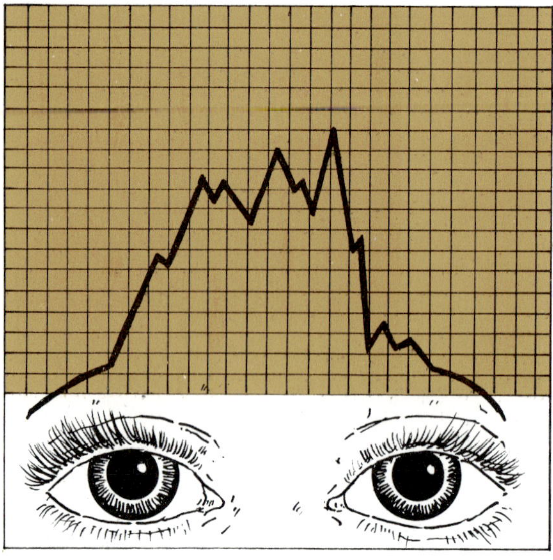

Test yourself: smoking? drinking? drugs? backache and palpitations? . . . how much do you eat, and what? . . . what risks do you take in everyday life? . . . how good is your sex life? Now add up – to what: good health, bad health, happy hypochondria?

A questionnaire in five parts, with scores and interpretations following.

PART ONE

Smoking, drinking and drugs

1 Do you smoke
(a) more than 40 cigarettes a day?
(b) 20–30?
(c) 10–20?
(d) only pipe, cigars or cigarillos?
(e) not at all, having given it up?
(f) not at all, having never smoked?
If you are still a smoker, proceed to questions (g)–(k); if you once smoked, answer all but (j).
(g) do you inhale deeply?
YES/NO
(h) do you smoke your cigarettes right to the end?
YES/NO
(i) can you honestly say you have no trouble with breathing when running or exerting yourself?
YES/NO
(j) do you reach for your cigarettes as soon as you wake, or whenever you see anyone else lighting up?
YES/NO
(k) do you smoke only low-tar cigarettes?
YES/NO

2 Do you
(a) drink heavily – say half to a whole bottle of hard liquor or more than five pints of beer a day?
(b) have two or three beers or glasses of hard liquor at lunchtime and perhaps again in the evening?
(c) take two or three beers a day, or a couple of glasses of hard liquor, or half to a bottle of wine?
(d) take one or two drinks only each day?
(e) take a drink occasionally for social reasons, at a party?
(f) never drink?
If you drink at all, go on to questions (g)–(j); if your answer was (e), answer only questions (h) and (i).
Do you
(g) ever drink alone?
YES/NO
(h) believe a drink or two gives you confidence?
YES/NO
(i) drink (1) before breakfast; (2) at mid-morning; (3) not until lunchtime; (4) not until evening or the end of the working day?
(j) do you tend to force additional drinks on people so that *you* can take another one yourself?
YES/NO

3 Do you rush for the aspirin at the slightest sign of a headache?
YES/NO

4 Do you take any drug regularly, for pleasure (not counting alcohol and cigarettes)?
YES/NO

5 Do you regularly take sleeping pills which are *not* medically prescribed for you?
YES/NO/SOMETIMES

6 If you regularly took sleeping pills under prescription and the doctor told you the time had come to do without them, how difficult do you think you would find this?
NOT AT ALL/SOMEWHAT/VERY

7 Would you try smoking marijuana?
YES, BUT UNDER PROPER ADVICE/YES, ANY TIME/NO

8 Have you ever been addicted to heroin or LSD?
YES/NO

PART TWO

Vulnerability

You are unlikely to be vulnerable to *all* the ailments listed below: check the list carefully and note which bother you, even occasionally.

1 Headaches: (a) often; (b) sometimes

2 Throat: sore throat, loss of voice, laryngitis: (a) often; (b) sometimes

3 Prone to have minor accidents: (a) often; (b) sometimes

4 Tension, nervousness: (a) a good deal; (b) from time to time

5 Worry: (a) constantly; (b) sometimes

6 Backache: (a) often; (b) sometimes

7 Palpitations: (a) often; (b) sometimes

8 Constipation or diarrhoea: (a) constant; (b) sometimes

9 Indigestion: (a) constant; (b) sometimes

10 Aches and pains: (a) continually; (b) occasionally

11 Poor circulation: (a) all year round; (b) chiefly in winter

12 Problem feet: (a) dropped arches, flat feet, hammer toes, etc.; (b) corns, shoes never comfortable.

13 Sleep: (a) sound regular sleep; (b) very variable

PART THREE

Diet and exercise

The amount of food you eat and the amount of exercise you need must depend to some extent on your occupation. So first grade yourself: are you

I *Highly active* (a professional boxer or gymnast, a labourer, a football or baseball player; someone who takes regular and heavy exercise at work)

II *Active* (taking regular but lighter exercise as a sports coach or instructor, a dancer, someone whose work is mainly outdoor and involves considerable moving about)

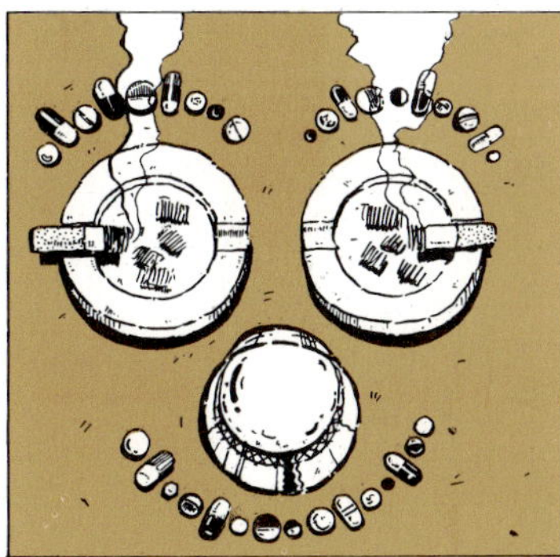

III *Semi-active* (working as housewife, teacher, salesman, sales assistant in a store; an occupation which keeps you on your feet)

IV *Sedentary* (clerk, receptionist, secretary, etc.)

The scoring will depend on which grade you are in.

1 Do you
(a) eat three cooked meals a day?
(b) eat two cooked meals a day, including breakfast?
(c) eat one cooked meal, with a snack breakfast and one other meal?
(d) depend on TV meals and frozen convenience food?

2 Do you raid the refrigerator at least once a day for cheese, cookies, a glass of milk or whatever?
YES/NO

3 Do you eat at least two chocolate bars or $\frac{1}{4}$lb of candies or sweets a day, or a similar quantity of peanuts, potato chips, etc.?
YES/NO

4 Do you eat (a) a large amount, (b) a moderate amount, (c) very little, meat?

5 Do you eat (a) a moderate amount, (b) very little, 'roughage' – i.e., fibrous food, wheat-bread, fibrous vegetables?

6 Do you take (a) regular, (b) some, (c) no, exercise every day?

7 If you exercise, is that exercise (a) very demanding (swimming, basketball, boxing, digging); (b) demanding (tennis, squash, sculling, sawing wood, fencing); (c) light (golf, walking, light jogging, archery)?

PART FOUR

Taking care

In scoring, maintain your grouping from Part Three.

Grade I

Do you
(a) always wear what protective clothing and safety equipment your job provides?
(b) wear protective clothing only in special circumstances, and not by the rule?
(c) not bother with it?

Grade II

Are you
(a) meticulously careful about checking equipment?
YES/NO
(b) careful to get the proper treatment for any minor injuries and as quickly as possible?
YES/NO
(c) careful to be sure you are in condition to cope with any demands made on you?
YES/NO

Grade III

Do you
(a) keep electrical or other equipment, step-ladders, stair-carpets, etc., in good order, checking them regularly?
YES/NO
(b) Make sure you have some interest to relax you if you feel pressures and tensions building up?
YES/NO
(c) always wear car seat-belts?
YES/NO

Grade IV

Do you
(a) ever walk or cycle to the office?
YES/NO
(b) take large 'business lunches'?
YES/NO
(c) worry?
YES/NO

PART FIVE

Sex

1 Do you
(a) have regular and rewarding sex?
(b) have sex quite often, once a week or more, and feel reasonably happy and fulfilled?
(c) feel sexually unfulfilled and restless?

2 Do you
(a) enjoy regular sex with one or two steady partners?
(b) have many partners and change them fairly often?
Men (c) like casual, impersonal sex with any willing girl?
(d) frequent prostitutes?
Women (e) sometimes have impersonal sex?
(f) consider yourself very promiscuous?

3 Do you enjoy violent sexual expression (ranging from slightly rough treatment of your partner to active or passive sadism)?
YES/NO

4 If you enjoy casual sex, do you watch carefully for any signs of sexual diseases?
YES/NO

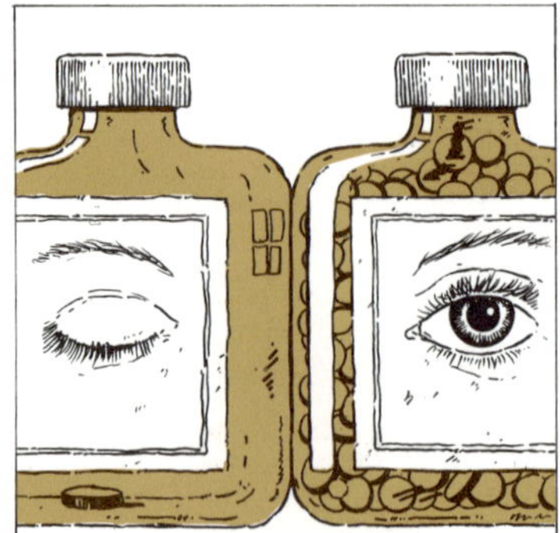

Scoring

Score 0 for any question unanswered.

PART ONE
Smoking, drinking and drugs

Work out your score for questions 1–2 (smoking and drinking) and 3–8 (drugs) separately.

1 (a) 5; (b) 4; (c) 3; (d) 2; (e) 1; (f) 0; (g) Yes 3, No 1; (h) Yes 2, No 1; (i) Yes 1, No 2; (j) Yes 3, No 1; (k) Yes 3, No 1.
2 (a) 5; (b) 4; (c) 3; (d) 2; (e) 1; (f) 0; (g) Yes 3, No 0; (h) Yes 2, No 0; (i) (1)–3, (2)–2, (3)–1, (4)–0; (j) Yes 2, No 0.
3 – Yes 1, No 0; **4** – Yes 3, No 0;
5 – Yes 1, No 0, Sometimes 0;
6 – Not at all 0, Somewhat 1, Very 2;
7 – Yes, under advice 2, Yes 3, No 0; **8** – Yes 5, No 0.

PART TWO
Vulnerability

1 – (a) 3, (b) 1; **2** – (a) 3, (b) 0;
3 – (a) 1, (b) 0; **4** – (a) 2, (b) 1;
5 – (a) 4, (b) 1; **6** – (a) 3, (b) 1;
7 – (a) 2, (b) 1; **8** – (a) 3, (b) 0;
9 – (a) 3, (b) 1; **10** – (a) 2, (b) 1;
11 – (a) 3, (b) 1; **12** – (a) 3, (b) 2;
13 – (a) 0, (b) 1.

PART THREE
Diet and exercise

1 **Grade I** (a) 2 (b) 1 (c) 3 (d) 4
Grade II (a) 3 (b) 2 (c) 3 (d) 4
Grade III (a) 3(b) 2 (c) 2 (d) 4
Grade IV (a) 4 (b) 2 (c) 1 (d) 4
2 **Grade I** Yes 1
Grade II Yes 2
Grade III Yes 2
Grade IV Yes 3
No score for a 'No' in any grade.
3 **Grade I** Yes 1
Grade II Yes 2
Grade III Yes 3
Grade IV Yes 4
No score for a 'No' in any grade.
4 **Grade I** (a) 1 (b) 2 (c) 2
Grade II (a) 2 (b) 2 (c) 1
Grade III (a) 3 (b) 2 (c) 1
Grade IV (a) 4 (b) 3 (c) 1
5 Each grade scores (b) 2, no score for (a)
6 **Grade I** (a) 0 (b) 0 (c) 0
Grade II (a) 0 (b) 1 (c) 1
Grade III (a) 0 (b) 2 (c) 3
Grade IV (a) 0 (b) 2 (c) 4
7 **Grade I** (a) 0 (b) 0 (c) 0
Grade II (a) 0 (b) 1 (c) 1
Grade III (a) 0 (b) 2 (c) 3
Grade IV (a) 0 (b) 1 (c) 4

PART FOUR
Taking care

Grade I (a) 0 (b) 4 (c) 6
Grade II (a) No 3 (b) No 4 (c) No 3
Grade III (a) No 3 (b) No 1 (c) No 4
Grade IV (a) No 1 (b) Yes 4 (c) Yes 3

PART FIVE
Sex

1 (a) 3 (b) 2 (c) 0
2 (a) 5 (b) 4 (c) 3 (d) 3 (e) 3 (f) 3
No score for a 'No' in (a)–(f) inclusive.
3 Yes 3, No 0
4 Yes 0, No 5

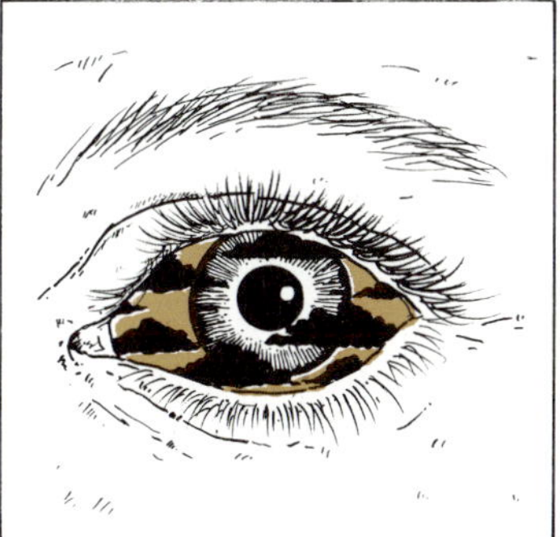

Interpretations

In general, in scoring this section, the lower your score the more healthy you are likely to be. Those with moderate scores need not relax into a comfortable haze of self-congratulation: quite a small effort to improve diet and physical well-being can pay off remarkably and show results in your appearance and general appetite for life. Those with high scores should perhaps look at their life-style and consider (at least) whether they should not think of making some reforms, or (at worst) whether they should not have a thorough medical check-up.

PART ONE
Smoking, drinking and drugs

Questions 1–2
Score 0–11
You obviously have an excellent basis from which to enjoy continual good health and a longer life than those who score higher in this section. Ignore suggestions that failure to smoke or take more drink than you want makes you in any way a wet blanket or spoil-sport; you can afford to laugh at the cigarette and drink ads.

Score 12–24
You are probably only a moderate smoker or drinker: but there is one catch – if most of your points come from either the drinking *or* smoking sections, you should examine that habit and how addicted you are to it! You can afford to think a little about the extent to which you may be abusing your body; if any of your points come from smoking, remember that that habit has nothing to be said for it. Even a moderate drinker should take certain precautions: always try to eat *something* when you are drinking, for instance, and watch the combination of drinking and driving.

Score 25–33
You may have tried to give up smoking and to drink less; you may even have succeeded for short periods of time. Your present habits may not be dangerous, but they could certainly become so. Don't think that *you* could not catch lung cancer or become an alcoholic: you could – a little extra pressure at work or at home could drive you over the top. Common sense is the answer. If you smoke, check your breathing, have regular X-ray checks, try to cut it out. If you drink heavily, try not to drink when you are alone, try to cut down gradually until you are drinking only with your meals. You are among the more vulnerable section of society in this respect.

Questions 3–8
Score 1–7
You have a healthy attitude towards drugs and the likelihood of your abusing them is low. It is silly not to use drugs legitimately, but the tendency to rush for the aspirin bottle at the slightest temptation is probably to be resisted: try a breath of fresh air instead!

Score 8–15
You probably have an above-average interest in drugs and may have gone through a period of experimentation; alternatively drugs may have been prescribed for you which you have continued to take rather longer than strictly necessary. Drugs are a medical tool: drop them as soon as you are advised. As to drugs for 'pleasure': well and good – but there is a fearful lack of evidence as to the dangers of even the most innocent-seeming of them.

PART TWO
Vulnerability

The maximum score in this section would be 33, but it is very unlikely that you will score so highly. Similarly, it is unlikely that anyone will score 0.

Score 0–6
You are obviously pretty healthy and have the right attitude to minor ailments – watch them carefully in case they get out of hand, but otherwise treat them as they deserve to be treated: with a certain respect, but without over-anxiety.

Score 7–15
This is about an average score and your points may have crept upwards from the previous category as you have grown older. You can live quite reasonably with the ailments you have, but they could tend to get you down from time to time and if you tend to grumble or worry they could assume oversize proportions. If you are seriously worried about any one of them, take yourself off to your doctor and discuss it with him; there may be a perfectly simple explanation and even a perfectly simple cure.

Score over 15
Look at yourself objectively: do you *really* suffer from all the ailments you have checked? If so, this may (again) be the result of age, illness or accident. But there is also a chance that it may be the result of poor diet and lack of exercise, so check those sections too! It is difficult to over-estimate the psychological origin of many illnesses: are you lonely, depressed, or do you perhaps want to attract attention to yourself? An engrossing hobby, more participation in

neighbourhood activities might be as much of a help as medical treatment. Try to convert your negative feelings about your body and its functions into positive mental channels.

PART THREE
Diet and exercise

Maximum scores: Grade I, 10; Grade II, 14; Grade III, 20; Grade IV, 25.

Common sense will explain the scores in this section. Anyone in Group I who eats three large meals a day may very well be engaged in work heavy enough to use up all the calories he consumes and may also not need any, or much, additional exercise – though the most active workman may not be exercising *all* his muscles and might benefit from specialized exercise. It is very important for Group I men and women that they do not suddenly stop work and stop taking exercise; the sudden deterioration of a previously well-exercised body is frightening and ignoble. If you place yourself in Group 4 and still eat three large meals a day, you are storing up trouble for yourself with every mouthful, especially if you take no exercise outside working hours: you will be specially vulnerable to heart disease and are more than likely to be very much over-weight.

A high score in any Group is a sign that something is probably wrong, somewhere, with your programmes of diet and exercise; sometimes insidiously wrong – the constant nibbling of chocolate bars, for instance, does no one much good (unless a sudden physical effort is needed on an otherwise empty stomach). Try to get at the *reason* for such nibbling: are the chocolate bars 'comfort food' because you feel lonely or under strain?

The real message of this section is *balance*: it is not always easy to get a balanced regime of diet and exercise going, especially when you have to fit it in with other activities. But it is very well worth trying. Remember, over-exercise may not be as bad as complete lack of exercise, but it is not especially good for the average man; a tendency to over-weight or sluggishness is not best countered by a starvation diet, but by sensible planning of meals.

PART FOUR
Taking care

As long as it does not result in slowing the pace of life to a stagger, it is hardly possible to be too careful in any activity. The greatest proportion of accidents occur in the home: the housewife is probably more vulnerable to such accidents as slight falls, burns, bruises and cuts, than a high-rise scaffolder is to a fatal fall. In each case the answer is a proper evaluation of the circumstances and reasonably careful precautions. It is, for instance, by general consent extremely silly not to wear a seat-belt even on the shortest car trip. It is as silly not to wear safety harness on scaffolding, or a helmet beneath it.

Once again, the higher the score, the worse the problem: in a sense, *any* score in this section, however low, is a black mark; anyone who scores should look again at the hazards of their work – if you work in an office, are electrical appliances switched off at night? Are you sure of the position of fire doors? And do you allow yourself to worry unduly about problems? The hazards of people in Group I are obviously different from those of Group IV, but are none the less important and, sometimes, fatal.

PART FIVE
Sex

Health surveys have stated that a happy and rewarding sex life can add as much as two years to our expectation of life; if this is the case, it is surely one of the most enjoyable ways of keeping healthy. But apart from physical health, there are obvious implications for your psychological health.

If you score between 0 and 8, your sex life is probably as rewarding and enjoyable as one could hope and sex is unlikely to be a physical or emotional problem in your life. If you score between 9 and 13, your sex life is probably varied and exciting enough; it is possible you need rather more variety than average and in seeking new experiences you might run into certain dangers – not only the obvious dangers of infection, but of having an incomplete relationship with those you love. You may not be abusing your body, but there are other abuses to which you may be susceptible. Anyone who scores between 14 and 22 is much more liable to disease and should watch carefully for signs of infection. Sadism and masochism are recognizable sexual conditions and, even if they are not to be condemned as such, remember that any practice of – say – flagellation or bondage can lead to abuse, however satisfying sexually. It is no longer the general belief that there is such a thing as 'over-indulgence' in sex: the amount of sexual satisfaction anyone wants or needs is a matter for their own personality and metabolism. Research into, for instance, the effect on football players or other competitive sportsmen on the eve of competitions has so far proved inconclusive, though there are many myths about it. A certain amount of prudence is probably as wise in this area of life as in any other.

Summing up

There are many ways of abusing the body and perhaps this series of questions has hinted at your predilection for some of them. The less the body is abused, the healthier it is and the longer, on the whole, it is likely to last. This is, of course, a generalization: give up smoking and drinking tomorrow and it may not add ten years to your life. Or it may. Is it worth the effort? Anyone with a mountainous total score in this series of tests may well benefit from thinking about the possible answer to that question.

7 You are your body

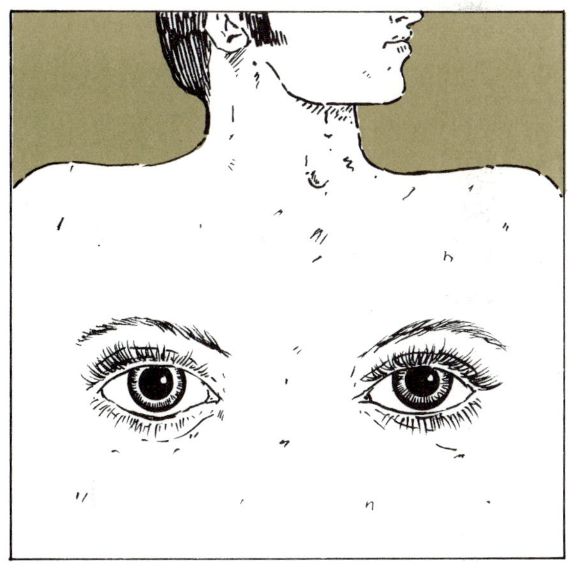

Are you lion or panther, choleric

or sanguine, eurymorph or mesomorph?

If your knees are slender, are you effeminate?

May the horse mate with the deer?

Centuries of experience have tried

to relate physical appearance to

the man or woman within the body.

THE NOTION THAT the human body is in some way a mirror of the human personality is an extremely ancient one. Pythagoras is sometimes said to have fathered physiognomy, the science which explored this theory, sometime in the sixth century BC; yet Galen, the Greek physician, believed Hippocrates (*c.* 460–*c.* 357 BC) to have been the first man to attempt to rationalize it.

However that may be, the first surviving book in which such an attempt is made is one ascribed to Aristotle (384–322 BC), published under the title *Physiognomica*. This describes the various parts of the body which allegedly reveal the character and goes on to show how, for example, bravery or cowardice, wrath or prudence are evident in the body.

The author or authors (almost certainly not Aristotle himself) collected the data by examining animals generally considered to have certain attributes and analysing what physical characteristics they also shared: their movements and gestures, colour, facial expressions, growth of hair, condition of the flesh, build of the body as a whole.

This sort of observation led them to a number of firm conclusions – that, for instance, a brave person would have an upright bearing, coarse hair, large strong bones, a broad flat stomach, a slim neck, a broad fleshy chest, heavy calves, eyes that gleam but are not too widely set, a rather dry skin and a straight small forehead, neither very smooth nor very wrinkled.

The ideal man was said to share many of the qualities of the lion: a good-sized mouth, a square, not too bony face, a rather thick nose, gleaming deeply-set eyes, neither too round nor too elongated, a square forehead rather hollowed at the centre and hanging like a cloud over the eyebrows. The head should be of moderate size, with a broad, long neck and a tawny mane neither too stiff nor too curly. The shoulders should be strong and the chest powerful, the trunk broad and easy moving. There should be no fat on the sides or haunches, the legs should be straight

and sinewy and the whole body well knit and without superfluous fat. Such a man should walk deliberately, moving gracefully and rolling his shoulders. This outward appearance inevitably denoted a generous, liberal, noble character, a lover of victory, but also someone gentle and just, and affectionate towards others.

The picture of the ideal man was reflected by another of the ideal woman, modelled on the panther, the bravest of the 'female' animals; the reader was warned that the brave woman would probably be, like the panther, small and furtive of soul and in general rather tricky of temperament. But this author also found in most cases that the woman was more cowardly and deceitful than the male.

The neo-Aristotelian writer went on to discuss other characteristics and what they signify: woolly hair indicates cowardice, for instance; those who walk stiffly, swinging their shoulders, are blusterers; those who stoop and roll the shoulders as they walk are 'great-minded'.

After the *Physiognomica*, the ancient author who won the highest reputation in the field was Polemon, who lived in the third century BC and became head of the Academy in Athens. He wrote a very comprehensive book (of some seventy chapters) on physiognomy, dealing with almost every conceivable aspect of the subject. In his second chapter he examines the similarities between human beings and no less than ninety-two animals. Then he goes on to devote separate chapters to almost every part of the human body – the nails, fingers, feet, shins, loins and thighs, hip-bones and so on up to the head. He describes the various shades of colour of the hair and skin and the importance of the growth or lack of growth of hair on various parts of the body; and he provides descriptions of various types of men and the outward signs their bodies show of inward characteristics. In his last two chapters he demonstrates with pride how the finest type of modern Greek is coincidentally the finest possible type of man and describes him in every detail with glowing praise.

Both the neo-Aristotelian book and Polemon's giant work take careful account of the theory of the 'humours', which was extremely important in early medicine and also in the theory of physiognomy. Alcemon of Croton in about 500 BC is said to have originated it; certainly he insisted that good health was dependent on a properly balanced mixture of the humours, which consisted of the fluids of the body – blood, phlegm, yellow and black bile. *Krasis*, or the ideal mixture, resulted in perfect health. But more often than not one of them predominated and the result was the phlegmatic man (in whom yellow bile predominated) or the sanguine man (in whom blood predominated). It was not until the ninth century AD that the great Arab

Charles le Brun, working in the 17th century, was one representative of a long tradition in comparing the physiognomy of men and animals.

physician Johannitius invented the terms *melancholici, phlegmatici, cholerici* and *sanguinei* to describe the types of men produced by the effects of the humours of the body. Long before that, however, specific physical characteristics were attached to each mixture of the humours, which were themselves each composed of two or four 'qualities' – blood was hot and moist, phlegm cold and moist, yellow bile warm and dry and black bile cold and dry.

It seems to have been Aristotle who first put forward the theory that the condition of the *mind* was also dependent on the mixture of the humours. Galen (c. AD 130–201) brought the theory of the humours together with the theory of physiognomy, making a serious attempt not only to relate the physique of a man to his character, but also the balance of the humours to his temperament.

These theories were repeated, elaborated and discussed at length by a great number of Greek and Roman physicians and philosophers – the Stoics and Epicureans in particular. Empedocles, about 400 BC, had proposed that not only man but all things were composed of the four elements, fire, air, earth and water, brought together as the result of the rival pressures of love and hate. When this theory was combined with those of the humours and of physiognomy in general, there seemed little in man left to be understood, at least little that could not be explained by reference to the total argument.

Fanciful though all this may seem today, in the earliest stage of medicine and science it must have seemed relatively convincing. After all, the humours are very real. Cut the body anywhere and blood flows. In response to certain drugs, the body will vomit yellow bile, and under certain other circumstances evacuate black bile. Phlegm is commonly seen, especially during the cold seasons of the year (it is, remember, cold and moist) – if you have a cold, do you not blow yellow phlegm from the nose? In the spring, the blood seems

to increase – dysentery, bleeding from the nose and other haemorrhages are not uncommon. Hot, dry weather sets the yellow bile in motion – fevers have a bilious character and the skin is often yellow; and in autumn black bile dominates in the dry, cold weather.

Thus a fairly complex relationship was established between the macrocosm of the universe and the microcosm of man's organism. By the time this had occurred, certain received ideas had also grown up about appearance and character: the infinite variety of human beings was roughly categorized – most roughly into two types, those in whom the horizontal proportions were on the whole greater than the vertical ones and those in whom vertical measurements were on the whole more substantial than horizontal ones. In fact, the 'psychosomatic constitutional types' of man, to be the subject of much scientific examination two thousand years later, had made their appearance. Experiments in the 1940s were to produce evidence to suggest that lean people were on the whole more intelligent than the heavier-built. Theophrastus (c. 372–287 BC) had already asked why men of genius were on the whole lean and melancholic, dominated by black bile. He concentrated on the melancholic temperament, which particularly interested him, as he believed that geniuses were almost invariably of the melancholic type – sad and depressed in cold weather, cheerful and genial in hot, in moderate weather working at their best!

Some Arabian scholars set themselves to describe equally fully men of the three other temperaments – sanguine, phlegmatic and choleric. Modern psychosomatic studies have shown their descriptions to be by no means fictitious. In the West, respect for the great classical period of the development of medicine ensured that the theories of physiognomy and the humours survived until well into modern times. In his giant *The Anatomy of Melancholy* (1621) Robert Burton paraphrased the writings on the subject by most of the great theoreticians, in the cause of explaining the effects and cures of melancholy, 'an inbred malady in every one of us'. His descriptions of the qualities of the humours sum up the theory more than adequately:

Phlegmatic people, he writes, are

> sleepy, sayeth Savonarola, dull, slow, blockish, asslike . . . they are much given to weeping, and delight in water, ponds, pools, rivers, fishing, fowling etc. They are pale of colour, slothful, apt to sleep, heavy; much troubled with the head-ache, continual meditation, and muttering to themselves; they dream of waters, that they are in danger of drowning, and fear such things. They are fatter than others . . . of a muddy complexion, apter to spit, sleep, more troubled with rheum than the rest, and have their eyes still fixed on the ground.

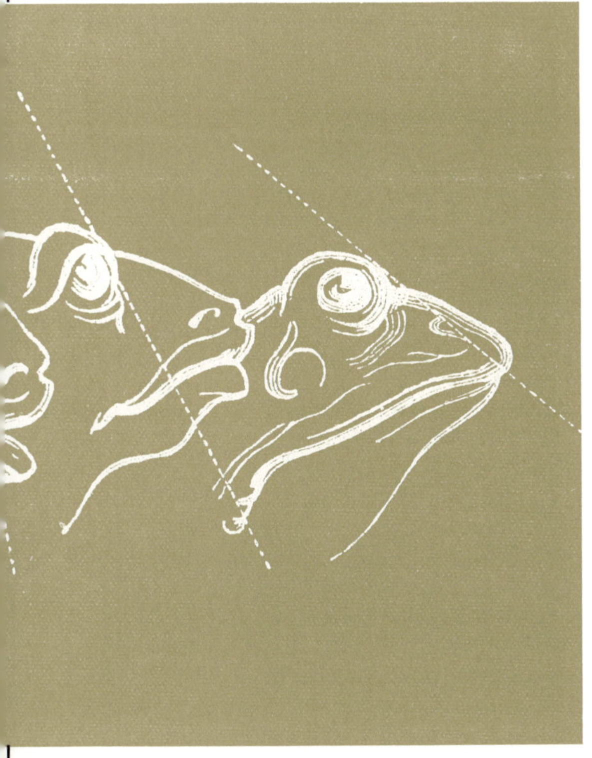

In the 19th century the caricaturist Jean Ignace Isidore Gérard, known as Grandville, illustrated the possible evolutionary link between a classical Greek face and that of a frog. His *Métamorphoses du jour* (1828) portrayed men with the faces of animals.

Das Achte Buch /
Das Erste Capitel.
Von dem Sal Solis.

Unter naß/ trocken/ heiß vnd kalt/
Wie fix vnd flüchtig hab ein gstalt/
Vermerck bey Man vnd Weibs figur/
Weiß ist der/ der erkennt d Natur.

Nim Wasser das aus Gold bereit/
Wie Archidoxa dich bescheidt/
Vier teil/ dasselbig digerier
Halb ein/ vnd darnach distillier

L. Thurneysser, in his *Quinta Essentia* of 1574 (above), illustrated the four humours and their relationship to the zodiacal signs. In *The Anatomy of Melancholy* (1621), ostensibly a medical work, Robert Burton claimed that melancholy is 'an inbred malady in every one of us', and contrived to apply his theory to all living persons.

The sanguine

are commonly ruddy of complexion, and high-coloured . . . the veins of their eyes be red, as well as their faces. They are much inclined to laughter, witty and merry, conceited in discourse, pleasant if they be not far gone, much given to music, dancing, and to be in women's company. They meditate wholly on such things, and think they see plays, dancing, and such like sports. . . . Wolfius relates a country fellow called Brunsellius, subject to this humour, that being by chance at a sermon, saw a woman fall off from a form half asleep; at which object most of the company laughed; but he, for his part, was so much moved that for three whole days after he did nothing but laugh; by which means he was much weakened, and worse a long time following.

Choleric subjects

are bold and impudent and of a more hare-brained disposition, apt to quarrel and think of such things – battles, combat and their manhood; furious, impatient in discourse, stiff, irrefragable and prodigious in their tenets; and if they be moved most violent, outrageous, ready to disgrace, provoke any, to kill themselves and others.

Melancholy people

are usually sad and solitary, and that continually and in excess, more than ordinary suspicious, more fearful, and have long, sore and most corrupt imaginations; cold and black, bashful, and so solitary that (as Arnoldus writes) they will endure no company; they dream of graves still, and dead men, and think themselves bewitched or dead; if it be extreme, they think they hear hideous noises, see and talk with black men and converse familiarly with devils, and such strange chimeras and visions, or that they are possessed by them, that somebody talks to them or within them.

The seventeenth-century authors of the West, in a great number of books on physiognomy, relied (as Burton did) almost exclusively on the ancient authors, though they sometimes embroidered considerably and had their own eccentricities of emphasis. Thomas Hill, in *A Pleasant History declaring the Whole Art of Physiognomy, orderly uttering all the*

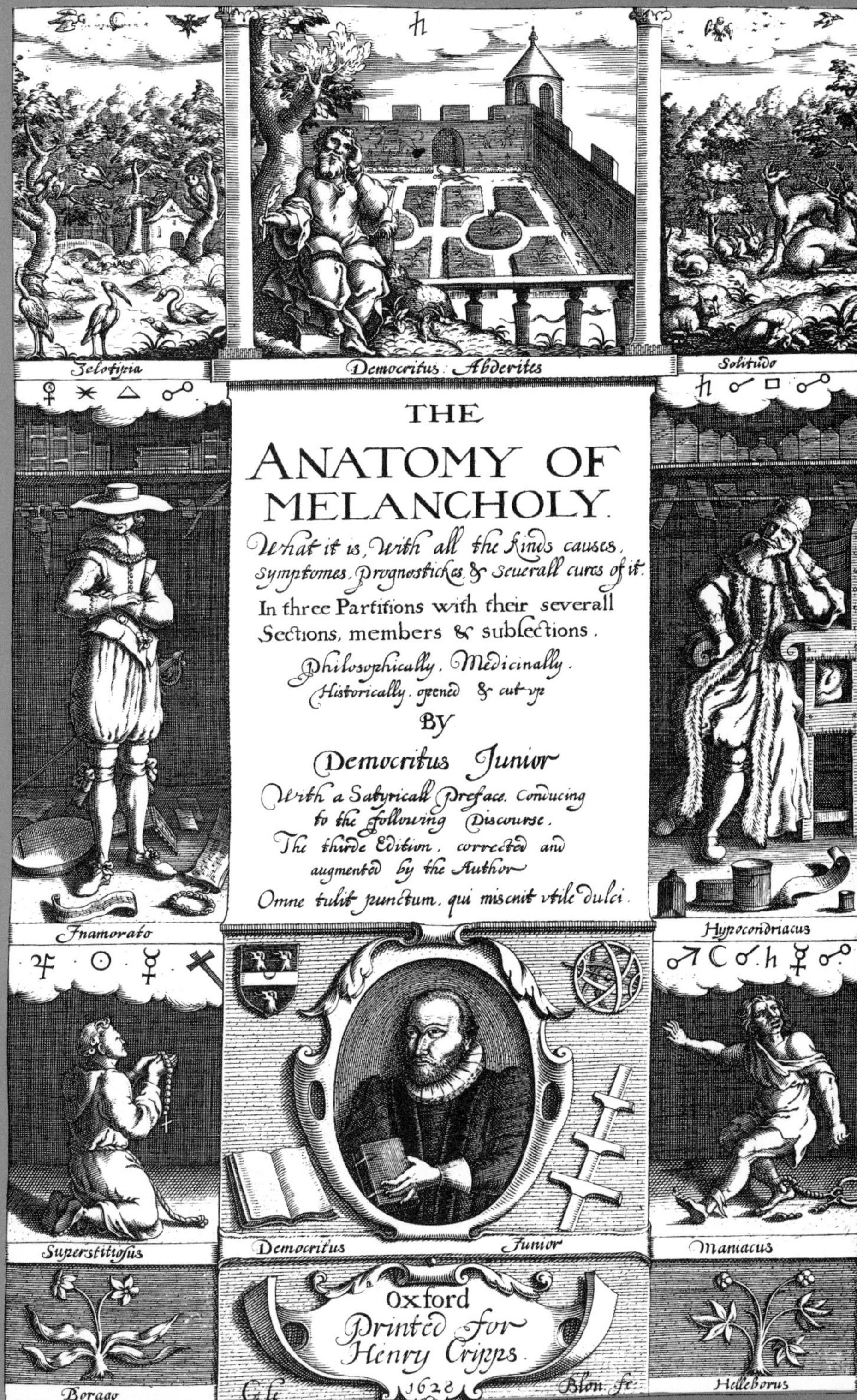
Zelotipia
Democritus Abderites
Solitudo
THE
ANATOMY OF
MELANCHOLY.
What it is, With all the kinds causes,
symptomes, Prognostickes, & severall cures of it.
In three Partitions with their severall
Sections, members & subsections.
Philosophically, Medicinally,
Historically, opened & cut vp
By
Democritus Junior
With a Satyricall Preface, conducing
to the following Discourse.
The thirde Edition, corrected and
augmented by the Author
Omne tulit punctum, qui miscuit vtile dulci.
Inamorato
Hypocondriacus
Superstitiosus
Democritus
Junior
Maniacus
Oxford
Printed for
Henry Cripps
1628
Cle
Blon fe.
Borago
Helleborus

Special Parts of Man from the Head to the Foot (1613), paid much attention, for instance, to the knees:

Such persons having the knees formed slender, are known to be effeminate . . . the knees full of fat flesh and fat do indicate a fearful person, liberal, vain and of small labour. The knees lean and thin of flesh do argue a strong person, bold, well enduring labour, secret, and a good goer on foot. Knees which in themselves are turned, as they (in a manner) do knock together are applied to a feminine property. . . .

But that was at the popular end of the market. There were more serious treatises, rivalling Burton's, and some of them earlier: Juan de Huarte's book relating physiology and psychology, for instance, first published in 1575 and translated into English by Richard Carew in 1594 as *The Examination of Men's Wits*. Based on Galen, the book examined the ancient proposition that cold had a bad effect on the mind, while dryness increased understanding, moisture made the brain pliant and impressionable and helped the memory, and heat was the source of imagination. It followed that if the qualities were to produce a major mind, they must be mixed in suitable proportions. Huarte believed that there were certain outward signs of these proportions. Baldness, for instance, was an infallible sign of too much heat and therefore too active an imagination; a moist hand or too much moisture in the eyes meant that the subject was likely to sway too much from one opinion to the other; cold hands or feet meant an almost certain paucity of brain.

Huarte took his theory to some lengths, including advice on the breeding of children. Since women were in general cold and moist (lacking, of course, in understanding and imagination) while men were hot and dry, fertility depended on a rather careful measurement of the degree of that heat and dryness, that cold and moisture, and the matching of those degrees in the copulating couple:

A woman cold and moist in the first degree, whose signs we said were to be wily, ill-conditioned, shrill-voiced, spare-fleshed and black and green coloured, hairy and ill-favoured, shall easily conceive by a man that is ignorant, of good conditions, who hath a well-sounding and sweet voice, much white and supple flesh, little hair, and well-coloured and fair of countenance.

J.K. Lavater (1741–1801, above) focused modern attention on the importance of physical appearance in interpreting character, but the furtherance of fashion continued to have a distorting effect – literally, in a machine of 1820 (opposite).

The problem of measuring the precise degree of the 'qualities' was an interesting one; one way of doing so, in man, was an examination of the temperature of the testicles or 'cods'. This did not necessarily mean an intimate medical examination, for there were other physiological signs. As Huarte pointed out:

The voice and speech much discovereth the temperature of the cods. That which is big and somewhat

sharp giveth token that a man is hot and dry in the third degree: and if the same be pleasant, amiable and very delicate, it purporteth little heat and much moisture, as appeareth in the gelded. A man who hath moist united with heat will have the same high but pleasant and shrill. Who so is hot and dry in the third degree is slender, hard and rough-fleshed; the same composed of sinews and arteries, and his veins big. Contrariwise, to have much flesh, smooth and tender, is show of much moisture: by means whereof it extendeth and enlargeth out the natural heat. The colour of the skin, if the same be brown, burned, blackish green and like ashes, yieldeth sign that a man is in the third degree of hot and dry; but if the flesh appeareth white and well-coloured, it argueth little heat and much moisture.

The hair and beard are a mark also not to be overslipped: for these two approach very near to the temperament of the cods. And if the hair be very black and big, and especially from the ribs down to the navel, it delivereth an infallible token that the cods partake much of hot and dry; and if these grow some hair also upon the shoulders, the same is so much the more confirmed. But where the hair and beard are of chestnut colour, soft, delicate and thin, it inferreth not so great plenty of heat and dryness in the cods.

The matching of men and women not only 'temperamentally', but also physically, was not peculiar to the West. In the *Kama Sutra* of Vatsyayana, composed between the first and fourth centuries AD, men and women were divided into three classes according to the size of their genitals – the men as hares, bulls and horses, and the women as female deer, mares or elephants. The ideal union was between like and like: that between a woman and a man with larger genitals than hers was known as high union, and with a man with smaller genitals as low union.

These categories were devised relative to sexual pleasure rather than the possibility of conception; and each of the categories was itself divided: the horse and the mare enjoyed high union, but the horse and the deer the highest union. On the other hand, the hare making love with the mare was in low union, and with the elephant in lowest union. Both men and women were also categorized as being of small, middling or intense sexual passion, and as being 'short-timed', 'moderate-timed' or 'long-timed'. Thus the union of hare and deer, of the same degree of passion and of timing, was likely to be the most perfect, while that of – say – 'long-timed' and 'short-timed' hare and elephant would be fairly disastrous. As with other physiological and physiognomical theories, this was all based on common sense (though the emphasis on genital size was misleading). As far as can be discovered, no Western writer considered the matching of lovers for the purposes of pleasure alone as being of the slightest importance – an aspect, no doubt, of the legacy of the Christian Church's teaching that sex as pleasure is not to be emphasized. As St Paul says, it is better to marry than burn; but only just.

It was perhaps Johann Kaspar Lavater, a Zurich clergyman, who focused modern scientific attention on physiognomy, with a book published in 1772 in which he contended that it was entirely possible to tell a man's character from his face and general presence. As he pointed out, 'there is not a man on earth who is not daily influenced by physiognomy . . . not a man who does not, more or less, the first time he is in company with a stranger, observe, estimate, compare and judge him, according to appearances.'

Influenced by him and his book, which was illustrated by almost six hundred portraits of subjects, several respectable scientists took up the challenge. Peter Camper, a Dutch anatomist, tried to measure intelligence by 'facial angles'; Sir Charles Bell, a Scottish anatomist, studied expression. The President of the Italian Society of Anthropology, Paolo Mantegazza, claimed in *Physiognomy and Expression* (1894) that moral, intellectual and physiological judgments could be made after a study of facial expression.

During the late nineteenth century numbers of instruction manuals were published which aimed to teach the layman to read the character of his neighbour in his face. C. Hartley's *Face and Form* (1885) was one of them, instructing the reader how to

Paolo Mantegazza allied natural expressions to certain temperaments: scorn, fright, wonder, hypocrisy, stupidity, intelligence, cynicism, irony, arrogance, modesty. . . .

observe the forehead, eyes and eyebrows, nose, mouth, lips and chin, hair, hands and form. Special attention was directed to the forehead:

> Observe the forehead more than any other part of the countenance when you would discover what a man is by nature, or what he may become according to his nature, and the motionless, closed mouth when you would know what he actually is. . . . The longer the forehead, the more comprehension; short, wrinkled, knotty, regular foreheads, pressed in on one side, and saw-cut foreheads with intersecting wrinkles, are incapable of durable friendship.

Even the eyebrows revealed valuable clues as to character– 'wild and perplexed eyebrows denote a corresponding mind . . . wild eyebrows are never found in a mild, ductile, pliable character. Men of intellectual force possess thick, shaggy brows' – though the observer was invited to note that 'some persons have spoiled their eyebrows by rubbing them very much in washing'.

One pleasant byway of physiognomy which survived into the nineteenth century, but had much earlier origins, was the study of moles and birthmarks – 'the stars of the body' – which, it was alleged, revealed character according to where they were placed. There was a strong connection between that theory and astrology; the positions of the planets at the time of birth were said to determine the positions of the moles. Indeed, the seventeenth-century astrologer William Lilly would prove his accuracy as an astrologer by working out a client's 'figure', or birth chart, and then informing him of the positions of the moles on his body. He taught this trick to a pupil, one John Humphrey:

> As we were at supper [Lilly wrote in his autobiography], a client came to speak with [Humphrey]; I called him before he set his figure . . . and instantly acquainted him how he should discover the moles or marks of his client; he set his figure, and presently discovers four moles the querant had; and was so overjoyed therewith that he came tumbling down the stairs, crying 'Four, by God, four, by God, I will not take one hundred pounds for this one rule!'

As late as 1894 textbooks on moles and birthmarks were still being published. Maud Wheeler wrote in one of them of such matters as the colour of the moles – honey-coloured ones being lucky, 'mitigating evil while confirming good', while dark moles, especially black ones, intensified evil. The moles placed on the face were most important and revealed much. For instance, a mole in the centre of the forehead showed that 'much interest will be felt for the opposite sex', while a mole under the middle of the right eye showed that the subject 'is vain and proud, but much loved. She will be fortunate, but if black her servants will prove dishonest and she may unintentionally cause the death of someone dear to her. To a man it announces a happy marriage but a short life.'

Such suggestions apart, during the nineteenth century and on into the twentieth certain scientists took physiognomy with a seriousness quite equal to that of the Greeks. C. G. Carus (1853) and F. W. Beneke (1878) in Germany, N. Pende (1924), J. Giovanni (1927) and G. Viola (1933) in Italy, and L. Rostan (1828) in France published major contributions to the study.

Among other theories it was suggested – in another recapitulation of a theory first suggested by Hippocrates – that certain diseases were more likely to attack people of certain body types. There appears to be fairly solid evidence to show, for instance, that people with slender, narrow-chested bodies are more likely to suffer from tuberculosis, pneumonia, dyspepsia and disorders of the brain, while those who are fleshy, broad, wide-chested may be more predisposed to diabetes, nephritis, apoplexy, dropsy, cerebral haemorrhage, cardiac disease and gall-bladder disease.

Ernst Kretschmer, in 1926, advanced the view that psychotic mental disorders could be related to specific body types in the same way. Schizophrenic illnesses seemed to tend to overtake the lean, while cycloid illnesses – characterized by oscillation between excitement and depression – were more prevalent in the stout. A vast number of influential authors from various countries produced evidence to support his view, though others disputed it.

One of the difficulties of following the many strains of argument attempting to draw conclusions from the physical characteristics of human beings is that different scientists tended to invent different terms in which to describe the various body types. For *leptomorph*, *mesomorph* and *eurymorph* (roughly, thin, normal and fat), for instance, Carus (1853) coined *asthenic*, *athletic* and *phlegmatic*; Brugsch (1918) endearingly used the simple terms *narrow-chested*, *normal*, and *wide-chested*; Kretschmer (1925) *asthenic*, *athletic* and *pyknic*; Huter (1928) *empfindungstypus*, *krafttypus*, and *ernährungstypus*; and Sheldon (1940) *ectomorph*, *mesomorph* and *endomorph*.

So much work has been done on the various theories that it is impossible to make a fair summary; but there seems to emerge some evidence that on the whole fat people tend to be better at practical work with their hands than thin people, but to be less well educated; to be more prone to illness but less anxious by temperament; to be much less obsessional than thin people and less prone to depression, to suffer less from headaches and much less from dyspepsia, to be a good deal less irritable and less apathetic. Far fewer of them are teetotalers and rather fewer of them get married.

In the concluding chapter of *Dimensions of Personality* (1947), in which H. J. Eysenck recorded extensive research carried out with a group of distinguished colleagues, a table appears (it is slightly shortened at the bottom of this page).

There is some reason to mistrust these results. The conditions under which the sample personalities were chosen left something to be desired and the examiners failed to make any attempt to look at the changes of body-structure which often occur in a lifetime (many people lose weight or put it on, start or stop taking exercise, and so on). But there is also something obvious about the starting-point of the theories: that any person whose shape or size is unusual, whether fat or thin, large or small, may tend to develop certain personality characteristics as a result.

There are various dangers in embracing any theory of physiognomy too wholeheartedly: no one would wish to be led in the direction of the theories of Cesare Lombroso, for instance, who could infallibly spot a 'born criminal' when he saw one, for he would have a receding forehead, a flat nose, large ears, a projecting chin, would be left-handed and would not have a keen sense of smell!

It is also true that our appearance will have an immediate effect on the people we meet; just as it will affect the way we live our own lives. The tendency to judge by surface appearances may be unfortunate, but it is indisputable. The pot-luck of birth, the

	INTROVERSION	**EXTROVERSION**
Constitution	Physique: leptomorph Effort response: poor high oxygen uptake high lactate level high pulse rate	Physique: eurymorph Effort response: good low oxygen uptake low lactate level low pulse rate
Intelligence functions	High intelligence Intell./vocabulary ratio low	Low intelligence Intell./vocabulary ratio high
Persistence	Good	Bad
Speed/accuracy ratio	Low	High
Level of aspiration	High	Low
Past performance	Underrated	Overrated
Sense of humour	Does not appreciate jokes Dislikes sex jokes particularly	Does appreciate jokes Likes sex jokes particularly

Bikinis, AD 400-style.

jumbling of the genes which makes one person strikingly handsome and another strikingly ugly, has its effect throughout a lifetime. Some men, however successful, never get over the fact that they are not, generally speaking, good looking. Charles Laughton, perhaps the finest screen actor of his generation, lived miserably under the impression that he was the ugliest man in the world and underwent torture when he had to appear in scenes (in *Mutiny on the Bounty*) with the ultra good-looking Clark Gable. It is a well-known popular theory that very small men need to compensate for their lack of size and often do so by being phenomenally successful or phenomenally offensive.

But what are 'good looks'? The West may still pay lip service to Michelangelo's David and the Venus de Milo as the ideally proportioned man and woman; yet through the last thousand years or so the proportions of the Venus, certainly, would scarcely ever have tallied with those of a woman regarded as distinctly beautiful. Compare, for instance, the boyish girls gaming on the beaches of Sicily in their bikinis in AD 400, those of the fifteenth century with their s-shaped figures, tiny breasts, long oval stomachs and large feet, the opulent charms of the Venetian women of Veronese's paintings, or of Rubens's fleshy lovelies, to say nothing of the flat-chested women of the 1920s and the huge-breasted American pin-up girls of the 1940s.

And non-Western races take a radically different view of ideal physical beauty. Place the ultra-thin Western model girl before the men of those aboriginal tribes who send their adolescent girls to fattening farms in order to attain the perfect gargantuan size for ideal beauty, and she would be a laughing-stock. Almost certainly the regard for fat women in some underdeveloped countries relates to the conception of them as members of families in which the women are well fed and do not have to work. Do the men who are attracted to them because of their evident singularity in that respect find them physically attractive? But, on the other hand, was Twiggy, the ultra-slim almost breastless model girl of the 1960s, ever an object of desire for men? She was admired by fashion photographers and became an image of elegance and beauty – but few people can have regarded her as very sensual or as a 'sex object' (the no doubt repellent fate to which so many women aspire).

The binding of the feet of infant Chinese girls to keep them tiny, the flattening of the foreheads of South American Indian girls with boards, the insertion of wooden splints into the lips or the stretching of the neck by means of rings – all may seem absurd, unattractive, or cruel to Westerners. But what of the Western women who force their feet into narrow, pointed shoes with heels raised at a permanent angle of 45 degrees? Or the nineteenth-century woman who laced her waist almost too tightly to be borne? What of the woman who thirty years ago might have

Do you see your ideal partner? Twiggy juxtaposed with *Pumping Iron's* Arnold Schwarzenegger, Miss World contestants with the wrestler 'Big Daddy'.

worn an enormously padded brassiere or had injections of silicone to enlarge her breasts?

Very few of these excesses in fact please men. The woman who even today laces herself into a tight corset obviously needs that corset, and not only for reasons of size – diet or strengthened stomach muscles will do as much. She wants to feel 'held in' and to that extent protected; the corset is a signal of inhibition as surely as the rejection of the brassiere by so many women in the 1970s was a signal of 'liberation', of whatever kind.

We live in a curious age. Most men and women are on the side of moderation in food and drink, of reasonable exercise (for the sake of health as well as looks); in theory, we are well on the way – in those fortunate countries in which most people are reasonably prosperous – to 'the body beautiful' as the norm.

Yet those bodies are constantly changing and not always predictably. While in 1894 the 'ideal' American woman was 5′ 4″ tall, weighed 140 pounds and was plump, in 1947 she was two inches taller, had lost weight and was thinner everywhere except at the ankles; and in 1975 she was two inches taller again, seven pounds lighter and generally thinner (34″ round the hips as opposed to 37″ in 1947 and 38″ in 1894; 19″ round the thighs as opposed to 22″ in 1894).

This increase in height is general throughout most of the world and there seems to be no dietary reason for it. Japanese children are now more than two inches taller, in general, than they were ten years ago and in Norway (where records have been kept for many years) there has been an average increase of something like a quarter of an inch in height every decade since 1760.

It is astonishing that the pull towards health, fitness and reasonably good looks has been tough enough to survive the continual campaign of advertisers pressuring Western men and women to eat more chocolate bars, drink more beer and otherwise indulge their

overfed bodies. As a result of indulgence, through the admen's imagination, everyone will automatically become rich and famous, handsome or beautiful, surrounded by lovely people with fast cars. The refusal of so many people to indulge in utter gluttony is a mark of the power of our need to look good.

In what that need consists is highly debatable. The vanity of men and women is served, certainly, by clothes, which look better on a good body. But sexual attractiveness is also a large factor and at least one authority asserts that both men and women now take more care of their bodies because 78 per cent of all Western couples (as opposed to only 34 per cent fifty years ago) now make love with the light on.

Some bodies – perhaps most – can at best only approximate to the ideal. Others are so tortured by their owners, for whatever reason, that they wildly overshoot the ideal and fall on the side of the distorted. The psychological obsession of *anorexia nervosa*, the dreadful compulsion to slim which can reduce some young girls to a starvation diet, is one side of the coin; the other shows the men or women with a glandular illness, or with a compulsion to eat which is in some cases so strong that they have actually had their teeth bonded together so that they can only take liquid, in a frantic effort to lose weight.

A few men put on weight for 'professional' reasons, like the Japanese sumo wrestlers, who can weigh as much as 350 pounds (yet conspire to remain extremely light on their feet). Those who study body-building, either in order to take part in certain sports or for narcissistic reasons, can also distort their bodies: weight-lifters have enormous shoulders and thighs, swimmers too have strong shoulder muscles (which can be most unattractive in women), professional tennis players sometimes develop the muscles of their playing arm to an extent which makes them appear positively one-sided.

The men who compete in male beauty competitions are among those who end up with a body distorted on the wrong side of the ideal. Their motive is obscure: they may triumph as 'Mr Universe', which in itself must be an achievement of a sort; but the many thousands who never reach even the lower slopes of that peak must have some reason for hours of painful effort. Oddly, most women tend to find the over-muscular man unattractive, despite the legends of the strong hero who gets the girl. There has been a homosexual tone about some male beauty competitions, though again this is not the reason for the extensive training involved. In the average gymnasium a certain amount of competition is inevitably involved. But the fact is very easily forgotten that the size of a muscle must match the general proportion of the limb, or of the body as a whole. As with the humours, proportion is all.

Perhaps the ultra-muscular male is trying to compensate for a deficiency in some other area of his life: poor grades at school, clumsiness at games? Perhaps he is shy or introverted, or has problems with his sex life? The average man who combines body-building with general exercises is probably vain and at the same time wants to keep fit. Well, vanity to that extent is a venial sin.

Women do not have the problem of distorting their body in order to win modern beauty competitions. The criteria for success – as Miss Blackpool or Miss Atlantic City, Miss France, Miss Australia or Miss World – are obvious, though the goal is also somewhat obscure both in promise and in reward. It is not a question of producing a body which is as nearly as possible approximate to some ideal womanly measurements (in the 1980s these would probably be in the region of 35″, 24″, 34″) but one which vaguely matches the general idea of what a beautiful woman should look like.

The very idea of the ideally beautiful woman is a nonsense (a degrading, merely amusing or flattering nonsense according to where one is sitting). Who would deny that Katharine Hepburn is one of the most attractive women in the world, though far from the accepted idea of physical beauty? Yet millions of television viewers all over the Western world watch with bated breath as a number of girls parade in dress and undress, answer a few undemanding questions and are then judged more or less exactly like cattle.

The body speaks in a general but limited fashion about the being that inhabits it. After all, we have only taken it on a lifelong lease and there is only a certain amount you can tell about a tenant by looking at his house. The general size and shape of your body may or may not indicate a predilection for tuberculosis or laughter, innate intelligence or an aptitude for all-in wrestling. Its physical shape is important, perhaps, at first meeting; but it is astonishing how quickly you forget the physical attributes of your friends, or, perhaps sadly, your lovers.

Our bodies are much more important to ourselves than to most other people. Models or film-stars may cultivate their bodies as a landscape gardener cultivates the surroundings of a house, enlarging the shrubbery here, rounding a curve here. For most of us, however, our bodies are machines for living in: by far the most important thing is not their appearance, but how well we can maintain them. An efficient and healthy body is the only sort of good-looking body that counts.

8 How young do you feel?

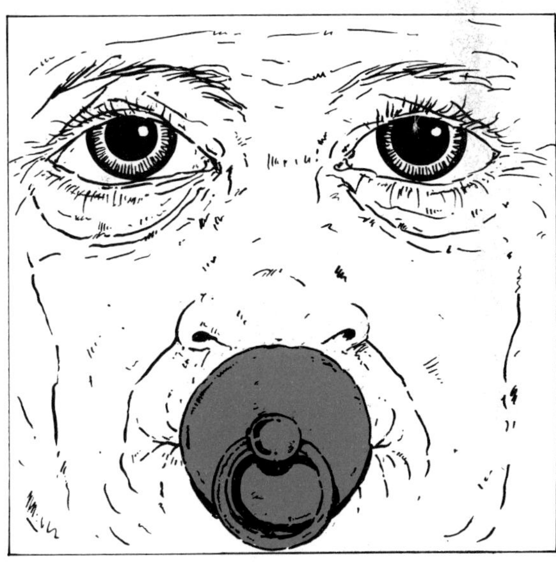

An 80-year-old can learn a new language as quickly as a 15-year-old. The East associates age with wisdom. And yet in the West a man can be too old at forty. How do you keep young – whatever the clock says?

VARIOUS ATTEMPTS HAVE been made to divide life into different periods. Shakespeare's 'ages of man' is one. But we commonly allude to other people as 'children', 'young people', 'middle-aged', 'elderly', 'old' – while on the whole disliking such epithets when they are applied to ourselves. Only a few of these terms, such as 'adolescents', refer to an actual physical condition; the others are extremely vague and often disliked by those to whom they are applied. Few people between thirty and forty like to be referred to as 'middle-aged', though the term would be accurate enough; and there seems now to be no acceptable word or phrase for those between the ages of, say, eight and eighteen: 'children' is thought insulting and 'young people' patronizing.

There is no 'golden age', of course. The old saying that 'schooldays are the happiest days of your life' affronts the intelligence of any schoolchild, and always has. (The only thing to be said about the phrase is that, if it is true, then the child in question is likely to have an exceptionally miserable life.)

Despite the fact that anyone who is no longer young speaks of 'youth' with something approaching a sneer, the cult of youth has become, in recent years, rather alarming. The feeling that once you are forty life is more or less over, that you must make your reputation or maneuver yourself into a position of power by your early thirties or it will be too late, is widely prevalent. It has resulted in many ridiculous actions, particularly in the world of big business – the sale of *toupées* has mounted, plump middle-aged men force themselves into trendy suits and ages are busily falsified for the gossip columns.

The reasons for the trend are various. It may have something to do with the enormous fortunes made by very young men in the pop music industry and the huge empires they have established. But it is not, on the other hand, solely a phenomenon of the twentieth century: the ancient Egyptians devised treatments supposed to transform old men into young men and the Greeks and Romans believed that one of the most enviable properties of the gods was that they could postpone old age.

Some of the reasons for the search for the fountain of youth are obvious. Apart from the fear of death, it has often been the general belief that old age can only offer weakness, impotence, incontinence and a fading of the mental powers. Naturally there are certain physical consequences of advanced age which are inescapable: compared to a person of thirty, a seventy-five-year-old has 70 per cent of the heart output, but only 56 per cent of the brain weight, 55 per cent of the strength of hand grip, 40 per cent of the maximum oxygen intake during exercise, and 36 per cent of the taste buds.

On the other hand an eighty-year-old can learn a foreign language for the first time as speedily and efficiently as a fifteen-year-old, and there are many examples to show that creative power can remain undiminished: Verdi wrote perhaps his best opera, *Falstaff*, when he was eighty; Tolstoy went on writing successfully into his eighties; Titian painted magnificently in his nineties. Precedents are not confined to the arts. General de Gaulle was sixty-eight when he became President of France in 1958 and he continued to steer his country through enormously complex political crises for over a decade; Churchill first became Prime Minister at sixty-five and was Prime Minister at eighty.

Comparatively little is known about the process of ageing. Many popular beliefs are mistaken: for some time, for instance, there was a fashion for the old and rich to be injected with supplies of male hormones under the illusion that this would keep them young. But this is not the case. Indeed, eunuchs on average tend to live longer than other men. There is some sign that there are genetic influences; but accident and disease make statistics difficult to correlate.

In the East, age has generally been associated with wisdom. Westerners tend to take the view that experience does not necessarily teach some men very much and have (especially within the past thirty or forty years) tended to neglect the old disgracefully, viewing every person whose physique has deteriorated as unworthy of anything other than minimal medical attention. This neglect can cause what some psychologists have called 'psychological death'. People who, after a lifetime of work, have found themselves suddenly unemployed and have in addition had to bear the normal shocks of age – change of environment, the death of contemporaries and society's apparent view that they are of no practical use – have convinced themselves that they would be 'better off dead'; the first step to senility.

An essential, if you are to avoid psychological ageing, is to keep in touch with the

Hairpieces subtract the years and, it seems, alter the personality. Opposite: Picasso at 84, Verdi at 87, both actively creative in old age, defied accepted processes of ageing.

'new' – to continue to read the newspapers with attention and to follow political and social developments, or at least those in which you have always been interested. It is equally important to make young friends, not to live in the past.

About that sad case, the 'old' young man or woman, there is little to be said. It seems a fact that some people are born to age prematurely, psychologically if not physically. There are various roots for this: often apparently insurmountable, as when someone is placed in a position of great authority and responsibility at an early age. But this fate seems to overcome those who are interested chiefly in a material goal – whether of money or power. On the whole, the placing of human beings in groups according to age says little about them, except statistically; the saying that 'you are as old as you feel' is one of the more reliable truisms.

Grouping by age is a statistical game played a great deal by census-takers in modern society; and in some cases some interesting facts are revealed. There are, for instance, some countries populated mainly by somewhat elderly people and others in which the accent is on youth. In Tunisia, Dominica and Togo, for instance, almost 50 per cent of the population is under fourteen, while only between two and six per cent are over sixty. Kenya, Libya, Morocco, Syria, Belize, Honduras, Nicaragua and Surinam are other 'young' countries in this respect.

On the other hand, Monaco (perhaps understandably) has a population 21 per cent of which is aged between sixty and seventy-four, and 9 per cent over seventy-five. Cyprus, Austria, Belgium, the Channel Islands, Czechoslovakia, East and West Germany, and Luxembourg are 'old' countries. The UK also has a current tendency to middle age: 24 per cent of its inhabitants are under fourteen, but 18 per cent between forty-five and fifty-nine, and 14 per cent between sixty and seventy-four. In the same categories, the figures for the USA are 28 per cent, 16 per cent and 10 per cent, and for the USSR, 30 per cent, 13 per cent and 11 per cent.

Nevertheless, these are arbitrary groupings. Few people avoid at least a momentary pang on, say, their thirtieth birthday; but the elderly person who, mentally and emotionally, still feels in his teens is much more common than used to be the case.

There are some simple guidelines to a hearty old age. Naturally, you must come to terms with any physical limitations. Some men and women can still jog or play tennis in their seventies; for others this may be impossible or unwise. But all except the very severely handicapped can take a certain amount of exercise (even isometric exercises, involving muscle contraction without body-movement, are better than nothing), and it is important to keep moving. Working in the garden is excellent; and at least get out of the house every day if you can.

Try not to lose interest in food. Vary your diet and try to take the right food for the various vitamins you need. At the same time, watch your weight! Unless you are ill, the less fat you carry the better. *Don't* get worried, as so many elderly people do, by the spectre of constipation. You may not need to move your bowels every day, and three days without a visit to the lavatory doesn't mean necessarily that you have any problem. And if you feel constipated, don't rush for a laxative; eat more 'roughage' (wholemeal bread and cereal, for instance); if that doesn't work, consult your doctor.

Nothing is more irritating than the failure of your senses, particularly your sight and hearing. Visit an oculist at least once a year if your sight is weakening and see your doctor if you are beginning to hear less well. It is very likely that all the doctor will need to do is syringe your ears to clear surplus wax; but a discreet hearing-aid is better than the irritation of having to ask everyone to repeat everything.

Finally, be careful in your movements (most accidents to the elderly occur in their own homes), keep warm, especially at night; and don't worry if you don't need as much sleep as you used to. A good book or a radio at your bedside are better than sleeping pills, for the only real danger of sleeplessness is boredom.

9 Coming to terms with age

How old are you,

and how old do you feel?

Test yourself: does TV rule your life?

. . . do you keep a dog? . . .

is every other motorist a fool? . . .

when did you last see your dentist? . . .

are you too bored for words?

THIS TEST FOR the elderly falls into five sections. The first covers general questions devised to cover your attitude to ageing; the second relates to your health, the third to those living alone, the fourth and fifth to preparation for retirement or retirement.

Everyone can answer the questions in the first two sections. Then go on either to section three or to four/five. Those who live alone can answer some of the questions in sections four and five, but should omit questions 4 and 5 in the section on pre-retirement, or question 4 in the section on retirement, and make the suggested adjustment in scoring.

SECTION ONE
General

1 Do you enjoy meeting new and different people of any age?
YES/NO/SOMETIMES

2 Are you willing (a) to listen to and to think about the opinions of young people, or (b) do you dismiss their attitudes and outlook on life almost automatically?

3 Is your pattern of TV viewing (a) so set that you would find it difficult to accept an invitation out for an evening when your favourite programme is showing; or (b) would you try to compromise?

4 Do you (a) enjoy going out and look forward to it; (b) make an effort to get out, knowing that it's good for you (and you're usually glad you did); (c) make excuses to yourself and others, because you can't be bothered to move?

5 Do you actively belong to the clubs or groups you have enjoyed

over the years? Or, if you've never been 'clubbable', do you actively keep up the hobbies and interests you have had?
YES/NO

6 Assuming that your family have built their own lives, is there someone in your immediate circle that you 'keep an eye on', or take an interest in, regularly visiting them and helping them?
YES/NO

7 Do you have a household pet? (a) dog, (b) cat, (c) caged bird, (d) fish, (e) none.

8 Do you feel (a) loved and wanted by the people around you, or (b) neglected and cast aside by your family and neighbourhood?

9 Can you honestly say that you (a) contribute something to your neighbourhood activities, or (b) do you feel it is time others amused and helped you?

10 Do you (a) enjoy making or finding out about things, and/or being generally creative? Or do you (b) think at this stage in your life it's enough for you to put your feet up or lie in the sun?

11 Driving, or as a passenger in a car, do you feel other motorists are usually wrong and constantly making misjudgments?
YES/NO

12 Are you basically (a) very happy, (b) happy, (c) mixed moods, (d) miserable, more often than not?

SECTION TWO
Health

1 Believing in taking as much exercise as is comfortable for you at this particular stage in your life, do you
(a) accept the fact that you aren't as young as you were, but keep up in a modified form any physical activities you've enjoyed – golf, swimming, ballroom dancing, walking or whatever?
(b) leave all that to younger folk, but continue to dig your garden, or do a fair bit of housework and walking?
(c) sit around as much as possible, artfully contriving that others do jobs in the garden or round the house; feel it's a bit undignified to be too active at your age?

2 How important is diet? (a) very; (b) you eat what you like, as you always have done.

3 Have you cut down on sweet foods and those with a high cholesterol content?
YES/NO

4 Do you (a) worry continually about your health; (b) worry somewhat, from time to time; (c) feel as fit as a fiddle and never think about it; (d) try to be aware that you need to watch your health?

5 Do you have regular check-ups with your doctor, optician and dentist?
YES/NO

6 At a dinner party, when the hostess produces a strange dish you haven't encountered before, do you (a) accept it, eager to try it; (b) make a discreet enquiry about its contents, then, if it seems happily digestible, accept it eagerly; (c) decline even to sample it?

7 Can you honestly say you seldom if ever moan to others about your health or how unwell and miserable you feel?
YES/NO

8 Do you (a) worry if you can't sleep well; (b) accept that you may not need as much sleep as when you were younger and provide yourself with a good bedside book?

9 Do you (a) watch your weight

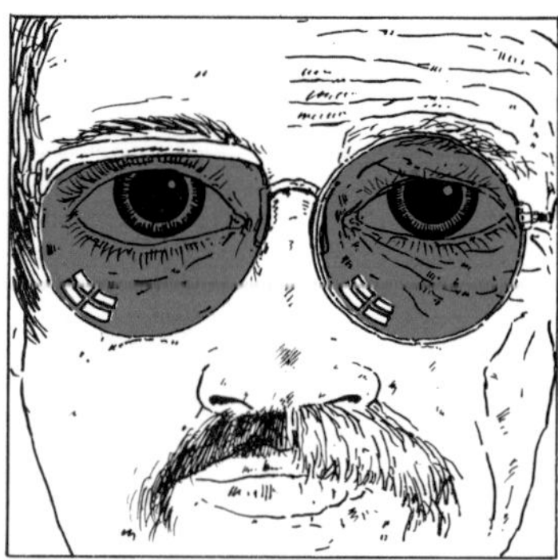

carefully; (b) take the occasional crash diet; (c) never climb onto the scales until your doctor makes you?

10 Do you follow a basic but flexible daily routine which includes a certain amount of physical activity?
YES/NO

SECTION THREE
If you live alone

1 Do you enjoy the company of good neighbours and exchange regular visits?
YES/NO

2 Are you sure that the security of your house is as good as it can be?
YES/NO

3 Are you on good day-to-day speaking terms with the milk-man, postman, paper-boy, and do the local police know you live alone?
YES/NO

4 Do you believe that the main essentials in old age are eating well and sensibly, and keeping warm in winter?
YES/NO

5 Can you honestly say you take good care of yourself?
YES/NO

6 Is there someone you can turn to if you feel lonely?
YES/NO

7 Do you enjoy going to the local shops?
YES/NO

8 Do you still enjoy light-hearted flirtations and jokes with members of the opposite sex?
YES/NO

9 Do you make excuses for regular little celebrations, asking your friends to join in, and are you happy to help anyone else who has some function to organize?
YES/NO

10 Do you enjoy the company of young children, perhaps telling them stories about when you were young?
YES/NO

SECTION FOUR
Pre-retirement

1 Do you plan to develop existing activities or take up new ones when you retire?
YES/NO

2 Are you thinking carefully about that presentation from the firm or present from the family? If so, will it be related (a) to an existing spare-time interest or some new activity, or (b) will you simply settle for a clock, watch or barometer?

3 Do you anticipate your retirement with excitement?
YES/NO

4 Perhaps for the first time since your marriage, you and your partner will be together all day and every day; over a period problems may result. Are you (a) talking about this, or (b) is your attitude, 'wait and see'?

5 When you retire, will you (a) move to a smaller house, so that you'll have more time to do the things you've missed out on so far; (b) stay where you are; the children will still need their rooms when they come to stay; (c) start an entirely new life far from your present home, hoping to make new friends in new surroundings?

SECTION FIVE
In retirement

1 Do you have a full and rewarding life?
YES/NO

2 Do you (a) continue to subscribe to magazines and journals about your favourite interests, or (b) have you given them up through lack of interest?

3 Do you enjoy making small improvements to your home?
YES/NO

4 Upon retiring, did you and your partner (a) come to terms easily with the additional time you now spend together, or (b) was the settling down phase trying for both of you?

5 Do you (a) feel you still have some interesting goals to work to; or (b) feel you've 'done your bit' and can now relax; or (c) are you bored to tears – while feeling you can't do anything about the fact?

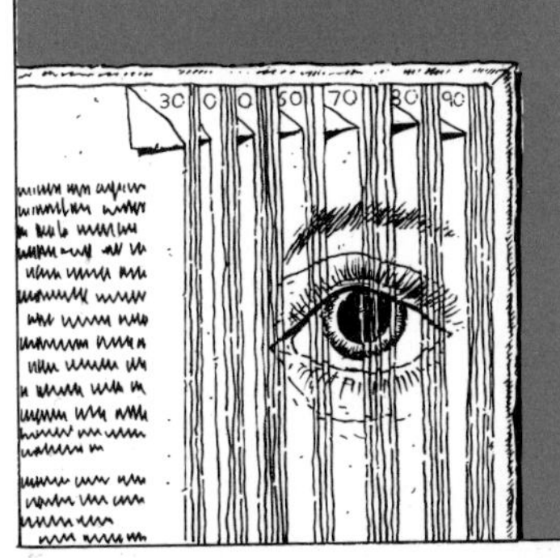

Scoring

Score as follows:

SECTION ONE
General

1 Yes = 3; No = 0; Sometimes = 1
2 (a) = 2; (b) = 0
3 (a) = 0; (b) = 2
4 (a) = 3; (b) = 2; (c) = 0
5 Yes = 3; No = 0
6 Yes = 3; No = 0
7 (a) = 4; (b) = 3; (c) = 2; (d) = 1; (e) = 0
8 (a) = 3; (b) = 0
9 (a) = 3; (b) = 0
10 (a) = 3; (b) = 0
11 Yes = 0; No = 3
12 (a) = 3; (b) = 2; (c) = 1; (d) = 0

SECTION TWO
Health

1 (a) = 3; (b) = 2; (c) = 0
2 (a) = 3; (b) = 0
3 Yes = 3; No = 0
4 (a) = 0; (b) = 1; (c) = 2; (d) = 3
5 Yes = 1; No = 0
6 (a) = 1; (b) = 2; (c) = 0
7 Yes = 2; No = 1
8 (a) = 0; (b) = 2
9 (a) = 3; (b) = 1; (c) = 0
10 Yes = 3; No = 0

SECTION THREE
If you live alone

1 Yes = 3; No = 0
2 Yes = 3; No = 0
3 Yes = 3; No = 0
4 Yes = 3; No = 0
5 Yes = 3; No = 0
6 Yes = 3; No = 0
7 Yes = 3; No = 0
8 Yes = 3; No = 0
9 Yes = 3; No = 0
10 Yes = 3; No = 0

SECTIONS FOUR AND FIVE
Pre-retirement and in retirement

The scoring for questions in these

sections is the same:

1 Yes = 3; No = 0
2 (a) = 3; (b) = 0
3 Yes = 3; No = 0
4 (a) = 3; (b) = 0
5 (a) = 3; (b) = 2; (c) = 0

Handicaps

If you are aged 75 +, interpret your full score.
If you are 65–75, deduct five marks from your score.
If you are single and retired, add 3 marks to your score.
If you are single and pre-retirement age, add 11 marks to your score.

Interpretations

High Scorers – married, 65–75; single, 100–110

Congratulations! – you're doing splendidly, living your life to the full and enjoying every minute of the extra time you've well and truly earned. The only advice we can give you is to encourage all those old people of thirty or forty to do the same! Keep up the exercise and all those compelling interests that keep your mind active and young, and you will continue to have a number of interesting experiences and adventures ahead of you. Whatever

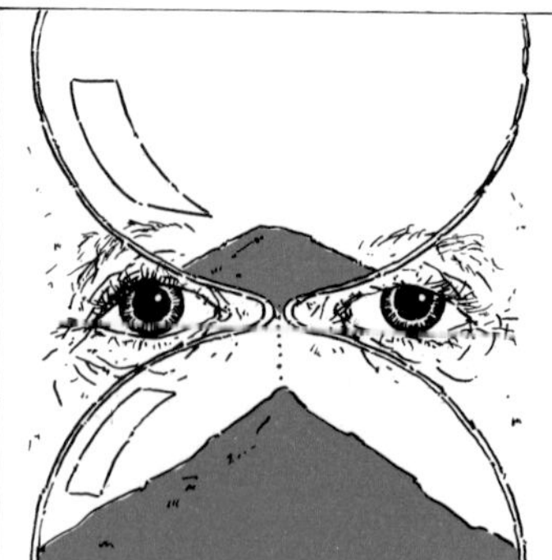

your actual age, you present to the outside world and to yourself the picture of a young man or woman, contributing as much to the community as you ever did.

Middle Scorers – married, 55–65; single, 90–100

While you are sensibly cautious, and have a basically sound attitude to growing older, it could be that you should think of spreading your wings a little more, and a little more often. It might be a good idea if you enquired about clubs and activities in the neighbourhood; people with similar interests to your own may live nearby and may be as shy as yourself about making the first move. You can probably give rather more to others than you do at the moment, and will enjoy that; don't be frightened to start a new interest if it attracts you – forget about TV for a while. And do try to maintain an interest in what's going on around you.

Low Scorers – married, 55 and below; single, 90 and below

You are a little too retiring even for someone who has retired! You still have much to offer the community, probably more than you think. When feeling 'down', you could be particularly sorry for yourself; you perhaps positively enjoy grumbling at the younger generation and continually remembering how much better things were when you were young. Is there someone to whom you can turn when you feel depressed? If not, have you ever asked yourself why? It may be you haven't been too quick to help and comfort others, or just to take part in the activities of your community. There are people around you who are worse off than yourself. Why not try to change the pattern of your life? Develop a different routine and make a few focal points in the week when you make an effort to exert yourself in some way on behalf of other people. If you are at all uncertain about your health, don't be nervous of asking your doctor for a full medical check-up, and believe what you're told; of course, everyone can fall ill and there are certain illnesses which affect the elderly. But you may be a great deal healthier than you think!

10 AC/DC?

Did the Y-chromosomes

or the X-chromosomes win the

race to make you male or female?

And win completely?

How easy is it to tell?

Is anyone wholly male or female?

WHAT APPEARS TO be the most basic human classification of all – that as male or female – is in fact one which has an almost infinite variety of shades of sexual ambiguity and emphasis. Everyone is bisexual, able to respond to people of either sex: and this is not merely the opinion of psychologists, but a physiological fact.

Every foetus starts out as female, exposed only to the female hormones – oestrogens and progesterones – produced by the mother's ovaries, the gonads. Before about six weeks after conception, the foetus is genuinely neither male nor female, with a shred of tissue that may develop either into clitoris or penis. Until a man dies, he carries within his urogenital system traces of a female womb.

At a crucial point in the growth of the foetus it must (if it is to become a male) receive a flow of male hormones, triggered by the so-called Y-chromosome in the original fertilizing sperm – an X-chromosome, on the other hand, inhibits the flow of male hormones and a girl will eventually be born. All ova (the female reproductive egg) contain an X-chromosome; some of the male sperms contain an X-chromosome, others a Y-chromosome. It is still not known what decides which will unite with the female cell.

Sometimes the process fails to work perfectly: it seems that X- or Y-chromosomes may split, or two X-chromosomes may join with one Y-chromosome. In extreme cases this has resulted in a child being born with both penis and vagina; more often a female may have a clitoris so well developed that it resembles a penis, or a male may develop breasts and lack facial hair. But apart from intersexuality, it remains true that no man or woman is wholly man or woman, totally lacking in any trace of the characteristics of the opposite sex.

For the vast majority of people there is no doubt about gender. Apart from the primary differentiation between the genitals and the obvious secondary sexual characteristics, such as facial hair and the development of the breasts, there are some strange superficial differences: at birth, a girl usually has the second finger of her hand longer than the fourth; in middle age a woman will tend to put on fat all over (though particularly on the thighs, breasts and buttocks) while a man, however lean and active, will almost always develop a pot-belly. Some physiological differences are obviously connected with woman's role as child-bearer – her pelvis is wider and set further back than man's, giving her buttocks the peculiarly female sway when she walks; her thighs are set wider apart from each other than the male's and are somewhat thicker; her belly is longer.

Differences in strength and musculature are as striking. At birth, a boy will tend to be five per cent heavier than a girl; by the time they are twenty, he will be on average twenty per cent heavier. Boys are in general taller than girls – two per cent at birth, perhaps ten per cent in maturity. Men tend to have larger feet and hands, broader shoulders and deeper chests with larger hearts and lungs; and, while at birth the sexes are equally strong, by adolescence or a little later boys are on average fifty per cent more muscular.

Most of the muscular differences are the direct result of cultures which insist on a disparate upbringing for male and female children. In the West boys still tend to have a more active, sports-orientated childhood and youth than girls and in some societies are given preference in feeding and diet. In Bali, where the men do very little physical labour and the women work extremely hard, the two sexes tend to weigh about the same; the men have very light musculature while the women have broad shoulders and small breasts; and in other respects the sexual differences are far less marked than in the West.

That the physical 'superiority' of the male is artificial seems to be underlined by the fact that many more male foetuses abort than female. Though in Western countries twenty-five per cent more males are conceived than females, only six per cent more male children are born alive. During the first year of life about 54 males die for every 46 females and at the age of 21 about 68 males die for every 32 females. In underdeveloped countries, it is true, the trend is reversed – but this is because so much less care is taken of female children than of male and even in adulthood the selfishness of the male is predominant.

The love of Greek warriors for young boys was long misunderstood and condemned by historians, but bisexuality may embrace narcissism, as when the American entertainer Julian Eltinge married himself in the trick photograph opposite.

To what extent the alleged superiority of the male in intellect is also due to the cultural inhibitions practised over many centuries is another matter. It has recently been suggested that if claims which can easily be explained in that way are ignored, there remain a few areas in which there seem to be distinct differences of ability between the sexes: males seem to be in general better at mathematics than females, seem to be more aggressive (even when they are not provided with the usual male aggressive games in childhood); girls seem to have a considerably greater natural ability to use and understand language than boys, to find creative writing

What sex are you? The sculptor Andrew Logan provides an ambiguous answer.

more natural and easier. And these abilities continue into adult life.

The determined dominance of the male in every known society is something of a mystery. It is obviously silly to assume that it is because of any natural superiority either of intellect or physique: there seems absolutely no reason why a woman-dominated society should not have developed in some part of the world. Yet the human equivalent of the hive, the Queen lording it over male workers, is unknown – those queens who may have had real power in the past have been masculinized by legend (the Queens of Egypt were often shown wearing beards, as neo-males, and Queen Elizabeth boasted that she had the 'heart and stomach of a king' but actually taxed beards in an attempt to reduce the contrast her bearded male courtiers provided with her beardless feminine self.) The women rulers who survived did so because they took care to behave as remorselessly as men.

In an age when female emancipation has not only been more generally approved (at least in theory) but has also become a cult, equality of the sexes has never been attained. Soviet Russia set out to achieve it at the time of the 1917 Revolution, when almost immediately a very radical line was taken – the law was changed to enable women to obtain divorce by consent and abortion on demand, there was free choice of marriage partners, equal pay was promised for equal work.

But after more than sixty years, women in Russia are still less equal than men. Gradually divorce laws have been tightened up again; and the award of various honours for child-bearing (the title of Mother Heroine for a woman bearing ten or more children may not seem entirely inapposite) is only one sign that women are now once more pressured towards a life in which their major task is the running of the home and the production of children.

Surveys have continued to show that women, as well as men, tend to believe that they are less intelligent, less competent, than men. When a woman does rise to a position of authority she has to prove herself not as good as but much better than her male equivalent before she is accepted; and even then her every mistake will be alleged to display a 'natural' feminine tendency to error. Though male politicians have shown often enough that they are susceptible to emotional disturbances it is still generally supposed that women are likely to make poor leaders because of the emotional changes they undergo during the menstrual cycle.

The same ingrained attitude – the male is the 'doer', the performer, the manager, while woman is the receiver, the passive one, the 'managed' – has in the past regulated sexual activity too. Nineteenth-century sex manuals insisted that 'the lady does not move'; and, if the often pervasive sexuality of the male in the same period was directed frequently towards servant-girls and prostitutes, it was more often than not because of that very attitude. The sexual frustration of women in such a male-orientated bedroom was inevitable.

Even today the need for sexual fulfilment in men and women is imperfectly understood. But one thing is clear. It used to be thought that because male sperm is from time to time released, if not in copulation then involuntarily, the sexual impulse in the male was in part the result of its pressure, and therefore irresistible. It is now thoroughly recognized (if not always by the ignorant male) that woman's need for orgasm is as strong as man's and that the difference between the nature of man's and woman's sexual drive is by no means as considerable as was once thought. Perhaps the most marked distinction noted by present theory is that the male seems to concentrate much more strongly on the achievement of orgasm, while the woman appears to take more pleasure in the build-up.

Between the obviously male male and the obviously female female (assuming, as we must, that gender does not always run parallel with sex) comes every shade of sexually orientated being. The most masculine male may well believe himself to be infinitely capable of hiding the slightest hint of female sexuality in himself, though the way in which he chooses to do this – by taking refuge, perhaps, in the ultra-male society of the sports

'Gay' and 'effeminate' have never been synonyms.

club, with often strongly sexual overtones in affectionate embraces on the field and skylarking in the changing-room – is sometimes highly suggestive.

At the other extreme come the homosexual and the transsexual – the man who is in gender masculine but whose sexual drive is directed and expressed towards other men, and the man who instinctively knows himself to be a woman, dresses as a woman and in these days sometimes undergoes a sex-change operation. The two categories also, of course, include the homosexual and transsexual woman.

This is not the place to discuss the very considerable variety of possible physiological or psychological causes of homosexuality. Briefly, there may be a predominance of female hormones in men or of male hormones in women; we would then speak of congenital homosexuality. Alternatively, the chief reason for a homosexual preference may be psychological. Yet again, homosexuality may be psychogenic. But, whatever the cause, the effect is extremely widespread. Kinsey reported that every third American man had

had at least one homosexual experience, in some cases purely experimental, the result of emergent adolescent sexuality, in other cases because of a lasting homosexual preference. More recent surveys have suggested that this would now be a very conservative estimate, while in some countries (such as Greece) homosexual activity before marriage, and sometimes after it, is very widespread indeed.

Look, then, at the shades of masculine and feminine sexuality and the various categories within each of those shades – the degree and intensity of sexual activity. And consider the fact that every kind of sexuality is 'natural' to the person who possesses it: no one can be 'cured' of homosexuality, or for that matter of other sexual behaviour which the majority of people might regard as distasteful or despicable (though a person of reasonably conventional moral sense might well be persuaded that that behaviour must be modified and controlled). It is difficult to avoid the conclusion that there is no such thing as the completely male or female human being.

Oddly enough, there are signs that this is unconsciously understood by most people. The biggest stars of the screen, for instance, have often been somewhat androgynous – Garbo, when dressed in boy's clothes, proved difficult to identify as positively masculine or feminine.

AC or DC? – three French princes of the late 16th century frame strongly masculine features in feminine coiffures and ruffs.

If the percentage of homosexuals in Western society has been variously estimated, the number of bisexuals is easy to estimate: it is one hundred per cent. And at least some psychologists have argued that until each human being recognizes and expresses his own bisexuality he cannot become a complete human being. This does not mean, of course, that bisexuality should be overtly expressed – but that, in the West, we should stop bringing up boys to be exclusively boyish and girls to be exclusively girlish. There should be no reason why boys should not play with dolls and girls with trucks; no reason why a girl should not read adventure stories and boys play 'girls'' sports; no reason why boys should not take cookery lessons and girls take woodwork in school.

In some Western countries, this is already happening; the boy who learns how to bake a cake or change a baby, the girl who learns how to mend a fuse, will obviously make a more useful and balanced adult than the child resolutely told that a particular activity is specifically 'tomboy' or 'girlish' and not for him or her. (Apart from anything else, how inconvenient for a man to have to wait about for his wife to sew a button on, or for a woman to fumble about in the dark because she does not know what a fuse looks like!)

If you grew up when boys were expected to be boys, and girls, girls, it may still seem odd that a young woman should want to drive a bus, or that a man should enjoy housework. If so, what you forget is the basic fact that men and women are only biological categories of humankind. You are a human being first, and a man or woman second – and the latter classification is increasingly less important. There is no reason at all why this fact, once you realize it, should not greatly enrich your life.

So the following test should be looked at not as an attempt to destroy your manhood or womanhood, but as an attempt to suggest that you may be less a man or woman than you think – that this may be an advantage rather than an insult.

11 So what sex are you?

If everyone is to some extent bisexual, what about you? Test yourself: do homosexuals, even slightly, embarrass you? . . . what term do you use? – 'gay', 'homosexual', 'fag'? . . . how often do you touch someone of your own sex? . . . and what about your fantasies?

ALTHOUGH WE ARE all to some extent bisexual, we are not equally able to recognize the homosexual elements in our own personalities. These questions are devised not to suggest whether you are or are not a homosexual, but in part to attempt to gauge your feelings of embarrassment about sexuality. In some acute cases such feelings may lead to open hostility to those whose sexual predilections are different to your own. It should not need saying that so elementary a test cannot reveal anything deeply significant about a single personality; but the resulting 'scores' may encourage an interesting and perhaps thought-provoking re-examination of your sexual personality.

Record the answer to each question nearest to your own attitude and total the suggested scores after reference to the table at the end. If you feel especially keenly about the answer to particular questions, add or deduct one from the stated figure.

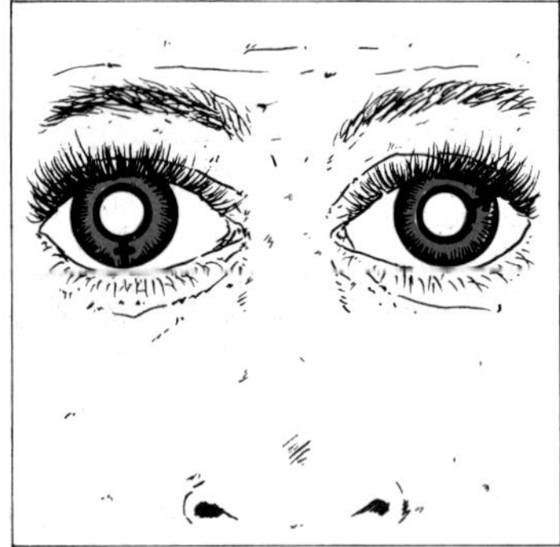

FOR BOTH SEXES

1 You had a homosexual experience in adolescence. Do you
(a) think of it as 'first love'?
(b) regard it as part of growing up?
(c) look back on it with embarrassed shame?

2 You are sitting in a sauna when a naked person of the opposite sex walks in and sits down. Do you
(a) panic and rush out?
(b) remain calm, but cover yourself with a towel?
(c) immediately start a conversation?

3 In a public place you see two young people of the same sex affectionately caressing each other. Are you
(a) embarrassed and annoyed?
(b) mildly curious?
(c) warmed by their obvious happiness?

4 You meet someone who makes it clear that he/she is homosexual. Do you
(a) feel embarrassed and wish he/she hadn't told you?
(b) feel sorry for and repelled by him/her?
(c) begin to speculate about his/her sex life?

5 If you have had a homosexual experience in adult life, did you
(a) enjoy it, but feel guilty afterwards?
(b) find it entirely repulsive and unpleasant?
(c) enjoy it without wishing to repeat it?

6 Someone of your own age and sex makes a pass at you. Do you
(a) make an excuse and leave?
(b) make it clear you are not interested, but go on talking?
(c) feel disturbed and worried?
(d) feel flattered and slightly interested?

7 Walking along the street, you are admiring the slim figure of someone in front of you, when you realize it is a person of your own sex. Are you
(a) extremely embarrassed and somewhat worried?
(b) amused at your mistake?
(c) amused and still admiring?
(d) annoyed and aggressive?

8 Your partner remarks on the sexual attractions of someone of the same sex as yourself. Do you
(a) entirely fail to comprehend?
(b) wholeheartedly agree, but fail to say so?
(c) join in enthusiastic praise?
(d) look hard for a point to criticize?

9 You have joined a group advertised as furthering a mutual interest, but discover that it is predominantly a homosexual social group. The members are lively and interesting. Do you
(a) remain a member, for your original reason?
(b) leave immediately?
(c) feel the group has an additional interest and stay with it?

10 A friend of your own age and sex is emotionally distressed and breaks down. Do you
(a) comfort him/her by making physical contact – an arm round the shoulder or an embrace?
(b) tell him/her to pull himself/herself together?
(c) feel bored and make an excuse to leave?

11 Half-asleep, you find your heterosexual fantasy world invaded by an attractive person of your own sex. Do you
(a) switch on the light and reach for a book?
(b) relax and let your unconscious continue to fantasize?
(c) make an effort to dismiss the new element from your dream?

12 An attractive person of your own sex, whom you suspect may be homosexual, invites you to take the place of a friend on a shared holiday. The accommodation comprises (1) two single rooms, (2) one room with two single beds, (3) one room with a double bed. In each case how would you sum up your thoughts?
1 (a) fine
(b) a rather 'distant' arrangement
(c) I don't think I'll bother
2 (a) I hope he/she doesn't snore
(b) how large are the beds?
(c) I don't think I'll bother
3 (a) fine
(b) fine, as long as it's a big bed
(c) I don't think I'll bother

MEN ONLY

1 You pick up a woman's magazine containing male nude pin-ups. Do you
(a) examine them with critical interest?
(b) think seriously about joining a gymnasium?
(c) find them totally uninteresting?

2 In a 'girlie' magazine, do you prefer photographs of
(a) beautiful girls beautifully photographed?
(b) the most explicit sexual poses?
(c) men and women love-making with evident enjoyment?

3 How do you refer to homosexuals in conversation: as
(a) queers, dykes, pansies, fags, or similar?
(b) homosexuals?
(c) gays?

WOMEN ONLY

1 You pick up a man's 'girlie' magazine. Looking at the photographs do you feel
(a) disgusted and repelled?

(b) irritated by the exploitation of the girls, while finding them attractive?
(c) decidedly sexually aroused?

2 An extremely handsome woman of your own age at a party reveals herself as a homosexual. Do you feel
(a) sorry for her?
(b) envious of her girl friend?
(c) fearful that she will approach you?

3 A woman candidate for political office 'comes out' as a homosexual. Would you
(a) admire her honesty to the extent of voting for her against your political judgment?
(b) withdraw your vote from her, whatever her party?
(c) vote for or against her as though she had never spoken out?

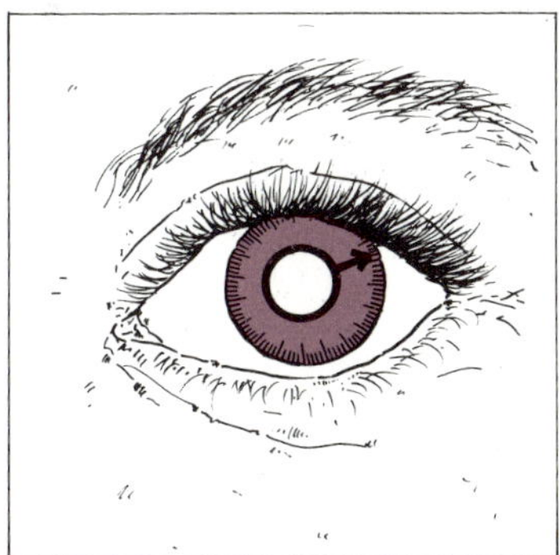

Scoring

Both sexes
1 (a) – 8 (b) – 5 (c) – 2
2 (a) – 1 (b) – 5 (c) – 8
3 (a) – 1 (b) – 4 (c) – 7
4 (a) – 2 (b) – 0 (c) – 6
5 (a) – 5 (b) – 1 (c) – 7
6 (a) – 1 (b) – 5 (c) – 3 (d) – 7
7 (a) – 3 (b) – 5 (c) – 8 (d) – 0
8 (a) – 0 (b) – 4 (c) – 7 (d) – 2
9 (a) – 6 (b) – 2 (c) – 7
10 (a) – 6 (b) – 2 (c) – 0
11 (a) – 1 (b) – 8 (c) – 3
12/1 (a) – 5 (b) – 7 (c) – 9
/2 (a) – 5 (b) – 7 (c) – 3
/3 (a) – 8 (b) – 5 (c) – 0

Men only
1 (a) – 6 (b) – 4 (c) – 0
2 (a) – 5 (b) – 1 (c) – 6
3 (a) – 1 (b) – 5 (c) – 8

Women only
1 (a) – 0 (b) – 5 (c) – 8
2 (a) – 4 (b) – 8 (c) – 2
3 (a) – 6 (b) – 3 (c) – 5

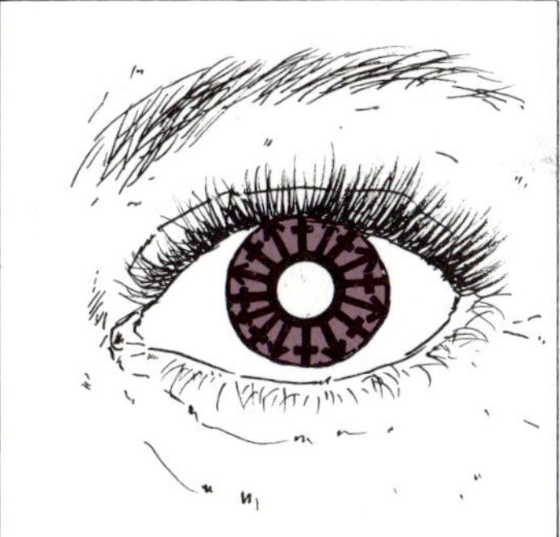

Interpretations

SCORE UNDER 65

You may be more purely heterosexual than is common, though if your score is below 25 there must be some doubt whether you have answered all the questions with complete truthfulness. In any event, if you have a very low score it may be that for some psychological reason you actively dislike and mistrust homosexuals and are on the defensive against anyone you suspect of being 'gay'. It would pay you to examine your attitude, which may result in inhibitions which will alienate you from people you would otherwise like and enjoy being with; you may suffer considerable embarrassment about sex in general (examine your score for question 2). You have a very clear-cut opinion of what constitutes 'manliness' or 'femininity': within a close relationship you may be less than considerate towards your partner because of your determination not to clean the car or pay for a meal while in male company, or to help with the housework or washing-up if you are a male. It is possible that you may be positively offensive in defending what you see as your most valuable possession – your gender. If you can persuade yourself to become more tolerant and easy in your attitudes the additional warmth and relaxation this will contribute to your personality will be rewarding in every aspect of your personal relationships.

SCORE 65–95

While by no means unsympathetic to homosexuals, you are probably slightly inhibited by conventional attitudes; you may inwardly feel that you would like to express yourself more affectionately to your friends of your own sex, but environment or upbringing perhaps militate against this – you would feel guilty if you felt yourself swinging too obviously towards a physical relationship. It is not necessarily true that the deepening of a friendship with someone of your own sex would lead to a homosexual relationship, or that you even unconsciously desire this; on the contrary, if you can persuade yourself to relax your attitude even more, this could considerably benefit your expression of your own sexuality, while also greatly strengthening the rapport and warmth you feel for friends of your own sex.

SCORE ABOVE 95

You are bisexual in the fullest meaning of the term. You have a radical attitude to sexual morality and have probably had and enjoyed homosexual experience. While you may live quite happily in a heterosexual relationship, you would be likely to respond to the advances of anyone, male or female, whom you found attractive. Not subscribing to the theory that homosexuality is 'wrong' or in any way abnormal, you accept it as a natural expression of human sexuality, and have the best of both worlds – with the reservation that unfaithfulness to a committed partnership is none the less painful because it is homosexual. You must remember that, however understanding your partner may be, not everyone has such a high level of sexual ambivalence as yourself. Otherwise you may have misunderstandings of a basic kind.

12 The 'real' you

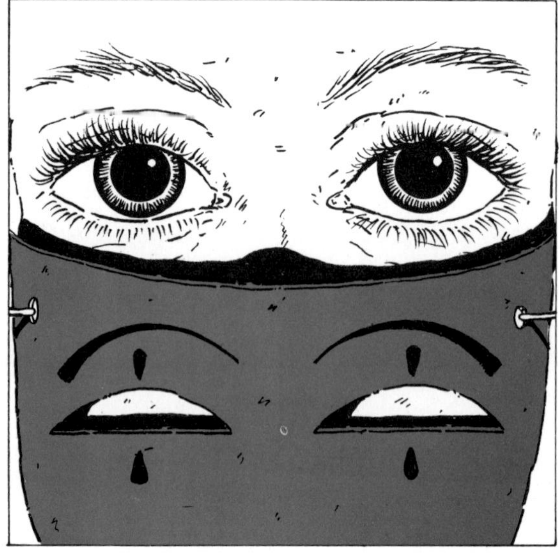

'Head-shrinkers' have been an easy laugh for almost a century, yet more and more people consult psychologists. How does psychology work? What are the different systems and can any of them truly help you?

WITHOUT SOME IDEA of how the man or woman next door, or standing next to you, working at the next desk or sharing the house, is going to behave, life becomes very difficult indeed. We need to know what sort of reaction there will be to a particular suggestion, or a particular action; whether the result of something we say will be approval or disapproval, agreement or disagreement, an embrace or an attack.

The attempt of one man to 'understand' another has been made ever since human thought began. A definition of 'psychology' might be that it is an attempt to study the behaviour of men and women under all sorts of circumstances, and to understand why it is that they behave as they do. Ever since such analyses began, people have disagreed about their interpretation. Yet disagreements between one psychologist and another (whether the professional, 'scientific' psychologist of today or his counterpart centuries or millennia ago) are theoretical, matters of opinion. Every man or woman is to some extent his or her own psychologist, attempting to understand his or her own motives: sometimes a very difficult task. Primitive man abandoned the effort to pass through the maze – at least to the extent that anything in his own behaviour he did not understand, he believed was governed by supernatural forces.

But that was too easy and gradually this animistic interpretation of existence gave way to more complex theories. A philosopher of the fifth century BC put forward the theory that body and mind might be two different entities. This was Anaxagoras, the Greek. Later, the Sophists went so far as to assert that experience was all, that man's knowledge depended on his own observations and explorations, that there was no such thing as objective truth.

Plato concluded that a man's 'ideas' were separate from his material existence; in an adult they became the *psyche*, the rational soul, which gave him intuitive knowledge. The

Epicureans put forward a theory of free will and Zeno the Stoic that of an individual and eternal human soul. St Augustine brought this theory into Christian philosophy when he said that human beings possessed an individual ego and will of their own.

These beliefs, or remnants of these beliefs, still flutter about in our twentieth-century minds: many of us find it difficult to believe that psychological tensions can have physical results, for instance; we like to believe in free will and in some kind of individual immortality. Some of the early ideas received support, while others were severely battered, as the various discoveries in physics and physiology led to a vastly increased understanding of how the body works. The separation of body and soul became more marked, reaching an extreme with Thomas Hobbes, who argued that man was only a machine, though admittedly a complicated one. A range of philosophers endlessly discussed how the human psyche might relate to God; while Locke believed that all ideas came from man's senses, Berkeley argued that they come from God. In the eighteenth century Hume, in a more complex theory, suggested that all knowledge comes from an association of ideas – and his theory was expanded by a long line of philosophers in England.

In Germany at the same time philosophers were evolving an equally intricate theory of 'mental faculties', classifying the mind into such categories as the emotions, the will, the intellect, and arguing that thought proceeds from one of these faculties or perhaps from a group of them detached from the others and working alone. In France, after some argument along the lines of Hobbes and Locke, Condillac insisted that all behaviour was a matter of instinct and association. *Sensationism*, as he called this theory, made a great effect: Rousseau and Pestalozzi were only two of those who insisted that children should be brought up to follow their natural instincts. (Many people believe that this is a peculiarly modern idea, hatched in the 1930s.)

Science continued to make discoveries about how the physical body worked. Research into the workings of the nervous system and various parts of the brain laid the foundation for 'scientific' psychology. In the early part of the nineteenth century experiments were already being made to measure speed of reaction (reaction to different colours, for instance), introspection and such physiological phenomena as the speed of the nerve impulses and the quality of the sensory nerves themselves.

One scientist has defined psychology as 'the scientific study of the behaviour of man and other animals'. But how far can the word 'scientific' be applied to such a study? Attempts have been made during the past century to draw up sets of rules which will explain, describe, classify human behaviour. But the brain has ten thousand million cells, each with a number of different connections – so the psychiatrist, medically qualified and concerned with the treatment of mental illness and emotional disorders, is nevertheless up against a very considerable problem if he attempts to treat them in a 'scientific' way. The most modern computer would have to be very elaborately programmed if it was to deal with such a vast number of possibilities and interconnections, let alone a fallible human being whose assumptions may be based in part on a very personal set of values and experiences.

The birth of modern psychology is often said to have taken place in 1879, when Wilhelm Wundt founded an experimental laboratory of psychology in Leipzig. He was attempting to analyze mental elements and discover how they worked together in the human psyche. Students from many countries, including the US, worked with him. More or less at the same time psychologists were working in Germany along similar lines, while in France Théodule Ribot began studying how physiology affected the workings of the mind. In England, too, Sir Francis Galton was studying heredity and working on a theory of eugenics, or the gradual elimination of unfit human beings from the developing race (naturally, of course, rather than artificially).

In America there were various influences at work, brought from Europe by students of

Wundt, Ribot and Darwin. William James was perhaps the first great individual American psychologist, whose textbook of psychology became a standard for American students and whose study of memory and the theory of emotions was very widely admired.

The business of psychology might be thought to be classification. Every theorist in the field adheres to one or other means of dividing men and women first into rough categories, then into increasingly more intricate individual categories, pieced together with such complexity that every human being ends up in a category of one.

However rough or minute classification may be, there are certain factors in common: we are all 'animal', for example. Each of us may react differently to a stimulus, but it works upon us, physically, in the same way. Stimuli are 'received' by the skin, the ears, nose, eyes, or whatever, and are conveyed to the nerve centre, whence instructions are sent out to the tear ducts, the muscles of the fist, or the face, or elsewhere. Although this mechanical system appears to be more or less the same for everyone, our reactions depend on our personality. It is the study of personality that is central to modern psychology – personality being the total *you* made up of all your various qualities and traits.

The reasons why one 'personality' differs from another have always been a matter for argument and discussion. Certainly a great number of elements play their part – heredity and environment, intelligence, learning, imagination, motivation (some of our motives are simple, such as pain, hunger, cold; some of them much more complex, such as sex, ambition, self-esteem, religion). Feeling and emotion play an important part: why are some feelings pleasant for some people, unpleasant for others? How do physiological effects – glandular or muscular changes – have their effect on our emotions?

There are various ways of studying our behaviour, of trying to find out how the human personality puts itself together and deals with the other personalities around it. They all have drawbacks: the experimental method, by which people's reactions are very carefully studied under laboratory conditions, has to contend with the fact that very few people behave naturally in a laboratory when they know their every move is being watched. This method, however, can be usefully combined with natural observation, when people are studied as unobtrusively as possible while living their ordinary, everyday lives.

Then there is the case-history method: the collection of as much detail as possible about an individual's life – environment, childhood, education, relationship to parents. . . . Though school records and medical histories may be fairly reliable, the statements of parents or friends, let alone the memory of the individual himself, are often suspect.

As for general psychology – the psychology of humankind rather than of a particular human being – this depends on general surveys which may be revealing but equally may be fallacious: the frequency with which political pollsters are wrong in their estimation of the way voters will behave at elections seems to indicate that a great many people positively enjoy hoaxing investigators who approach them with complicated forms and long lists of questions.

The questioners who work for pollsters are interested in our motivation – our motivation for voting as we vote, buying what we buy, behaving as we behave. Their methods are often based on what seem very questionable criteria. Our basic desires – for warmth, food, love – may seem simple enough, but in modern society, especially, they are difficult to isolate. Most people want some kind of social recognition – which is why so many of us join clubs: we want to 'belong', though in a way 'belonging' to a group seems a denial of our personal identity. At the same time we want to be independent, to feel free of undue influence – which is why there is always a tendency to grumble at authority, at 'them', the amorphous officials who tend to treat us as though we are not individuals.

Every individual is motivated by a complex system of drives and motives: three men may go to the movies at the same time – one because he has an hour to kill before catching a train, one because he is interested in the film being shown, one because it is a fashionable film which he feels he 'should' see. But even this classification is not simple: the man waiting for the train may have made a choice between the film, a drink in a nearby bar and a walk in the park. The cinema fan will have chosen between this film and several others; and there may be all sorts of reasons for his choice. The third man will have decided whether it is more important to his image to have seen the film, or an equally fashionable exhibition or concert.

Then, of course, in at least two of these cases there are other reasons behind the choice made: environment and upbringing, some kind of motivation, is in a sense responsible. The psychologist would want to look at it. Motivation drives us forward, but our motives are changeable, infinitely complicated and intensely difficult to analyze.

Motivation is often the result of 'learning' – we act as we act because we have 'learned' at some time in the past, and for some reason, that our action will give us pleasure, or bring us reward, will avoid punishment or add to our self-esteem, or satisfy some other criteria. Everything we learn, from childhood on – to say nothing of inherited 'knowledge' in the form of instinct – affects the way we behave.

The way we behave illustrates, or helps to reveal, our attitude to life in general and to any given situation or person. Some of these attitudes classify us as representatives of a trend or as members of a large group of people: in the West, for example, a man who approves of low taxation, the support of medical services by charity rather than the state, rigorous means tests applied to those in need of state assistance, strict treatment of all offenders, would be described on the whole as a conservative (whether or not he was a member of the Republican Party in the US, the Conservative Party in the UK, or similar parties in other countries).

The opinions of large groups of people are usually collected by means of opinion polls, the first of which were conducted in England by an organization called Mass Observation, founded by Tom Harrisson in the 1930s. George Gallup's first opinion poll in the US took place at about the same time, in 1935. Mass Observation attempted to discover what 'ordinary people' thought about this subject or that. It is now generally recognized that opinion polls are a pretty rough way of gauging public opinion: they have failed too often to be trusted. One of their most notorious failures was in America in 1948, when the Gallup Poll firmly predicted, right up to the last moment, a victory for Thomas E. Dewey in the presidential election. In fact, Harry S. Truman won the election with a massive majority. 'I don't know what happened', moaned Dr Gallup; and Truman happily appeared waving *The Chicago Tribune* with the banner headline DEWEY DEFEATS TRUMAN. Angry publishers cancelled their subscriptions to the polls and the public has been a little wary of them ever since, though newspapers still give them vast publicity (which says something about human gullibility and about man's eternal ambition to see into the future).

Psychologists continue to believe, rather against the evidence, that accurate predictions of group behaviour can be made. One of the emotions which makes such prediction difficult is individual frustration, which often provokes uncharacteristic behaviour. There does not seem much doubt, for instance, that much of the tension between black and white in both the US and the UK, and between immigrant and host communities elsewhere, has arisen because of frustration about jobs, housing, school places. Frustration provokes tension and tension leads to 'abnormal' behaviour in otherwise 'normal' people.

The preoccupation of psychiatry today, as the layman sees it, is with 'normal' and 'abnormal' behaviour. These two terms are by no means clear-cut. If you are living in a primitive tribe and a stranger moves his family into your hut, your 'normal' reaction may well be to seize your club and hit him over the head with it. A more 'normal' reaction in, say, Boston, in 1980, may be to hold a more or less rational argument, which will only degenerate into violence under particularly exasperating conditions. Again, it is quite clear that a large number of people, our neighbours, whom we think of as being normal rational human beings, are under certain circumstances capable of extremely unreasonable behaviour: some people are abnormally possessive of their property or their wives, others abnormally sensitive about politics or religion. There are innumerable ways in which 'abnormal' behaviour can occur – we only call it 'abnormal' because it seems unusual to us within a certain social set-up. Sometimes a whole population may seem to behave abnormally, especially in time of war.

And yet we do have a concept of what it is like to be 'normal' where our own mental health is concerned. The 'normal' man realizes that in order to live comfortably and easily in society he must in general conform to accepted behaviour patterns. Though he may have various conflicts, he will know how to regulate them so that they do not disturb his neighbours; he knows what is 'real' and what is 'unreal' in those terms; he is more or less physically healthy and enthusiastic about his everyday life and his work.

Those of us who are, or from time to time become, mentally ill (and a high proportion of people – about five in every hundred, in the West – need some kind of treatment for mental illness during their lives) are classified as suffering from *neuroses* or *psychoses*. If you are neurotic, you find it difficult to cope with the problems of everyday life and suffer unduly from fears and anxieties. This may cause physical symptoms – nausea, sweating, general tenseness. The 'abnormality' is that these fears have no rational cause. The psychotic person suffers not from irrational fears but from positive delusions – that he is being controlled by the men from Mars, perhaps – and behaves as though the delusions were real. If he thinks that wireless waves are being used to govern his actions, he will wrap himself in insulating material to deflect them; if he believes that he is Nero, he will go around condemning people to be thrown to the lions and perhaps setting fire to buildings. He may hear imaginary voices, or see imaginary people or things. Within this irrationality, however, he will behave rationally.

Psychotics are themselves classified according to the violence of their illness. A manic depressive will become either magnificently elated or terribly depressed, swinging from one extreme to the other without obvious cause (though particular circumstances may trigger his reaction). A schizophrenic (the most common psychotic type) withdraws from reality, sometimes so completely that it seems impossible to reach him. A paranoic suffers from acute delusions.

There seems to be a steady proportion of the population of any Western country which at any one time suffers from psychoses. It seems possible that the symptoms are inherited. If an identical twin has a psychosis, the chance of the brother or sister being mentally ill is as high as 85 per cent, and in ordinary twins the chance is something like 15 per cent. Neurosis is even more common than psychosis, but not as damaging except in its most extreme form. Nevertheless, a neurotic person is not likely to be a completely happy person. He will be in a state of uncertainty, unable to make a normal balanced decision, constantly worried about it. Fortunately a number of people cure themselves of this – or are cured by their daily life, for it seems that neuroses are 'learned'. If you punish a dog for sitting when you command him to and then reward him for doing the same thing, you will turn him into a neurotic. The human personality seems capable of learning or un-learning neuroses in much the same way. While drugs have been successfully used to treat psychotics' close personal relationships, love and kindness seem the best way to treat neurotics; and these are to the fore in psychoanalysis.

It was Sigmund Freud who developed the idea of psychoanalysis. In a close relationship between the patient and the analyst the patient becomes ready to reveal himself completely: the analyst may be able to explain to him those areas of his life which are obscure to him and possibly at the root of his problems.

The aim of psychoanalysis cannot be said

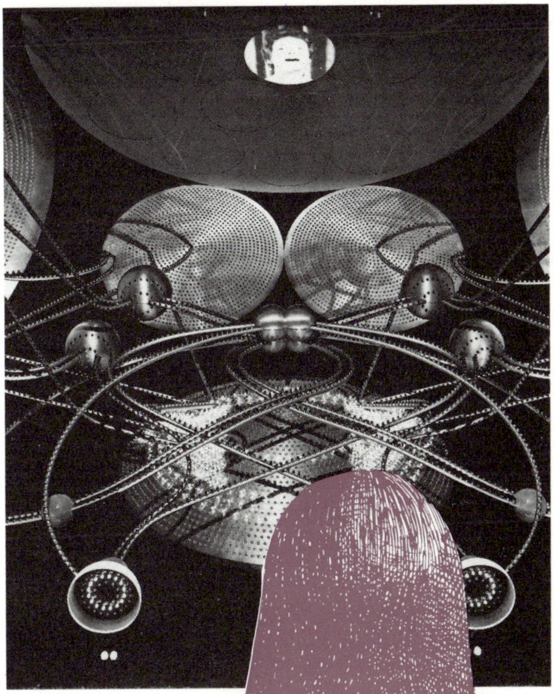

None of us can go through life without some understanding of our own and other people's behaviour. Freud (above) offered psychoanalysis. Scientists, as in the mechanical model of the brain (above right), have contributed to our understanding of the workings of the mind by illustrating its physical aspects. Whether the mind and body work as mechanically as suggested in the caricature of *The New Eve* (right) or not, we can all explore the many roads to human self-discovery.

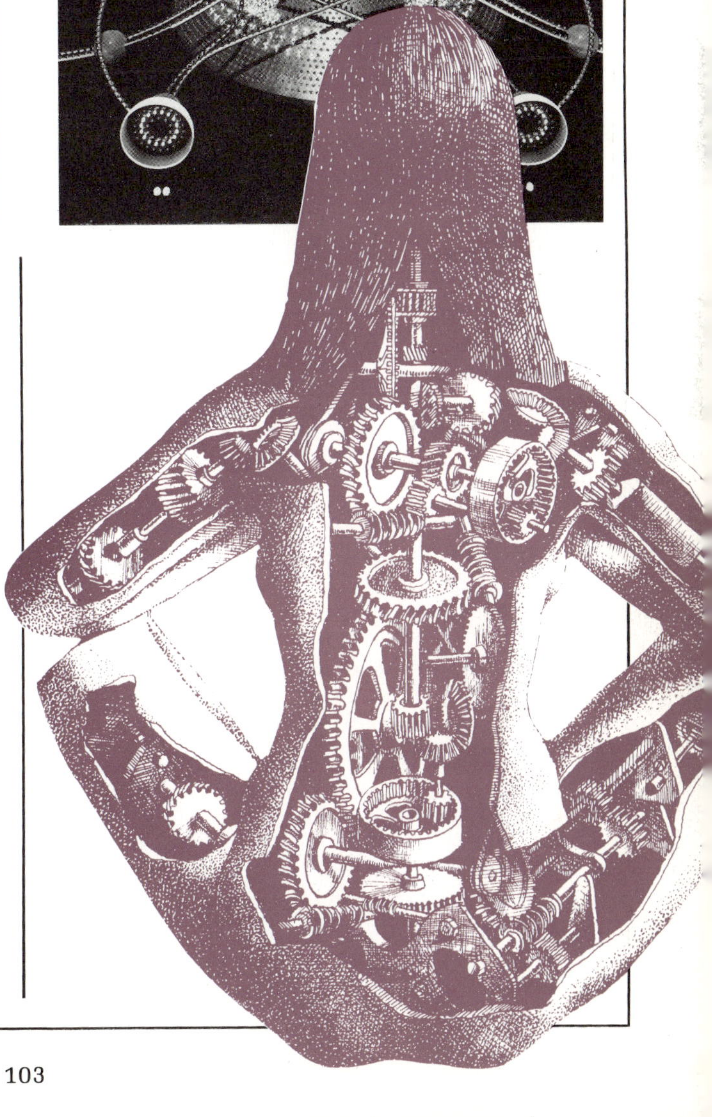

to be to 'cure' anyone, but by explaining his or her life more fully, to enable him or her to understand why he or she acts in this way rather than that. So it can be argued that none of us would fail to profit from psychoanalysis, as it leads us through our more recent or superficial life back to the earliest and darkest memories, to repressions of our childhood and influences on our development which we have long forgotten.

There are various schools of psychology which favour somewhat different approaches to analysis. Carl Rogers in the US, for instance, laid a heavy responsibility on the patient, who chose how the interviews should go, what the problems were and substantially how to solve them. His system is known as 'non-directional therapy'. The Behaviourists, founded in the US by John B. Watson, study observable human behaviour, responses to stimuli, movements that can be measured; they exclude everything that cannot be explained by reference to stimulus and response.

The Gestalt psychologist believes that the nature of the parts of a person is determined by the nature of the whole, so that he will not believe that a true picture of his patient can be obtained by listing a number of characteristics, but only by looking at the total personality, the organized whole, the *Gestalt*. In Japanese Morita therapy the patient is positively discouraged from exploring his own personality or feelings and concentrates on re-learning social behaviour. In group therapy, when six to ten patients participate together, a therapist will guide people into revealing themselves through mutual discussion. From this, 'encounter groups' have developed, some of them gimcrack and amateur, even somewhat dangerous, geared to action rather than mental introspection. Some people have claimed benefit, but on the whole they have been people who have not been emotionally disturbed, but interested in heightening their responses to other people, sexually and otherwise.

These schools of psychology have evolved various ways of classifying their patients. Chapter 7 has shown how some people have attempted to do this by relating the mind to the body. Psychiatrists have more recently tried to examine the workings of the mind itself, affected by the body, certainly, but substantially on its own.

One of the sensational ideas of Freud, which caused much scandal in the early years of psychoanalysis, was that our actions are almost exclusively directed by our sexual drives and that sexuality in infancy provokes many behavioural traits which later cause us difficulty. At the end of the nineteenth century there was still a prevailing view of childhood as the age of innocence and there was a great outcry when it was supposed that Freud was imputing sexual motives to infants.

What was misunderstood was that, although Freud came to the conclusion that unconscious conflicts over a young child's sexual attitude towards its parents (often jealous and hostile – Freud called it the Oedipus conflict) – were central to the development of psychosis in an adult, by 'sexual drive' he meant not only the need to make love, but other basic needs connected with food, the experience of pain, loneliness, even religion.

Freud divides human personality into three basic structures. The *id* is the human organism and the mass of energies and forces which make up the unconscious personality – the part of us that craves physical comfort and satisfaction. The *super-ego*, on the other hand, is the force which makes us behave not as we might wish but as others wish – the instinctive feeling which, acting through anxiety and guilt, persuades us to act in accordance with the general attitudes of the society we live in. In effect, this is the force most of us would refer to as conscience.

The *ego* balances these two forces: it is the part of us which is in contact with reality, recognizes the reactions of our senses and in the normal, healthy person governs the swings between the *id* (pleasure-seeking, ambitious, self-centred) and the *super-ego* (unselfish, idealistic, disinterested).

Carl Jung broke away from Freud, rejecting his idea of sex as the basic human drive, and built up a somewhat similar theory in which a number of drives – sex, but also fear, shame and so on – are responsible for conflict. It was he who classified people into introverts (those people who look at everything in terms of their own feelings) and extroverts (those who constantly reflect outside influences). He believed very strongly that man's behaviour not only reflects the conflicts which are a relic of racial history (the personal and collective unconscious), but also his aims and aspirations.

Alfred Adler was another of Freud's close associates who broke away, believing that self-assertion rather than sexual drive was at the base of human conduct. The helpless infant, with all its feelings of inferiority, could grow up, he believed, into a man or woman with a natural 'inferiority complex'; and if he or she did not make a success of life, this complex could cause endless trouble. Adler concentrated on trying to make people aware of their own inferiority complexes and their way of becoming, in their own eyes, 'superior'.

Other psychiatrists have devised terms in attempts to classify personality. An American psychiatrist, Raymond B. Cattell, for instance, developed a 'scientific' method of boiling down the infinitely subtle emotional characteristics of a great number of different people to come up with a list of personality traits from which some kind of pocket description of a personality could be produced. He listed sixteen pairs of human characteristics which he had found to be the most common basic personality traits to be assessed in a human personality:

A Goodnatured or Aloof
B Intelligent or Dull
C Mature or Emotional
D Assertive or Submissive
E Happy-go-Lucky or Sober
F Conscientious or Expedient
G Adventuresome or Timid and Shy
H Realistically Tough or Sensitive
I Trusting or Suspicious
J Practical or Imaginative
K Shrewd or Simply Kind
L Self-Confident or Insecure and Anxious
M Liberal or Conservative
N Self-Sufficient or Dependent
O Self-Controlled or Unreliable
P Relaxed or Tense

From this list it is possible to build up a rough picture of a personality, much as a police witness may build up a picture of a suspect by choosing one at a time the features he thinks he saw – big nose, small nose, wide mouth, narrow mouth (see chapter 24). Several pairs of characteristics can be used, roughly, to illustrate various characteristic traits.

If you are wondering, for instance, how balanced your general emotional state is, you could look at items C, I, K, L, O and P. Introvert or extrovert? – A, D, E, G and N might well have something to say about that. Tender-minded or tough-minded? – see H and K.

But this is all very simple, if not simple-minded. Personality is as volatile as mercury, as amorphous as steam. Psychologists have to use other means of measuring it, or attempting to measure it. Behaviour will be sampled, both at home and at work, there may be extensive interviews, stress tests, the life-history will be analyzed, there will be questionnaires, intelligence tests. . . . It is a long and taxing process.

Full analysis, involving at least a weekly visit of an hour or two to an analyst, is one of the most thorough ways in which anyone can learn who he really is. It may go on for several years. Most people will not want to go that far. You may have a healthy curiosity to know whether you always behave reasonably, or as you *think* you behave; how you appear to others. For you, if you have no problem, a mild interest in psychology probably does no harm and may do a little good – it is always salutary to discover your own selfishness, inherent violence or sentimentality. There are now a number of books which can help you to know yourself better; 'encounter' groups, if approached with caution, can sometimes be revealing. Considerable emotion can be generated at such groups and they need to be led by someone of experience and emotional balance.

Psychology as a study is still in its infancy. It is obviously open to the weirdest theories and the weirdest theories have been applied to it. It is not yet a true science; but gradually new truths based on scientific methods are replacing hypotheses and speculation, and falsehood is being driven out by positive, accurate knowledge. Eventually men and women may be offered the opportunity to understand themselves, their characters, their motivations and minds as thoroughly and empirically as they understand their car or their washing-machine. Whether that will be a good thing is a question for the future.

13 Introvert/extrovert test

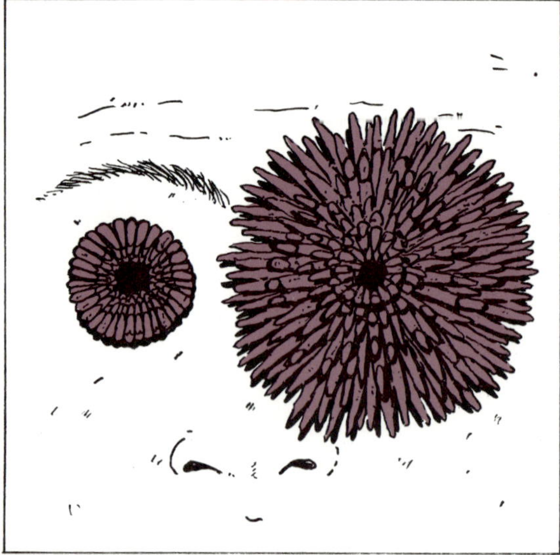

Is the world your oyster, or have you made a world in which to hide? Extrovert or introvert? Test yourself: do you like practical jokes? . . . enjoy crossword puzzles? . . . stay in bed in the morning, read the small print, always use the same perfume?

THE FOLLOWING QUESTIONS have been devised to suggest whether you are basically an introvert or an extrovert personality. Note a 'yes' or 'no' answer to each question, then check your score according to the checklist that follows and relate it to the interpretation offered.

1 Do you usually feel well and healthy?

2 Do you find it easy to introduce yourself to strangers at a party?

3 Are you a 'plodder'?

4 Are you 'careful' about money?

5 Do you like playing practical jokes?

6 Do you react well when you are the victim of a practical joke?

7 Do you live for today and let tomorrow take care of itself?

8 Are you constantly afraid of making a fool of yourself?

9 Do you like staying at home in the evenings?

10 Would you prefer playing the flute to the trumpet?

11 Are you easily excited when watching competitive sport?

12 Do you constantly blame others for dangerous driving?

13 Are you always in a hurry, whether or not you have plenty of time?

14 Do you procrastinate?

15 Do you pour out your troubles to your friends?

16 Do you live each day as though it were your last?

17 Do you allow for traffic hold-ups or other delays when catching a train or plane?

18 On holiday, do you prefer the bright lights to rural peace and quiet?

19 Would you prefer to read a biography of a famous person rather than to meet him or her?

20 Are you versatile?

21 Can you come to snap decisions?

22 Are you often forgetful?

23 Do you enjoy crossword puzzles?

24 Do you prefer writing letters to making phonecalls?

25 Do you consider yourself more reserved and shy than most people?

26 Can you be ready in fifteen minutes, and looking good, if you get a sudden invitation?

27 Do you believe in doing 'one thing at a time'?

28 Do you never forget a face?

29 Are you always keen to start new projects?

30 Faced with the unfamiliar, do you observe others, then do as they do?

31 Do you always look before you leap?

32 Do you enjoy being in large crowds?

33 Do you sometimes speak out of turn?

34 Do you prefer 'inspirational' music to music that may make you want to get up and dance?

35 Do you prefer the planning stages of a project to its realization?

36 Do you practice preventive medicine and believe in self-preservation?

37 Have you good powers of concentration?

38 Do you cope well in emergencies?

39 Do you like to dawdle through a day, lying in bed in the morning?

40 Do your friends tell you that you never relax?

41 Do you like to take part in demonstrations, street parties, parades?

42 Do you consider the pros and cons before coming to a decision?

43 Do you find it difficult to express your true feelings on paper?

44 Do you find others painfully slow in thought and action?

45 Do you take world problems seriously?

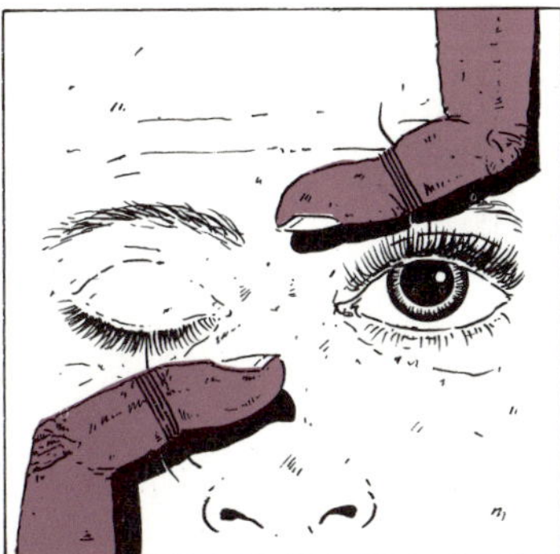

46 Do you take the initiative in organizing activities in your district?

47 Do you find it interesting to track down information, to do painstaking research?

48 Are you upset when you hear about disasters in foreign countries?

49 While there may be things you would like to do, do you find it difficult to muster the energy to do them?

50 Do you lose your temper easily?

51 Do you keep a promise once you have made it?

52 Can you keep a confidence?

53 Are you often late?

54 Might 'anything for speed' be a maxim of yours?

55 Do you smile easily and freely?

56 Would you 'bite your tongue' rather than upset someone by disagreeing with them?

57 Are you generally speaking reliable?

58 Before signing any contract, do you always read the small print?

59 Do you always look forward to tomorrow, even if it's Monday?

60 Are you easily bored by dull, routine work?

61 Do you get pleasure from taking unnecessary risks?

62 Have you ever seriously thought of opting out of society?

63 Do you enjoy gambling?

64 Do you dislike being touched by strangers?

65 Do you find quiet periods restorative and necessary to your psychological wellbeing?

66 Do you tend to drift off into your own private world?

67 Do you tend to stick to one familiar brand of cosmetics or after-shave?

68 Do you prefer dogs to cats?

69 Do you agree that 'East, West, Home's Best'?

70 Do you prefer your fried eggs 'sunny side up'?

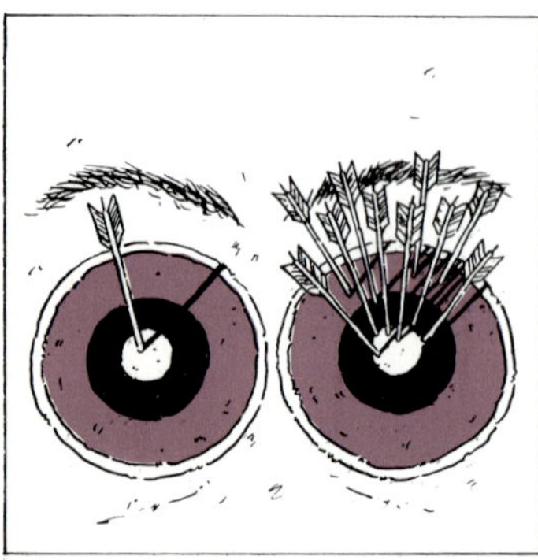

Scoring

Start with a basic score of 70. For every + answer add one point, for every – answer take a point away.

1 yes +, no –
2 yes +, no –
3 yes –, no +
4 yes –, no +
5 yes +, no –
6 yes +, no –
7 yes +, no –
8 yes –, no +
9 yes –, no +
10 yes –, no +
11 yes +, no –
12 yes +, no –
13 yes +, no –
14 yes +, no –
15 yes +, no –
16 yes +, no –
17 yes –, no +
18 yes +, no –
19 yes –, no +
20 yes +, no –
21 yes +, no –
22 yes +, no –
23 yes –, no +
24 yes –, no +
25 yes –, no +
26 yes +, no –
27 yes –, no +
28 yes +, no –
29 yes +, no –
30 yes –, no +
31 yes –, no +
32 yes +, no –
33 yes +, no –
34 yes –, no +
35 yes –, no +
36 yes –, no +
37 yes –, no +
38 yes +, no –
39 yes –, no +
40 yes +, no –
41 yes +, no –
42 yes –, no +
43 yes +, no –
44 yes +, no –
45 yes –, no +
46 yes +, no –
47 yes –, no +
48 yes –, no +
49 yes –, no +
50 yes +, no –
51 yes –, no +
52 yes –, no +
53 yes +, no –
54 yes +, no –
55 yes +, no –
56 yes –, no +
57 yes –, no +
58 yes –, no +
59 yes +, no –
60 yes +, no –
61 yes +, no –
62 yes –, no +
63 yes +, no –
64 yes –, no +
65 yes –, no +
66 yes –, no +
67 yes –, no +
68 yes +, no –
69 yes –, no +
70 yes +, no –

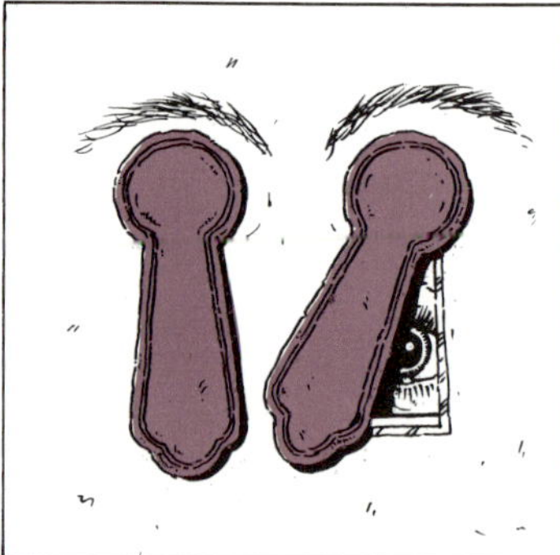

Interpretations

SCORE 0–35

Very introvert
You seem to be extremely introverted. The familiar offers you security, so you are at your best in your own home environment and among a small circle of intimates. You may tend to withdraw, even from those dear to you, into a world of your own. While you need to do this, and in many ways it is good for you to have your own private world in which to be yourself, you should try to realize that those who love you want to help you face your problems – it is not a good thing for you to bottle up any negative feelings you may have. It is helpful to talk problems over with someone sympathetic and it is more than likely that there are people close to you who would be only too glad to listen.

You are very much a contemplative kind of person, with considerable depth of feeling, who thinks seriously about the important issues of mankind and the world's problems in general. Because of this you may well have a good deal more to give than you may realize; your absorption of detail and emotion gives you considerable inner strength and this is worth remembering when you feel shy or inhibited in the company of those you believe to be cleverer, wittier, superior to yourself.

Since you are shy, you may find it a temptation to be over-talkative or over-anxious to please. Remember that your best way to develop as a person is through the strength of your inner calm and tranquillity. Aim for serenity: contribute a few meaningful statements from time to time rather than act out a twitchy sort of gaiety which is definitely not you.

SCORE 36–69

Introvert
Books, quiet evenings at home with the family or a small group of friends, holidays on a peaceful stretch of river or in the deep countryside are the kind of things you enjoy. You are not the kind of person to take unnecessary risks, believing that prevention is better than cure; you plan your life carefully, in your own quiet way. You are a plodder and accept the fact that to achieve your modest ambitions you will probably have to make gradual progress.

You can feel very uncomfortable: noisy clubs, rowdy nights out with the girls or boys are not for you. The best thing is to try not to get caught up in such circumstances, in which you will be miserable and may well communicate your misery! But there are plenty of suitable substitutes.

You will probably favour calm occupations where your brain has to work; but try not to cut yourself off too much from other people – if, for instance, you enjoy listening to debate, try occasionally to join in the discussion or argument.

You may be inclined to worry. No use telling you not to do so, if it is part of your nature. However, remember there are other approaches to problems than continually revolving them in your mind. Perhaps you should analyze them in as much detail as possible; or, if you have a strong intuitive instinct, it may not be wrong to exercise it. Either approach may be rewarding, whether it leads to a long list of pros and cons, or to a sudden decision to follow a strong instinctive impulse.

SCORE 70–104

Extrovert
You like to accept people at their face value and expect others to do the same. You probably enjoy life and get a lot out of it in a fairly obvious, lively way. Ambitious, you are by no means shy about seizing any opportunities that come your way. Being in a large crowd of people presents no problems for you: while you no doubt enjoy cheering on your own team or competitor you may well like to compete yourself – if not on the field, then in business or in your social life, where your natural exuberance and enthusiasm will find positive expression.

You do need, though, to be careful to quell a tendency to take on too much, whether at work or in your spare time – to have too many interests, so that your genuine versatility in the end expresses itself in a rather superficial way. The feeling that the grass is greener over the hedge should not persuade you to throw away achievements that could bear riper fruit given time.

You may need to work to develop patience; you may be able to control a tendency to take short cuts, but your strong will-power and high energy level may take over a little too forcefully at times. Take a few psychological deep breaths from time to time; give yourself a little time for contemplation; where are you going, what do you want out of life? A firm point of reference applied to your sprightly, expressive qualities will enable you to get the best out of them.

People probably look to you to get things organized; and you do. But attention to detail may not be your strongest suit. If you are involved in committee work, for instance, you may hold a key position – but you should delegate the work involving small detail to those of a more careful, analytical frame of mind. In many ways you can be a breath of fresh air to other people; but it is important that you should not miss out on listening to what they have to say.

SCORE 105–140

Very extrovert
As far as you are concerned, the world is your very own oyster. You are incredibly assertive and go-ahead; nothing is going to stop your progress. Your ambitions are sky-high and you certainly have what it takes to achieve them. If you are in business, your competitors fall by the wayside like an exhausted army.

You will very likely put yourself first most of the time and your will to win – a motor race, a huge Arabian contract, or the partner of your choice – is all-important. Because you are so strong-willed and determined, you need to be very careful that in attaining your objectives you do not hurt other people along the way. You could very easily do this, without as much as noticing; when your partner complains that he or she is not getting enough attention, it will be a tremendous shock. There will be no question of neglecting them purposely, but of not thinking of them at all! The time which your many commitments swallow will be very considerable.

You will have many excellent qualities which others admire and envy: you will be brave and daring, and your abundant enthusiasm is admirable. But because you are so positive and assertive, there may be areas of your life in which you will miss much. You will have no time for contemplation, for instance (except of your energetic business schemes); the more inspirational aspects of your emotional and intellectual life may be a closed book to you. If you pause, from time to time, to question your own basic psychological motivation, it is just possible that a deeper and more meaningful area of your personality will open out, giving a more sensitive dimension to your personality as a whole. Such sayings as 'Fools rush in' could have been coined for you; do try occasionally to 'look before you leap'.

14 Testing your sexual libido

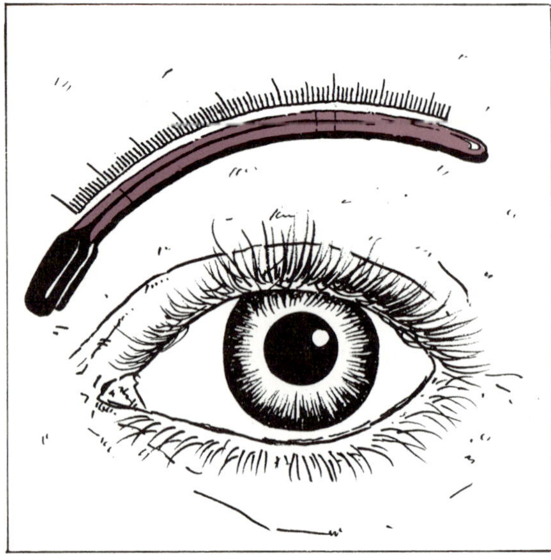

Is sex a part of life, or the most important part of life? Test yourself: should all overtly sexual films be banned? . . . is obscenity always disgusting? . . . is your sex life as good as it used to be?

THE FOLLOWING QUESTIONS have been devised to suggest the strength of your sexual libido. Needless to say, this differs very much from one person to another; and although those with extremely low or extremely high libidos may have problems (the former because of difficulty in having a satisfactory sexual relationship with a partner, the latter because of a continual need to govern what may seem an all-embracing sexual need) there is no need to assume that any criticism is implied.

Answer the questions with agree or disagree, then check with the scores and suggested interpretations at the end.

1 Friendship between a man and a woman can be much more satisfactory than a sexual relationship.

2 You could never make love to anyone the first time you met them.

3 No man wants to marry a girl who is not a virgin.

4 You become sexually aroused, to some extent, almost every day.

5 You could never make love to anyone you did not love.

6 You enjoy caressing your own body.

7 You feel slightly disappointed if a novel or film has no sexual content.

8 The nude pin-ups in newspapers and magazines are a waste of space.

9 You keep an eye open for the sexual possibilities of any situation.

10 It is a good thing for everyone to have sexual experience before marriage.

11 You are disgusted at the idea of organized prostitution.

12 You would welcome the opportunity to make love with a partner ten years younger than yourself.

13 You can understand how sexual passion can lead people to murder for love.

14 It is especially exciting to seduce a virgin.

15 The pornography of sex is as dangerous as the pornography of violence.

16 The banning of explicitly sexual material is long overdue.

17 Nude scenes on stage and screen are almost always unnecessary.

18 Explicit love-making in films is never justifiable.

19 You have never made love to two different people within twenty-four hours.

20 When someone is described as immoral, you think first of sexual immorality.

21 All expression of sex outside the marriage bed is by definition wrong.

22 You have never wondered what it would be like to make love with your best friend's partner.

23 No one has ever been faithful to one partner in thought, word and deed.

24 The thought of a stranger's hands caressing you is exciting.

25 Making love to one person, you often fantasize about making love to another.

26 A harem must be a very embarrassing institution.

27 Arriving at a party to find that it was an orgy, you would make an excuse and leave.

28 You could only think of joining an orgy if the others involved were close friends.

29 The average, healthy human being should not need sex more than twice a week.

30 Over-eating is as disgusting as over-indulgence in sex.

31 Masturbation is disgusting.

32 Obscenity is always disgusting.

33 The thought of homosexuals making love is disgusting.

34 You would decline an offer to see *Deep Throat.*

35 Any sexual stimulus not based on spiritual love is wrong.

36 Wife-swopping disgusts you.

37 You would enjoy watching another couple making love.

38 You prefer to make love with the light on.

39 You would like to have a mirror on your bedroom ceiling.

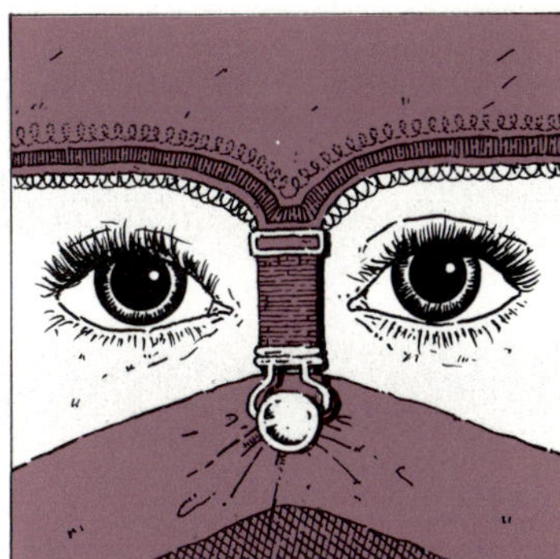

40 You would not like to make love in the open air.

41 You would be sexually aroused if your partner bought you a sexy garment.

42 You find the touch of certain materials sexually arousing.

43 You are quick to recognize sexual signals from others.

44 Advertisements often have a high symbolic sexual content.

45 You have a strong fear of sexual rejection.

46 Sexually speaking, anything goes.

47 The age of consent should be lowered to fourteen.

48 Your parents' attitude to sex has inhibited you.

49 Your sex life is more rewarding than it used to be.

50 The thought of making love with someone of a different colour disgusts you.

Scoring

Start with a basic score of 50. For every + answer add one point, for every – answer take a point away.

1 Agree –, disagree +
2 Agree –, disagree +
3 Agree –, disagree +
4 Agree +, disagree –
5 Agree –, disagree +
6 Agree +, disagree –
7 Agree +, disagree –
8 Agree –, disagree +
9 Agree +, disagree –
10 Agree +, disagree –
11 Agree –, disagree +
12 Agree +, disagree –
13 Agree +, disagree –
14 Agree +, disagree –
15 Agree –, disagree +
16 Agree –, disagree +
17 Agree –, disagree +
18 Agree –, disagree +
19 Agree –, disagree +
20 Agree –, disagree +
21 Agree –, disagree +
22 Agree –, disagree +
23 Agree +, disagree –
24 Agree +, disagree –
25 Agree +, disagree –
26 Agree –, disagree +
27 Agree –, disagree +
28 Agree –, disagree +
29 Agree –, disagree +
30 Agree +, disagree –
31 Agree –, disagree +
32 Agree –, disagree +

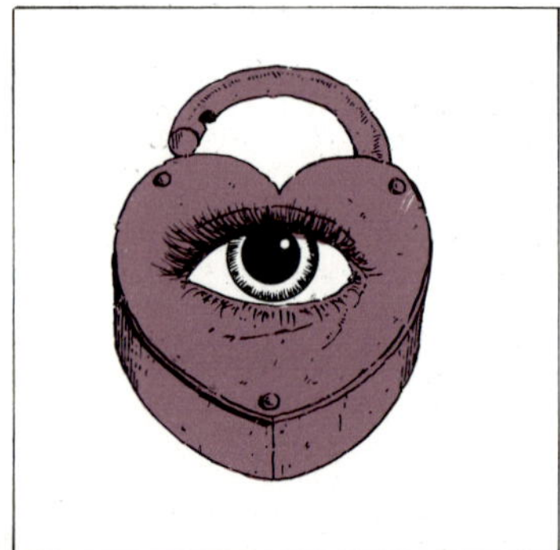

33 Agree –, disagree +
34 Agree –, disagree +
35 Agree –, disagree +
36 Agree –, disagree +
37 Agree +, disagree –
38 Agree +, disagree –
39 Agree +, disagree –
40 Agree –, disagree +
41 Agree +, disagree –
42 Agree +, disagree –
43 Agree +, disagree –
44 Agree –, disagree +
45 Agree –, disagree +
46 Agree +, disagree –
47 Agree +, disagree –
48 Agree –, disagree +
49 Agree +, disagree –
50 Agree –, disagree +

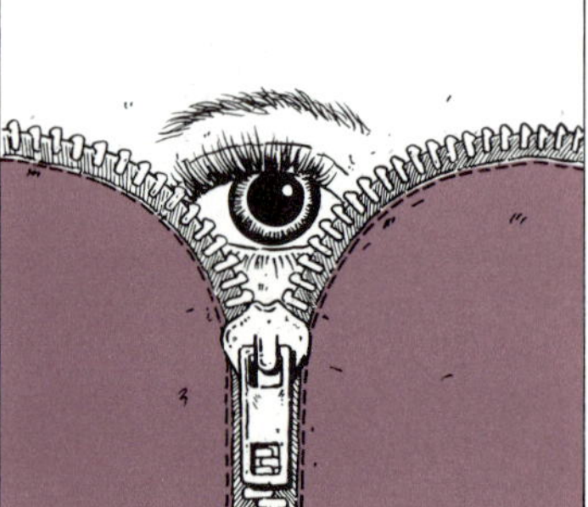

Interpretations

LOW SCORE 0–24

Sex is probably unimportant to you. If you are asked why, you may say that you have 'no time for it', that it is 'over-rated'; on a deeper level, you may even feel that there is something slightly disgusting or even 'dirty' about sex. Perhaps you were turned against it by some specific incident in the past which you did not fully understand at the time and which you may or may not actually remember. If at one level of consciousness you feel you could be more interested in sex, but cannot communicate your feeling to a partner – if you feel you are missing something – you might benefit from specialist therapy. On the other hand, there is absolutely no law that sex must be an important part of everyone's life: if you feel that your life is complete and fulfilled and that there is no gap in it, there is no reason why you should not be content as you are.

MEDIUM/LOW SCORE 25–49

You may well feel somewhat inhibited, not getting as much enjoyment out of sex as you would like to, or feel you should. You could also feel that sex is *very* over-rated and may tend to blame an unsympathetic partner. But perhaps you should look at yourself and your attitudes a little more closely. You may well take the tensions of the day to bed with you and think of your career, the children, or problems of any kind, when you should be in a more relaxed frame of mind. Sheer physical tiredness, perhaps especially for women, really does sap your sex urge (but don't use this, or bedtime headaches, as an excuse!) Try not to rush or be rushed. Quick sex can be a relief of tension for a man, but is not really satisfactory, and for the woman can be at best a bore and at worst an unbearable frustration. If you feel that your sexual life could be improved, you might well get greater satisfaction from new forms of love-play and benefit from developing your technique by experimenting. Do not underestimate the help you can get from the new and outspoken books on sexual techniques now available. These are sneered at by some people, but can improve your sex life just as much as a good cookbook can improve your cooking; you don't have to follow the recipes meticulously. Above all, relax more – much more. Does the form of contraception you use get in the way? Then try another. Don't put off a visit to a clinic because you feel shy about it. Specialists are used to dealing with people who are apprehensive and will be far more sympathetic than you may realize. A great number of people are finding that sterilization is both the practical and psychological answer to their problems. You can do a great deal to improve your sex life and from your score it seems likely that you want to do so.

MEDIUM/HIGH SCORE 50–74

You have a healthy and lively attitude towards sex, which will be expressed most rewardingly and fulfillingly with a partner whose score is similar to your own. You are willing to experiment and expand your sexual techniques, but you are not irresponsible. You could do much to improve the sex life of a less responsive and active partner. Sex is great fun for you. You are unshocked by sexy films and stage shows and by soft porn (which is not to say you go in for the hard stuff). You are not likely to lack partners; but you are not on a constant sexual rampage, for your strong sex drive is very well balanced.

HIGH SCORE 75–100

The higher your score, the more preoccupied you are with sex. Just as the lowest score may indicate that you are missing something, so the very highest score seems to hint that your constant preoccupation with sex may be over-taxing for you and for other people. Your basic desires and needs are undoubtedly higher than average and it may be that some of that abundant sexual energy could be profitably redirected. You certainly need a very sympathetic and understanding partner to enjoy your sex life with and, even so, you may find it difficult to restrict yourself to one relationship. This will bring its problems. If you can organize your life and cope with multiple relationships – fine. But try not to 'use' your partners; consciously give them a little more consideration, since your drive could tend to make you a selfish and over-demanding partner.

15 Ambition and you

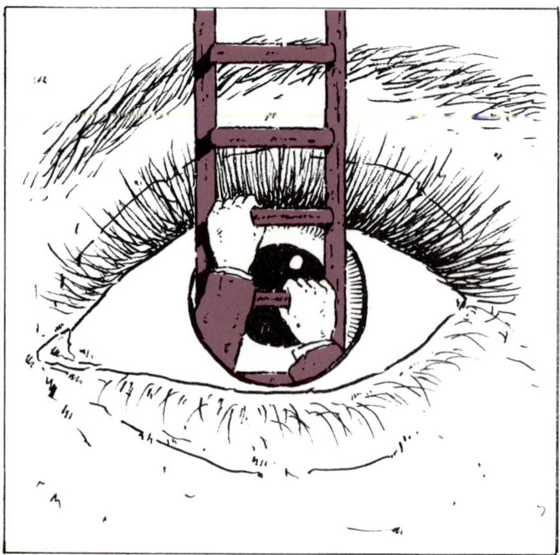

Are you ambitious? For what? Test yourself: would you rather have a large diamond or a healthy share portfolio? . . . do you enjoy using the executive washroom? . . . how well do you know your wines?

THESE THREE LISTS of questions together indicate to what extent you are an ambitious person. The total score for the three lists applies to ambition in general. But ambitious for what? – money, power, social advancement? The separate score for each list give you a hint.

MONEY

1 An admirer gives you an elaborate piece of jewellery. Do you
(a) accept it, delighted and proud?
(b) accept it, but immediately think: 'They can't afford it – it must be false'?
(c) get it valued and insured?
(d) sell it?

2 You have some stock and are given the option to purchase additional shares at a favourable rate. You have a heavy household bill to pay. Would you do all you can to take up the option?
YES/NO

3 You have to visit a capital city on business. Your firm pays expenses, but a friend also lives in the city. Would you phone and ask if you can sleep on his couch, in spite of discomfort and inconvenience, then pocket the expenses?
YES/NO

4 Do you
(a) give large tips for exceptional service?
(b) give as little as possible, or nothing if you can get away with it?
(c) only give large tips when you are with people wealthier than yourself?

5 Is 'money makes money' one of your mottoes?
YES/NO

6 At Christmas or on your birthday would you rather be given
(a) a cheap but original gift?
(b) an expensive, useless gift?
(c) a sum of money?

7 Do you give to charity
(a) by regular subscription?
(b) on impulse?
(c) only when directly asked?

8 Do you agree that to give is better than to receive?
YES/NO

9 Which would you like to own:
(a) a large diamond?
(b) a country or seaside home?
(c) a healthy stock portfolio?

10 You have £100 ($200) to spend. Would you
(a) buy an article of clothing?
(b) buy a minor antique?
(c) send all or part of it to a charity with which you identify?
(d) buy blue chip stock or add it to your savings account or insurance policy?

11 Do you enjoy taking financial risks?
YES/NO

12 Whom would you most like to befriend:
(a) a member of a very wealthy family?
(b) your bank manager?
(c) a businessman on the way up?

13 Would you buy a painting because
(a) you thought it beautiful?
(b) it would be a good investment?
(c) it would impress your friends?

14 Do you instinctively mistrust foreigners?
YES/NO

15 Do you always check the cashier's arithmetic at restaurants?
YES/NO

16 Do you study the stock market
(a) regularly?
(b) from time to time?
(c) not at all?

17 Do you wish you could
(a) invest more money?
(b) buy more consumer products?
(c) or does neither apply: you have all you want?

18 Do you nearly always admire people who are wealthier than yourself?
YES/NO

19 Do you positively enjoy spending money?
YES/NO

20 Do you
(a) always think twice before making a financial commitment?
(b) have decided opinions about children's pocket money?
(c) consciously consider whether your purchases are 'a good investment' or 'a dead loss'?
(d) believe that 'money makes the world go around'?
(Answer all four questions)

POWER

1 When you give a dinner party, do you
(a) entertain friends for the pleasure of their company?
(b) invite your worst enemy, among other guests, and make sure he feels very uncomfortable?
(c) go all out to impress your guests?
(d) invite people who can put in a good word for you?

2 You have applied for a job. The company phones you prior to an interview and asks if you have knowledge of a technique not mentioned in the advertisement. You haven't. Do you say
(a) no?
(b) yes, of course – then rush to the public library to look it up?

3 A good worker in your firm is trying hard for promotion. He asks for your help, but you are not in favour with the man he wants you to approach. Would you nevertheless do your best for him?
YES/NO

4 When going through heavy swing or revolving doors, do you
(a) make a point of helping the elderly, or people with heavy baggage?
(b) never give others a thought?
(c) take a quick glance to see if anyone is approaching behind you?

5 Do you find it difficult not to mix business with pleasure, even on holiday?
YES/NO

6 As a senior member of the firm, you are entitled to eat in the executive restaurant; most of your friends are not. Do you
(a) enjoy your solitary state?
(b) regret your isolation, but feel you 'must' put up with it?
(c) eat wherever and with whom you like?

7 You have two young children. Would you
(a) discipline them to the standards of behaviour when you were a child?
(b) let them come and go as they please?
(c) make sure they understand the problems they may face in their lives and come to a happy compromise?

8 Do you immediately realize when someone is trying to get the better of you and invariably come out on top?
YES/NO

9 You are enjoying dinner at a plushy and very reputable restaurant, as host to a small group of friends. One of the dishes is totally unsatisfactory. Do you
(a) call noisily for the waiter who served the dish and blame him, making a fuss which disturbs the other diners?
(b) discreetly ask for the head waiter and complain firmly but tactfully?
(c) make excuses to your guests and do nothing?

10 Would you be most likely to spend time and energy
(a) with the local committee of the political party in which you have electoral ambitions?
(b) with a sick friend?
(c) with a young person who is developing a skill of which you have expert knowledge?
(d) working on an elaborate scheme to put to your boss?

11 Can you cope with loneliness?
YES/NO

12 Who would you most like to entertain:
(a) your boss and his wife?
(b) the spiritual leader you most sympathize with?
(c) an influential local politician?

13 Asked to join a charity committee, you accept because
(a) you see yourself as President or Chairman?
(b) you truly admire the cause?
(c) it will improve your social status?

14 Would you be furious if someone in a subordinate position to yourself was given a superior new piece of office furniture?
YES/NO

15 When driving, do you always make a conscious effort to be first away from the traffic lights?
YES/NO

16 Would you say you were
(a) very assertive?
(b) assertive?
(c) easy come, easy go?

17 Which would be of most advantage to you:
(a) developing new interests?
(b) taking a course in business management?
(c) learning a language?

18 Will you get to the top if it kills you?
YES/NO

19 Do you feel deliciously smug when you know you have got the better of a rival – even if you know that he or she has suffered by it?
YES/NO

20 Do you
(a) assess your progress every year and make New Year resolutions?
(b) keep those resolutions?
(c) always exercise your vote in elections?
(d) feel yourself to be a pillar of the community?
(Answer all four questions)

SOCIAL ADVANCEMENT

1 You receive an invitation to an Embassy cocktail party. Do you
(a) refuse, realizing you would feel awkward and out of place?
(b) turn up in your best clothes and enjoy living it up while you can?
(c) tell everyone about it, before and after, in a loud voice?
(d) force your company on the Ambassador?

2 Someone has, unexpectedly, a spare ticket for the theatre. Your first thought is
(a) what's on?
(b) which part of the house?

3 You and your partner want to buy a puppy. Your partner has fallen for an attractive, scruffy mongrel. You want a terrier with championship pedigree. Do you give way?
YES/NO

4 You have spent a lot of time and money improving your house or apartment. You gradually realize that new neighbours are less socially acceptable than you would like. Do you
(a) ignore the situation?
(b) worry about what your friends will think?
(c) move?

5 Can you produce from your wardrobe exactly the right thing to wear for any occasion?
YES/NO

6 Arriving on your cruise liner, you find that it is 'one-class'. Are you
(a) furious?
(b) disappointed, but angle for a seat at the captain's table?
(c) unconcerned?

7 At a formal gathering, do you wear
(a) what you think is most correct?
(b) what you think will make most effect?
(c) whatever is most comfortable and will 'get by'?

8 Have you ever formed a close relationship with a partner from a different social class to yourself because you knew this would improve your own social standing?
YES/NO

9 Where would you most like to be:
(a) at a large social gathering at Buckingham Palace or the White House?
(b) a film première or gala performance of opera or ballet?
(c) a large Halloween or Thanksgiving party in your neighbourhood?

10 On whom do you spend the most money at Christmas:
(a) someone with whom you identify?
(b) someone who has done you a good turn?
(c) someone you know who may be rather famous or 'ahead' of you in some way?
(d) a pleasant elderly relative?

11 Do you feel really sure of yourself at all types of social occasion?
YES/NO

12 Would you most like to meet
(a) Jackie Kennedy?
(b) Jack Nicolson?
(c) Your Senator or MP?

13 Would you find someone less appealing because
(a) they had fallen on hard times and had to change their life-style?
(b) they had become involved in a strange religious cult?
(c) they had purchased an ostentatious limousine?

14 When compiling a list of guests for a party, do you ask
(a) mostly close friends?
(b) people whose life-style you identify with?

15 Do you keep abreast of best-selling book lists and book reviews?
YES/NO

16 Would you say your knowledge

of wine is
(a) very good?
(b) reasonable?
(c) poor?

17 From the following, do you feel you should
(a) improve your golf, tennis or bridge?
(b) invest in a set of solid silver cutlery?
(c) learn a new skill, or to play a musical instrument?

18 Can you honestly say you do not look down on people of any other race, colour, or social stratum?
YES/NO

19 Do you feel *particularly* satisfied when you have entertained people who are important to you (as opposed to close friends) and things have gone exactly as you hoped and planned?
YES/NO

20 Do you
(a) get annoyed when friends' dinner tables are not set to your liking?
(b) always phone or write 'thank-you' notes after a visit or dinner party?
(c) thoroughly enjoy a big night out?
(d) hate to be seen in an hotel that has less than a four-star rating?
(Answer all four questions)

Scoring

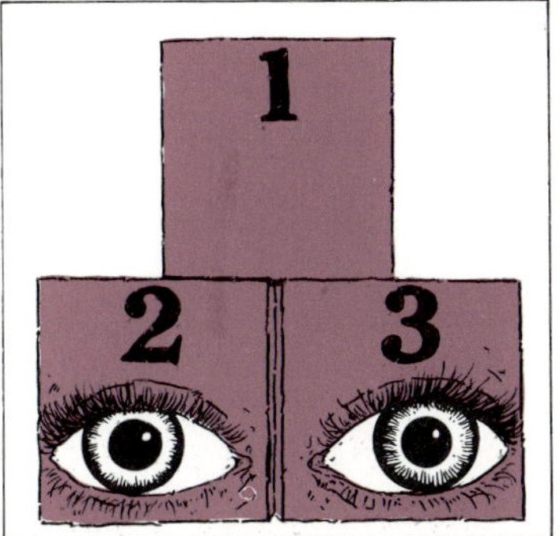

MONEY

1 (a) – 1; (b) – 2; (c) – 4; (d) – 3
2 Yes – 2; no – 1
3 Yes – 2; no – 1
4 (a) – 1; (b) – 2; (c) – 3
5 Yes – 2; no – 1
6 (a) – 1; (b) – 3; (c) – 2
7 (a) – 1; (b) – 2; (c) – 3
8 Yes – 1; no – 2
9 (a) – 2; (b) – 1; (c) – 3
10 (a) – 2; (b) – 3; (c) – 1; (d) – 4
11 Yes – 2; no – 1
12 (a) – 2; (b) – 1; (c) – 3
13 (a) – 1; (b) – 3; (c) – 2
14 Yes – 2; no – 1
15 Yes – 2; no – 1
16 (a) – 3; (b) – 2; (c) – 1
17 (a) – 2; (b) – 1; (c) – 3
18 Yes – 2; no – 1
19 Yes – 1; no – 2
20 For each answer score
Yes – 2, no – 1

POWER

1 (a) – 1; (b) – 4; (c) – 2; (d) – 3
2 (a) – 1; (b) – 2
3 Yes – 1; no – 2
4 (a) – 1; (b) – 3; (c) – 2
5 Yes – 2; no – 1
6 (a) – 3; (b) – 2; (c) – 1
7 (a) – 3; (b) – 1; (c) – 2
8 Yes – 2; no – 1
9 (a) – 3; (b) – 2; (c) – 1
10 (a) – 1; (b) – 2; (c) – 3; (d) – 4
11 Yes – 2; no – 1
12 (a) – 2; (b) – 1; (c) – 3
13 (a) – 3; (b) – 1; (c) – 2
14 Yes – 2; no – 1
15 Yes – 2; no – 1
16 (a) – 3; (b) – 2; (c) – 1
17 (a) – 1; (b) – 3; (c) – 2
18 Yes – 2; no – 1
19 Yes – 2; no – 1
20 For each answer score
Yes – 2, no – 1

SOCIAL ADVANCEMENT

1 (a) – 1; (b) – 2; (c) – 3; (d) – 4
2 (a) – 1; (b) – 2
3 Yes – 2; no – 1
4 (a) – 1; (b) – 2; (c) – 3
5 Yes – 2; no – 1
6 (a) – 3; (b) – 2; (c) – 1
7 (a) – 3; (b) – 2; (c) – 1
8 Yes – 2; no – 1
9 (a) – 3; (b) – 2; (c) – 1
10 (a) – 3; (b) – 1; (c) – 4; (d) – 2
11 Yes – 2; no – 1
12 (a) – 3; (b) – 1; (c) – 2
13 (a) – 3; (b) – 2; (c) – 1
14 (a) – 1; (b) – 2
15 Yes – 2; no – 1
16 (a) – 3; (b) – 2; (c) – 1
17 (a) – 3; (b) – 2; (c) – 1
18 Yes – 1; no – 2
19 Yes – 2; no – 1
20 For each answer score
Yes – 2, no – 1

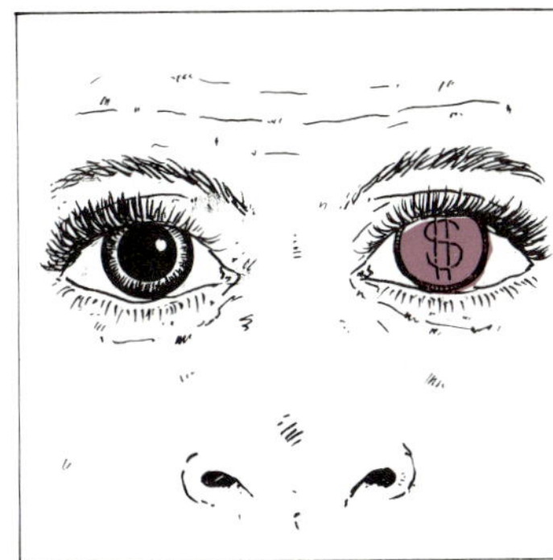

Interpretations

Total the scores for each section and for all three together. In the individual sections the maximum score is 58 points and the minimum 23. The total score maximum is 174; the minimum 69.

Grading
In each section, a score of 23–32 is rated 'low', 33–45 'middle' and 46–58 'high'. For the total, 69–96 is 'low', 97–135 'middle' and 136–174 'high'.

MONEY

Low score 23–32
From a purely aesthetic point of view your attitude to money may be admirable, but you need to be made aware that, through your lack of concern for it, you may run into difficulties. Possibly what money you have slips through your fingers all too easily. You are not over-concerned about it, to say the least; your attitude to it borders on the unworldly and you could be accused of being 'dizzy' or impractical. Try to be a little more constructive and perhaps, too, more realistic about your financial affairs – and above all else get sound professional advice before committing yourself to any sizable outlay or apparently attractive financial scheme or investment.

Middle score 33–45
You probably enjoy the money you have and, while you would welcome with open arms any improvement in your finances, it is quite likely that generally speaking you get by – and have enough to do what you really want to do, when you want to do it! This is excellent; and what is better, it seems likely that you *enjoy* the money you have and believe that it should be used, not just kept as a pleasant display of black figures in your bank account. If you felt like it, you could learn a little more about money and how to make it grow, since you may well not always opt for the best bargain, or get the most out of what you have. Possibly you enjoy owning beautiful things and get pleasure from them, knowing that at the same time they are an investment (this is your justification for having spent money on them). If you were shrewder, or put money first, you might invest more, or think in terms of stocks and shares rather than home comforts and the odd work of art. But good luck to you; we think you've got it about right!

High score 46–58
You attach great importance to your financial affairs: the higher your score the more likely you are to think of money as all-important. At times you could tend to be avaricious and you need to be a little on the defensive, since you would probably hate others to think of you in that way. You may well not get quite as much fun from the fruits of your labours as you ought to; while you may think that a little more spent for the sheer pleasure it would give yourself and other people would be simple unjustifiable extravagance, do watch others' reactions when you give them an unexpected present. Having a healthy bank balance gives you a great sense of security and this of course is fine; but there are other ways of feeling secure and the spontaneous show of affection – given and received – is one of them. Try just occasionally to forget to buy *The Wall Street Journal* or *The Financial Times*!

POWER

Low score 23–32
You probably like – indeed love – people for what they are and not for what you can get out of them or what they can do for you. You have no ambition to be President, whether of the PTA, your local debating society, or the US of A. You think about other people's needs and are unselfish in your attitude towards them. They will love you for this; but it is possible that they will also ask you to do too much for them, thus taking advantage of you. It is obvious that you are a kind, delightful person in very many ways, but because you do not want power you may be rather less assertive than you should be – some care is needed here. Don't be too backward in coming forward. Do what *you* want to do and don't be pushed around or listen quite so much to other more assertive types. You have plenty to offer.

Middle score 33–45
You wouldn't consciously harm anyone to get yourself into a more powerful position in life; that just isn't your way. You make progress through self-confidence and use your brain constructively and positively. You can give orders charmingly and if necessary correct a subordinate in a fair and reasonable way (knowing that in the long run this will be to your advantage). You would not say no to a seat on the board or any committee of your choice; you know that if in due course you are elected to an officer's chair on that committee you will not only cope, but will enjoy the responsibility and concomitant power. You deal well with the cut and thrust of twentieth-century life and probably thrive on it. Keep your horizons broad and avoid getting bogged down with worrying details. At most times you will be able to do this; but remember that you might not adapt too well if, towards the end of your career, you find yourself in a very high position, for the loneliness that this would almost inevitably bring is simply not for you.

High score 46–58
You are very assertive and have excellent powers of leadership. Certainly the rest of humanity needs people like you; but, while you have a great deal to contribute, it is possible that in achieving a powerful and prominent position you would be ruthless towards others, causing them more injury and upset than you may fully realize. You are determined and it seems unlikely that many people will be able to get the better of you. While you may well have considerable ability for leaving no stone unturned, don't let yourself down in others' eyes by carping over petty slights or worrying if a competitor is getting ahead of you. This could sap your energy and interrupt the overall progress so important to you. On a personal level you could appear to others either as very cool and calculating or as a fire-brand. Decide which, and ask yourself if you need either to warm up or cool down a little!

SOCIAL ADVANCEMENT

Low score 23–32
You couldn't care less about social climbing. It is not important to you what others have or what you haven't. You expect people to take you as they find you and would never do anything merely to impress another human being. You would consider this a waste of time. You may even feel a little disgusted at times, when people you know try to impress you about where they've been on holiday, the size of their car, or whatever. Name-dropping, too, will have a similar effect. You are most unpretentious and may hate to dress up, even on formal occasions. Because you accept people at their face value, you expect others to react to you in the same way. This may well not always be so, since other people are more affected and could think of your low profile on the snob scene and your basic honesty as a sort of inverted snobbery. It is important that while you are being yourself – with no false values – others should recognize you as genuine. So don't be self-effacing and continue to be yourself even if you don't want to be caught up in the social whirl.

Middle score 33–45
You certainly keep half an eye on what's about to happen – who and what is 'in' and 'out' of fashion, in the news or limelight – and enjoy doing so. When you get the chance to see how 'top people' live, you take it and enjoy every minute. You don't let other more socially 'advanced' people get the better of you; you know exactly what to do and when to do it, feeling excited and exhilarated but at ease on all occasions. You like to talk about your social life because you genuinely want others to enjoy your more interesting experiences with you. However, to less fortunate people this could seem like showing off and you might be accused of snobbishness and social climbing. An element of jealousy might be provoked. In your enthusiasm, you could get carried away; some soft-pedalling might be necessary. The great thing is that you have the ability to enjoy life; if you do have a bigger car than your neighbours you'll take pleasure in it and wouldn't be averse to filling it up with their kids – or their garden refuse!

High score 46–58
If you're not 'the top' yet, you're all set to be – but be very careful that you're not taking the smart set and the social scene too seriously. If you do, you could well seem very 'pushy' to others – 'pushy' in the sense that you monopolize your host and hostess, insist on talking for too long to the guest of honour at a reception. Even worse, you may go on repeating stories of your own social successes for far too long afterwards, becoming a social bore. You genuinely like *real quality*; you like things to be 'right and proper'; and other people may sometimes lose sight of the fact that, whether you intend to or not, you do raise the standard of the general quality of life. Many people could learn a great deal from you; but you must question your motivation. Are you just a social climber? Or have you a real love of the best things in life (which of course are not, nor ever have been, free)? Look again at individual questions in this section and your answers to them. While we would never suggest that you lower your standards or your sights, you might like to reassess your *reasons* for all that aspiration . . . perhaps a little philanthropic work for a cause that inspires you would help you along the way.

OVERALL AMBITION

Low score 69–96
It seems very unlikely that you will ever suffer from a stomach ulcer – you are not sufficiently interested in getting to the top, either socially or in your career. You plod on – unperturbed by what the neighbours have, or by seeing others overtaking you in your career. You have a kindly, gentle attitude and are probably very philosophical in outlook; but it is important that you realize that in your somewhat un-twentieth-century approach to life you could get trampled by others who might take advantage of your good nature. Try, if you can, to be a little on your guard against this – you might well be an over-willing slave. While you enjoy helping others and get considerable pleasure from doing so, don't allow yourself to be treated like a doormat. It may well be that your partner or friends tell you that you are unambitious and even lackadaisical. Listen to what they have to say. While the world can do with a few more of your nice, kind, generous sort, it is no good giving your cloak to a beggar if you need it for the children's bed next winter!

Middle score 97–135
While you are well able to enjoy worldly pleasures and progress and are by no means sat on by other people, you probably feel that you would like to earn a bit more and rise a little further up the social ladder. There are plenty of modest but possible ambitions for you to attain. You have a healthy attitude to material advancement and, though you work hard, you also have an excellent capacity to enjoy the fruits of your labours. It is possible that you might over-reach yourself sometimes – but, because you are basically well balanced, you are most certainly the type to learn by experience. You will take calculated risks, but the longer you live and the more experience you gather, the more you will learn that your best progress is made by steady application. This sounds dull, but isn't, because you see to it that it is enjoyable and fun. You probably get a few pats on the back from partners and colleagues at work and you will deserve them; but, should things go wrong, you will be willing to admit that you were wrong and take positive action to set things right. Contentment probably comes for you when you realize you have completed a job and know that your expertise, in whatever field, has made it a job well done.

High score 136–174
Your basic motivation in life is to progress on all fronts: the higher your score the greater your ambition. You are very likely to have what it takes to get to the top; your will is so strong that you have to be out in front and, let's face it, BE SOMEONE. You probably ought from time to time to think about the reasons for this very powerful basic motivation. Perhaps you are fighting off miserable memories of your childhood? If so, you are succeeding. But with such a powerful exterior energy-force and will, you may be missing out on some of the simple and inexpensive pleasures of life – in some ways, life could be passing you by. Enjoy your position of power – but use it gratefully and kindly. Make sure your marriage or partnership is a two-way, alive thing; bear in mind that you could be the archetypal heavy father. While it may not be easy, it is very advisable for you to relax – and not in the artificial atmosphere of an expensive health farm, or a five-star hotel at a fashionable resort. If you don't, your health will suffer.

16 Identifying intelligence

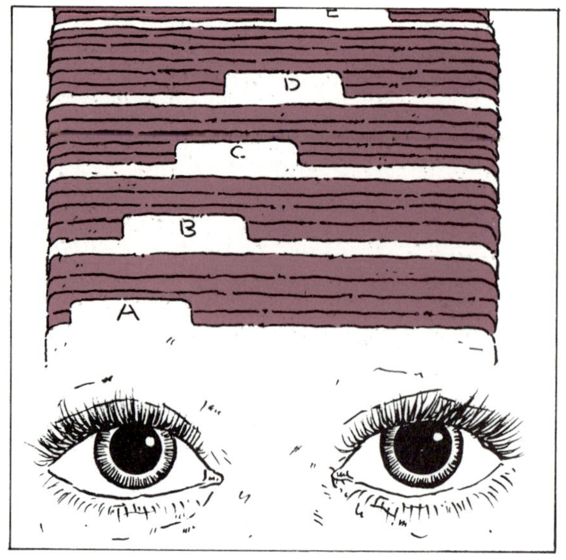

Divide your mental age by your calendar age and multiply by a hundred. Does your IQ tell you anything useful? How reliable are the tests? How do they relate to age, heredity, nationality, language . . .?

DO YOU CONSIDER yourself intelligent? Of course, that depends on what you mean by 'intelligent'. In general, psychologists seem to mean 'able to learn and able to adjust to new circumstances' – a capability shared by many animals. In which case it would be a mistake to assume that 'intelligence' is of supreme importance to, say, the creative artist, while it is of the utmost importance to a parking-lot attendant whose work consists of fitting a large number of cars, appearing at irregular intervals, into random spaces.

The great disadvantage of 'intelligence tests' – and especially of the best known of them, the IQ, or 'Intelligence Quotient' test – is that they only relate to somewhat mechanical skills, skills some of which at least can be learned by some animals and have not a great deal to do with the kind of intelligence that separates man from beast. International MENSA, the organization which monitors the IQ of its members, experimented at one time by publishing anthologies of poetry written by people of high IQ. General critical opinion was that this poetry was for the most part of an abysmally low standard.

It was Dr Alfred Binet who first, in 1905, attempted to devise a practical means of measuring human intelligence. He had been instructed to classify 'bright' and 'dull' children in Parisian schools and, working with other researchers, he devised a series of tests which could be applied to the children's normal, everyday behaviour. These were rather different for each age group and the theory was that a 'dull' child would perform them adequately later in his life than might be expected, while the 'bright' child would

Intelligence and genius: do they match? The infant Mozart and the ten-year-old Yehudi Menuhin. The first, a creator; the second, a great interpreter.

deal with them earlier. If between sixty and ninety per cent of children in one age group could perform the task satisfactorily, then it was considered a norm for that age group.

At the age of three, for instance, a child was expected to be able to point to his nose, eyes and mouth, to know his surname and to repeat two numbers. The six-year-old child was expected to be able to count up to thirteen coins, to tell the difference between morning and afternoon and to be able to copy a diamond shape. A twelve-year-old would be asked to make up a sentence containing three given words and to make sense of a sentence in which the words had been jumbled.

When Dr Binet discovered that a child had a mental age lower than his calendar age, he was classified as 'dull'. An attempt was made to express this in a figure by dividing the mental age by the calendar age and multiplying by one hundred. So a ten-year-old child with a mental age of 8 had an 'intelligence quotient' of 80 ($8 \div 10 = 0.80 \times 100 = 80$). But an eight-year-old with a mental age of ten had an IQ of 125 ($10 \div 8 = 1.25 \times 100 = 125$).

In adult terms, there have been rough attempts to classify IQ scores: L. J. Cronbach's *Essentials of Psychological Testing* suggested in 1960, for instance, that while someone with an IQ of 130 'can achieve post-graduate university degrees, and usually fills professional, administrative or executive jobs', someone with an IQ of 90 could only 'perform jobs requiring some judgement, such as operating a sewing machine or assembling parts', and someone with an IQ of 40 would be reduced to 'learning how to mow lawns or do simple laundry'. About half of the population seems to fall within ten points of the average, which of course is 100.

Dr Binet's tests now seem pretty rough; on the other hand they were in practice reliable in that the children he classified as 'dull' had been generally regarded as such by their teachers and their friends. IQ does relate, however, to a great extent to what people have been taught – in school, at university or work, and simply by observation. An extremely quick and intelligent African

native, able to stay alive under devastatingly hard and difficult conditions which would kill the 'educated' Westerner in a matter of hours, would come out of a Western IQ test with an extremely low score. There is evidence to suggest that IQ tests are only fair when applied to people of the same culture, and even the same social status, as those who set the tests.

Modern intelligence tests for adults are complicated, because they attempt to evaluate

Relaxation for Albert Einstein (opposite), who revolutionized 20th-century man's view of the universe; and concentration for the Russian Grand Master Spassky as he faces a group of ten-year-olds: is the sum of their wits equal to the weight of his experience?

various kinds of intelligence (some more amenable to testing than others). There are tests of verbal ability, the understanding of numbers, general reasoning power, the ability to see relationships between one object or concept and another. Other tests measure potential rather than present ability (variations of these are used in vocational guidance tests to help career choice). Some of these tests are given to one person working alone, others to several people at the same time.

There are further problems. The time limit usually set on such tests can defeat people who are temperamentally incapable of sustained effort, who give up too easily when they would be capable of providing answers with more steady attention. Carelessness is another factor which can falsify results – knowing the right answer, but setting down the wrong one. Extrovert people are notoriously good at undervaluing themselves in IQ tests. The more original, inventive and creative a person, the worse he is at 'closed' tests, in which *one* answer (the right one) is demanded, but the better at 'open' questions, in which there might be several 'right' answers and a choice has to be made between them and several 'wrong' answers. Age also has an effect: people under eighteen or over fifty-five or so will normally score lower than others.

Within their restricted area, IQ tests have nevertheless provided some fascinating insights into intelligence. Are you, for instance, a first-born child? These children are, as a matter of statistical fact, generally more intelligent and successful than their younger brothers and sisters. More than half the Presidents of the United States were first-born sons and a study of the IQs of 400,000 Dutch males has recently shown that elder children score higher than their younger brothers (who in turn score higher than *their* younger brothers).

The first-born may be more intelligent than his (or her) siblings as a result of attempts to retain the interest and affection of parents preoccupied with a new baby, or because of the exclusive attention received from the parents before the birth of a brother or sister. The phenomenon does not seem to be related to heredity – though it is certainly true that high or low IQs do seem to run in families and identical twins tend to score very similar IQ ratings – more similar than chance would suggest – even if they are brought up by different people and in different environments.

There is no evidence that certain races are inherently more or less intelligent than others. A large-scale experiment organized in the state of Israel has shown the opposite to be true: the chances of your being more or less intelligent than average remain the same whether you are Irish, Polish, African, Jewish or German or French. . . .

There are many questions to be answered about how intelligence is developed and even precisely what it is. Measuring it is still a very rough science – but IQ tests of various kinds may provide some answers to the question, 'How intelligent am I?', and enable one questioner to match skill with another.

17 The IQ test

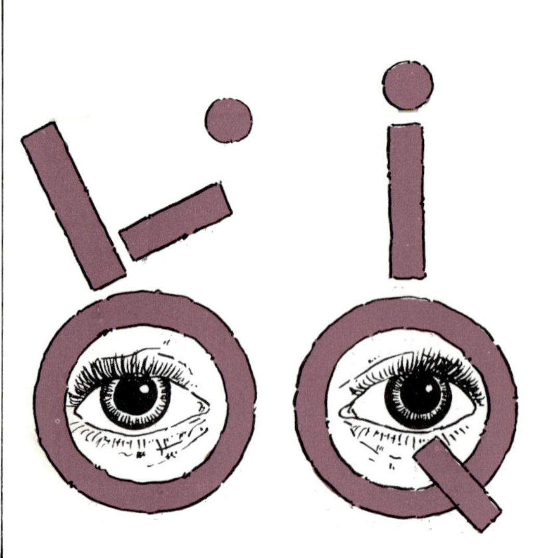

Words – numbers – spatial conceptions. . . . Score 80 in this test and you could probably make a better one yourself.

TESTS DEVISED TO measure your 'Intelligence Quotient' vary considerably, often consisting of a great number of questions covering visual as well as verbal and numerical skills.

But shorter and rather simpler (not necessarily 'easier'!) tests have been shown to be capable of assessing IQ and one of these (devised by A. E. Davies for British Mensa) follows.

There are eighty questions and you should allow yourself forty minutes in which to answer them. Do not spend too much time on a question you don't immediately understand; press on and come back to it later, if you have time. It is best to set an alarm timer, or to have someone to tell you when the forty minutes is up. Having completed all eight sets of questions, then turn to the answers given at the end and check. Mensa's interpretation of your results follows. And good luck!

TEST 1

On each line below, underline the two words which mean most nearly the same.

Example: person, man, lad, youth

1 Absurd, logical, preposterous, popular
2 Receive, deceive, accept, disown
3 Negligent, unimportant, careless, cautious
4 Comparable, intricate, comprehensible, understandable
5 Conquer, achieve, find, accomplish
6 Soft, fragile, severed, brittle
7 Serene, seething, mobility, tranquil
8 Subservient, menial, manly, morbid
9 Stupid, idle, activity, inactive
10 Transient, immutable, transport, momentary

TEST 2

Write, at the end of each line below, the number which continues the series.

Example: 2, 4, 6 (8)

11 3, 5, 7 (. . . .)
12 28, 21, 14 (. . . .)
13 3, 7, 11 (. . . .)
14 45, 36, 27 (. . . .)
15 2, 4, 8, 16 (. . . .)
16 2, 3, 5, 8 (. . . .)
17 81, 27, 9, 3 (. . . .)
18 1, 4, 9, 16 (. . . .)
19 3, 6, 5, 10, 9 (. . . .)
20 288, 144, 148, 74, 76 (. . . .)

TEST 3

In each sentence below two words have changed places with each other: underline each pair of words.

Example: <u>clothes</u> wear <u>men</u>

21 A is air gas.
22 Sugar from not obtained is sea water.
23 Has triangle every three angles.
24 Making mistakes of a part is human nature.
25 Of people are worthy intemperate trust.
26 Any never employ debaters irony.
27 Envy traits malice are bad and.
28 Finds the summer one in sparrows in pairs.
29 Is comprehend cause to to forgive error.
30 It is other aimless as any as.

TEST 4

In each set of six numbers below, each of the three numbers on the bottom line, including the missing number, is formed by starting with the corresponding number on the top line.

In each set, the same method of arithmetic (e.g., adding two or dividing by three) is used to make the numbers on the bottom line. Find what the different rule is for each different set and write in the missing numbers.

Example:

1	3	4
2	4	5

31

3	5	1
5	7	

34

4	7	9
11	14	

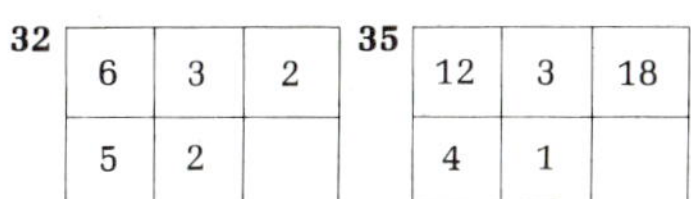

32

6	3	2
5	2	

35

12	3	18
4	1	

33

3	4	7
6	8	

36

2	9	3
6	27	

37

24	100	144
6	25	

39

27	75	9
18	50	

38

3	7	4
−2	2	

40

45	24	12
60	32	

TEST 5

On each line below write one letter to continue the series.

Example: AA BB CC D (D)

41 AXY BXY CXY (. . . .)
42 FEDCB (. . . .)
43 ECDDCEBF (. . . .)
44 ABBCBDEFBGHI (. . . .)
45 DVCWBX (. . . .)
46 GRCDEGRFGGRH (. . . .)
47 BHCDGEFGFHIJ (. . . .)

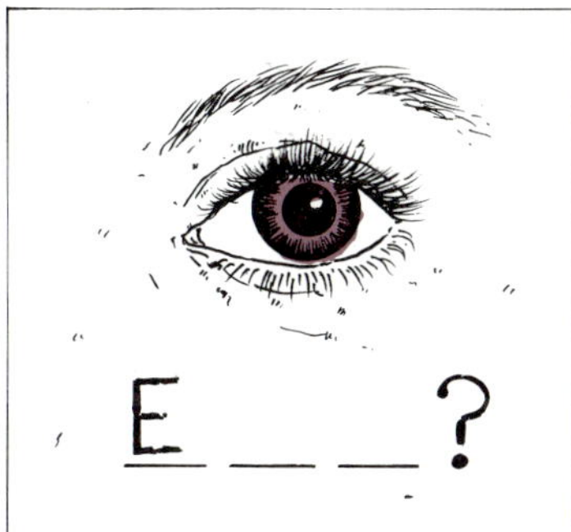

48 ADGBEHCF (. . . .)
49 LOMPN (. . . .)
50 CDECGHIHKLMM (. . . .)

TEST 6

Example: '*Up* is to *down* as *above* is to *below*.' This example was a complete analogy. In each analogy below the third and fourth of the main words are missing and you have to select from the group of words on the right the missing words. In each case underline the two words needed to complete the analogy.

Example: up is to down . . . <u>above</u>, beyond, near, <u>below</u>

51 Second is to time . . . ounce, return, minute, weight
52 Prediction is to future . . . past, absence, memory, present
53 Clumsy is to deft . . . ugly, clever, awkward, stupid
54 Hook is to eye . . . flange, nut, screw, bolt
55 Dynamic is to static . . . politic, active, erg, inert
56 River is to brook . . . plateau, mountain, hill, hillock, pile
57 Farmer is to vegetable salesman . . . cutter, weaver, cloth, tailor, hatter
58 Where is to room . . . which, when, there, now, hour
59 More is to again . . . often, repeat, continue, time, still
60 Manner is to matter . . . say, frown, custom, word, message

TEST 7

On each line below, the words run in pairs. Write the missing word at the end of each line to complete the series.

Example: no, never; perhaps, sometimes; yes (always).

61 Line, two; square, four; pentagon . . . .
62 Here, now; nowhere, never; there . . . .
63 Canoe, paddle; steamer, screw; yacht . . . .
64 Taxicab, taxi; luncheon, lunch; blossom . . . .
65 Memory, memorize; courage, encourage; guile . . . .
66 Analysis, analyse; agreement, agree; danger . . . .
67 Legal, illegality; ready, unreadiness; illegible . . . .
68 Explanatory, explain; breathy, breathe; facile . . . .
69 Division, divide; amendment, amend; peril . . . .
70 Angry, anger; abstract, abstraction; irate . . . .

TEST 8

71 How many miles will a plane fly in 7 hours at an average speed of 500 miles per hour?
72 If there are 5 kinds of chocolates what is the least number a child must buy to be sure of at least three of the same kind?
73 If six machines make 1000 boxes in three days, how many machines could make 1000 boxes in half a day?
74 A bin (with all its corners

square) holds 400 cubic feet. If the bin is ten feet long and five feet wide, how deep is it?

75 A man spent one-eighth of his money on rent and four times as much on food and clothes. He then had £9 (or $9) left. How much did he have at first?

76 A ship has food to last her crew of 250 men for six months. How long would it last 600 men?

77 Mick shared five rolls and Will shared three with Tim, who brought no food but paid eight pence. They all ate equal amounts. How much should Will get from the eight pence?

78 A snail climbed up a twelve-foot wall at a rate of three feet each day, but slipped down two feet each night. How many days did it take him to reach the top?

79 How many miles does a fly travel flying non-stop from end to end of a sixty-foot carriage at sixty miles an hour in a train leaving station A at 6 p.m. and reaching B, 90 miles away, at 9 p.m.?

80 Write the way in which you could arrange three nines to equal eleven.

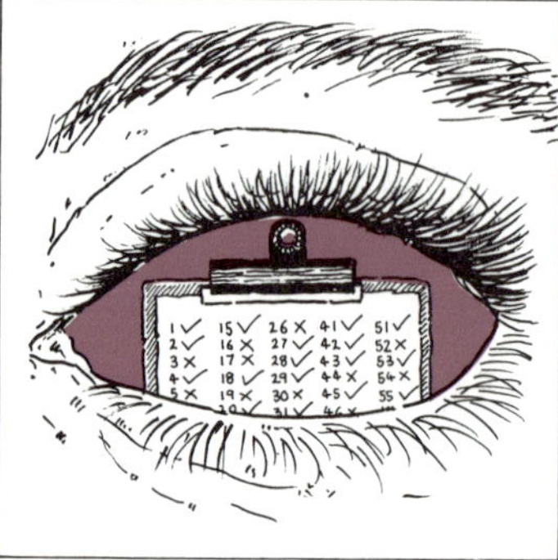

Answers

1 Absurd preposterous
2 receive accept
3 negligent careless
4 comprehensible understandable
5 achieve accomplish
6 fragile brittle
7 serene tranquil
8 subservient menial
9 idle inactive
10 transient momentary
11 9
12 7
13 15
14 18
15 32
16 12
17 1
18 25
19 18
20 38
21 a air
22 from is
23 has every
24 of is
25 of intemperate
26 any debaters
27 traits and
28 finds in
29 is to
30 other [the 2nd] as
31 3
32 1
33 14
34 16
35 6
36 9
37 36
38 −1
39 6
40 16
41 D
42 A
43 A
44 J
45 A
46 G
47 K
48 I
49 Q
50 O
51 ounce weight
52 past memory
53 clever stupid
54 nut bolt
55 active inert
56 mountain hillock
57 weaver tailor
58 when hour
59 repeat continue
60 word message
61 five
62 then
63 sail
64 bloom
65 beguile
66 endanger
67 legibility
68 facilitate
69 imperil
70 ire
71 3,500
72 11
73 36
74 8
75 24
76 $2\frac{1}{2}$
77 1
78 10
79 180
80 99/9

Interpretations

British Mensa's comments on your possible scores are:
With 10 marks or less: you are suffering from a hangover or something.
With about 20 marks: approximately average adult standard.
With about 30 marks: in Britain or America you would have deserved a selective high school education.
With about 40 marks: in Britain you could probably have passed the school-leaving certificate in a few subjects or in America achieved a High School Diploma.
With about 50 marks: you would probably benefit from further education after leaving school.
With about 65 marks: you would stand a fair chance of passing Mensa membership entrance tests.
With about 70 marks: about the level reached by only one per cent of the population.
With about 80 marks: you could probably make a better test yourself.

18 *The prison of the family*

Imprisoned by the family?

But how large a family?

Perhaps 40,000 genes told your

body how to grow and develop.

Did they make you Aryan,

Jew, Negro, Anglo-Saxon?

Does it make any difference?

OUR KNOWLEDGE OF genetics is still in its infancy, but it seems that every human body contains between six and forty thousand genes, each of which probably has tens of thousands of codes which tell our bodies how to grow and develop. All this information is passed down from parents to children in the tiny sperm and egg from which the human embryo is formed; as the cells of the egg double and redouble, they divide themselves according to the genetic code into muscle and blood cells, kidney and liver cells, nerve and skin cells, and the hundreds of others which construct a human being. The genes rule over them all.

The chromosomes, threads on which the genes are strung, are already present in the fertilized egg: 23 from the father, 23 from the mother, making up the total of 46 – individual to humans; a chimpanzee has 48, a gibbon 44. The embryo child inherits a random selection of genes from each parent, so that the genetic make-up of one man or woman is individual: the chance that you could have the same genetic make-up as someone else is 1 in 1 followed by three thousand zeros. If you are to some extent imprisoned within a genetic pattern, a genetic family pattern, the prison is a pretty big one. Yet there are some compartments into which you can be locked.

Contained in our bodies are both dominant and recessive genes and, in a complex system of juggling for position, they may inflict physical disabilities on a child. Eight to ten of the recessive genes in our bodies are likely to be 'lethal', passing on to us in a double dose disabilities which may not have shown themselves in our parents. About 150 recessive diseases are known, varying from quite severe mental defects to common blindness and deafness. The male and female chromosomes present in all of us are also sometimes at odds, so that the male element in a man may sometimes be stronger than normal, or vice versa (see chapter 10).

In an attempt to defeat these possibilities humanity has evolved taboos, which have resulted in the broadening out and development of human characteristics. The definition of incest is now narrower than it once was: cousin marries cousin without too much fuss. In the past, the incest taboos were so strong that they constantly sent man in search of a woman sufficiently far enough from his home to be completely unrelated to him. Genes were thus exchanged between tribe and tribe, population and population and, later, between race and race. It is interesting, on the other hand, that there seem to be some forces (social pressures among them) which incline us to marry people rather like ourselves – a short man will tend to marry a short woman, for instance, a deaf man marry a deaf woman; plump people, thin people, people with the same skin colouring tend to get together.

Darwin's theory of evolution – the theory that the men and women with the most healthy genetic make-up survive – has been severely dented in recent years by advances in medical care and knowledge, which have kept alive men and women who a century ago

would have died in childhood or adolescence. We may by this means be carefully nurturing certain weaknesses in the human race – though these weaknesses are relative, for the results would only become dangerous if modern medicine for some reason was unable to cope with them.

The genes you received at the moment of your conception were outside the control of you or your parents; in many ways they were as random as a deal of cards from a vast pack. Within the tiny family unit of father, mother and one child the range of chance is astronomical enough; within the family of parental relatives there is an increase in the odds; within the family of a single country, an unthinkable proliferation; within a whole race, the possibilities become too complex for the mind to grasp.

If we are in the genetic 'prison of the family', the rest of the human race is in there with us. The passion of some people for attempting to set themselves apart as members of a relatively small family (the attempt of the German Nazis to see themselves as peculiarly 'Aryan', for example) is as stupid as it is pejorative. A race is only a breeding population in which certain traits tend to appear more often than in some other populations. These traits may include colour of skin, which was originally dependent on a race's ability to adapt to a very sunny environment. We might as well object to (or congratulate) all fair-haired or left-handed people, people with blood group A, or homosexuals, as being in some way inferior (or superior) to the rest.

David Hockney frames his own image between portraits of his parents (opposite). Nazi Germany forced its citizens into a 'family' of a different kind, from which the 'impure' were excluded.

Those who are deeply prejudiced about their own race's superiority forget, too, that today there is no such thing as a pure race – certainly not in Europe or the USA. Individuals have interbred continually over the past hundred or two hundred years and there can be very few people living in Europe or North America who have not somewhere in their family tree a black person, or a Jew, or an ancestor from a 'foreign' country. When Hitler tried to insist on Germans being 'pure-blooded', he was barking up a non-existent tree. Medical authorities in Sweden, for instance, have recently found that only 10.1

"THE THING WON'T MELT"

per cent of men drafted into army service are 'pure-blooded' Nordics – and that in a country which most people would think archetypally Nordic.

There is another sense in which it is futile to think of the blood as either 'pure' or 'impure'. Blood-group characteristics are certainly passed down from one generation to another but, just as it is impossible to tell whether the child of a blonde mother and a dark-haired father will have brown or blue eyes, so it is impossible to foretell what blood group the child of parents of different blood groups will have.

The blood groupings most usually used today depend on the different types of proteins present in the red cell membranes. Your blood group is determined by the presence of A or B proteins or both; if you have neither, you will be in O; and there are four groups in all – A, B, AB, or O. Blood tests are sometimes done in an attempt to prove or disprove paternity of a child. But positive proof cannot be obtained, though there are certain blood groups to which the child of two parents could not possibly belong. The only evidence is negative: the suggestion that it is very unlikely that a child with a particular blood group could be born of two parents of other groups.

Blood grouping is especially important when blood transfusion takes place. In some cases when a recipient is of one blood group and the donor of another, the red cells of the donated blood cling together in clumps and clog up the small blood vessels, then disintegrate to release haemoglobin which may seriously injure the cells of the kidneys and even cause death from kidney failure. So blood transfusion must take place between people of the same blood group, or people whose blood has at least been tested for compatibility before transfusion. A useful short-cut is available: you can wear a bracelet or carry a card with your blood group on it.

There is another factor which may cause trouble at transfusion: the so-called Rhesus factor, an antigen to haemolytic disease of the

new born which forms antibodies, that will react upon the red blood corpuscles of about 85 per cent of the population of white people, and may be dangerous during a second transfusion, or when a woman has given birth to a child not long before the transfusion.

It is now a cliché to talk about ourselves as members of 'the family of man'; but it is none the less true. You, reader, share the same store of genes as the Australian aborigine, the American Indian, the Sicilian peasant, the African tribesman, the Eskimo, the Ethiopian. . . . You will have about 30 per cent different genes from your neighbour of the same race and social circumstances. If you are compared with a man as different as possible in race and circumstances, the difference might rise to as much as 35 or 40 per cent. But that is all.

Biological analysis begs some enormous questions: questions of environment, temperament, social and political background and attitude, for instance. And then there is the question of the smaller, more personal prison of our own immediate family circumstances, with the attendant psychological pressures put upon us by our parents, brothers and sisters – pressures which may well affect our every action and thought.

But as to race: that is only skin deep. Our skin, the shape of our body and face, mark the outline where 'we', our bodies, meet 'life', the environment in which we live. The colour and shape they take on may resemble the colour and shape of our parents, our tribe, our race. It may be a colour and shape which is attractive or unattractive to others – but, on the evidence of biology, nothing could be more foolish than to suppose that it imprisons us in any kind of cage but that artificially built by prejudice.

A *Life* cartoon of 1915 (opposite) suggested that Germans, then soon to become the enemy, alone resisted assimilation into the multinational American melting pot. By contrast, Tom Torlino, a Navajo who attended the first Indian school in the 1880s, proved quickly responsive to the pressures of his new environment.

19 You are what you worship

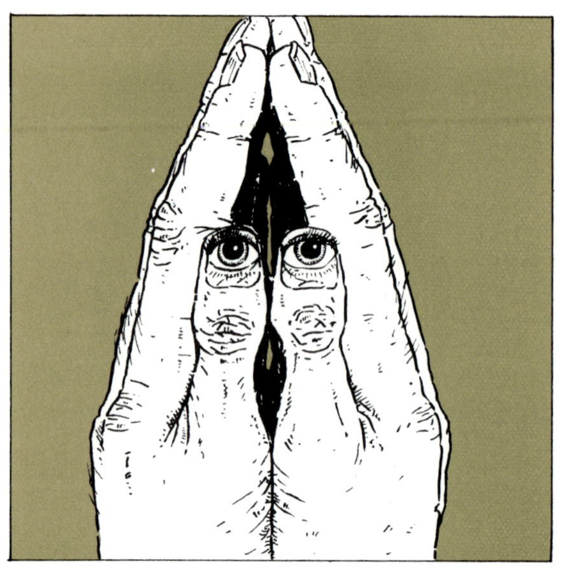

What is religion, and are you religious? High Church – Low Church – Broad Church? Test yourself: would you go to church dirty and in rags? . . . be cremated . . . argue with a priest about religion? . . . is everyone sinful?

THE AMERICAN PHILOSOPHER William James defined religion as 'the belief that there is an unseen order and that our supreme good lies in harmoniously adjusting ourselves thereto'. It is perhaps the most satisfactory definition of religion available; it is probably true that the great majority of people, whether or not they believe in a supreme Being, at the very least have a feeling that life cannot be completely meaningless, that morality must have some spiritual basis.

A greater number of people than ever before, at least in the West, no longer subscribes to the beliefs of organized religion. But a very large number of individuals are still members of one or other of the churches – Roman Catholic, Baptist or Presbyterian, Armenian or Methodist, Islamic or Mohammedan, Anglican or Hindu.

Most of them are drawn to a particular church by circumstance. Just as in politics many people vote just as their parents voted, so in religion the tendency is for children to be taken to church by their parents and for a variety of reasons – social or psychological – to continue going to that church until they die. On the other hand, some individuals do eventually begin to question the beliefs, customs or rituals of their churches; some become so disturbed by the conflict between these and some aspects of their own personality that they change churches, or are even forced out of their church by their fellow-worshippers.

Here is where personal predilection has a role. Some people, for instance, are temperamentally attracted by ritual and high ceremony, by handsome vestments and ornaments; seeing their god as God the King rather, or at least as well as, God the Father, they feel that they should treat Him with the same kind of honour they would treat an earthly monarch. Others see their god as at once greater than, and more humble than, any earthly head of state, and believe that He should be approached simply, and with a total lack of meaningless ceremonial; they

Religious impulses are not always expressed in complicated ritual, nor always divorced from politics and everyday life. Amsterdam Quakers (below) held services with no formal shape, in which worshippers 'waited before God' in silence and equality of fellowship. In our own time there have been wholly informal prayer meetings in unusual settings: above, a Roman Catholic priest leads prayers outside the White House in a protest against Civil Rights violations in Alabama.

CENTAUR

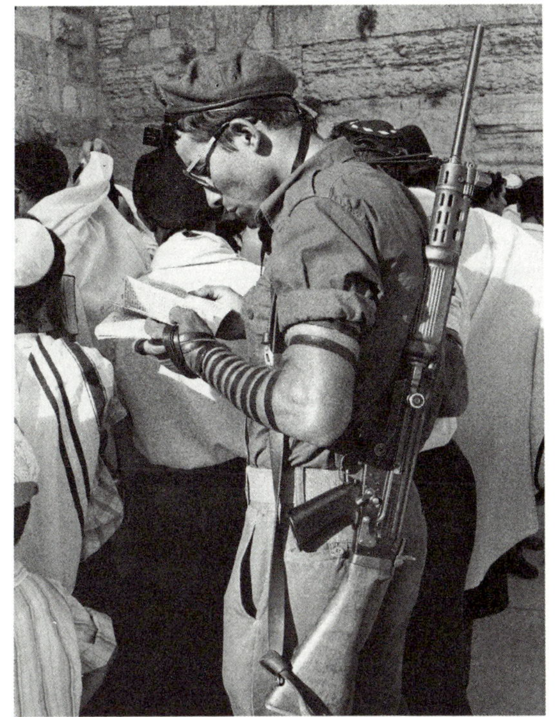

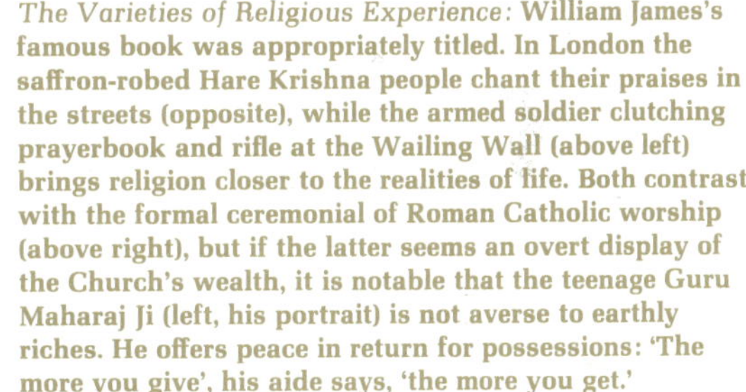
The Varieties of Religious Experience: **William James's famous book was appropriately titled. In London the saffron-robed Hare Krishna people chant their praises in the streets (opposite), while the armed soldier clutching prayerbook and rifle at the Wailing Wall (above left) brings religion closer to the realities of life. Both contrast with the formal ceremonial of Roman Catholic worship (above right), but if the latter seems an overt display of the Church's wealth, it is notable that the teenage Guru Maharaj Ji (left, his portrait) is not averse to earthly riches. He offers peace in return for possessions: 'The more you give', his aide says, 'the more you get.'**

prefer silent prayer to the use of ancient forms of prayer in out-dated, formal language, and relative solitude to the bustle of corporate worship.

So forms of worship differ from the meditation of the Hindu to the silence of the Quaker, from the wild whirling of the Dervish to the stately ballet of the Catholic Mass, from the whirring of the prayer-wheel to the lighting of a candle.

There is a parallel to be drawn between man's approach to religion and to politics. It would be rash to assert that right wing = extrovert = High Church, while left wing = introvert = Low Church; there are far too many exceptions for any such simple equation. There have been many left-wing churchmen who have enjoyed and practised the most extreme forms of ritual, just as there have been right-wing men and women who have been at home in dissenting churches. But there is perhaps a general tendency for those who are reactionary in politics to enjoy elaborate ceremonial, in church as elsewhere, while radicals have often been closely identified with nonconformist churches, and lately, in the West, with some forms of Eastern religion.

It may be, too, that those generally of the right in politics also tend to accept the religion of their fathers unconditionally and unquestioningly. The following test is directed at discovering roughly where in the hierarchy of religious attitudes you are placed and how much you have asked yourself about the nature of your religious beliefs. All our attitudes have a pervasive effect on our characters or, alternatively, display those characters; to some extent we are what we worship (and this applies, of course, outside the immediate sphere of religion – health-worshippers, money-worshippers, power-worshippers are immediately recognizable). In religion, the person who accepts the doctrine of papal infallibility may be much more likely than his agnostic neighbour to accept the authority of his boss, his trade union, his political party. The person who asks herself whether Buddhism may not, after all, be as credible as Christianity may be more likely to see both sides of a political argument, to accept the different social behaviour of her immigrant neighbour, to realize that her children will have different – but not necessarily less proper – moral attitudes than herself.

The way of meditation: here, an exercise in prolonged mental discipline rather than in worship.

1 Should the church sell all its treasures and use the money for the relief of poverty?

2 Is the idea of 'worker priests' a contradiction in terms?

3 When you pray, do you prefer using biblical language to the language of today?

4 Have you ever seriously thought of changing your religious allegiance?

5 Did your parents ever offer you the option of not attending church?

6 If you had to attend church in casual or dirty clothes, or not at all, would you stay away?

7 Have you ever deeply weighed the arguments for and against your beliefs?

8 Would you resign from your church if it decided to contribute money to a political organization?

9 Are those who accept the Commandment, 'Thou shalt not kill', but are prepared to fight for their country, to some extent hypocritical?

10 Your boss is an atheist: you are a keen churchgoer. Do you carefully conceal the fact?

11 You are on a jury. A witness chooses to affirm rather than take a religious oath. Do you treat him with some suspicion?

12 Do you believe that believers in other religious systems will be punished by your own God?

13 Is the Bible (or the sacred text of your religion) literally true?

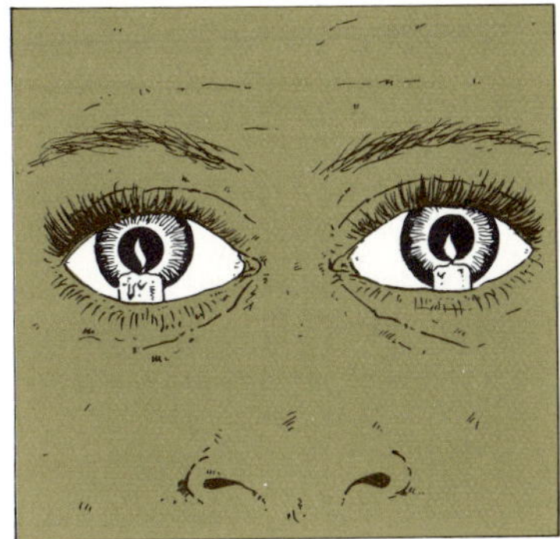

14 Should a devout Christian be cremated?

15 Should the church ever be concerned with politics?

16 Is it *particularly* important to go to church at the time of the great religious festivals?

17 Have you ever had a religious argument with a priest?

18 If scientists produced positive proof that the sacred writings of your religion were forged, would you still believe?

19 Someone of whom you thoroughly disapprove is seriously ill. Would you urge repentance under the threat of eternal punishment?

20 Would you be lonely without your religion?

21 Were the people of ancient Greece, who worshipped the gods of the ancient world, (a) gullible fools, (b) as rational as modern Christians?

22 Is it possible for any human being to keep all the Ten Commandments?

23 Are the Hare Krishna people, who shave their heads and chant their prayers in city streets, (a) harmless eccentrics, (b) believers expressing their religion in their own way?

24 Do Billy Graham and other modern evangelists appeal as strongly to man's hidden psychological fears as to a religious sense?

25 Is it necessary in any religion (a) to follow all the ancient tenets of the faith, or (b) can a modern worshipper choose those parts of ancient tradition he wishes to follow?

26 Since the existence of a god cannot be proved, is religion a waste of time?

27 Are sex and true religious behaviour incompatible?

28 Is meditation as useful as prayer?

29 Is every individual naturally sinful?

30 Is earthly suffering inevitable?

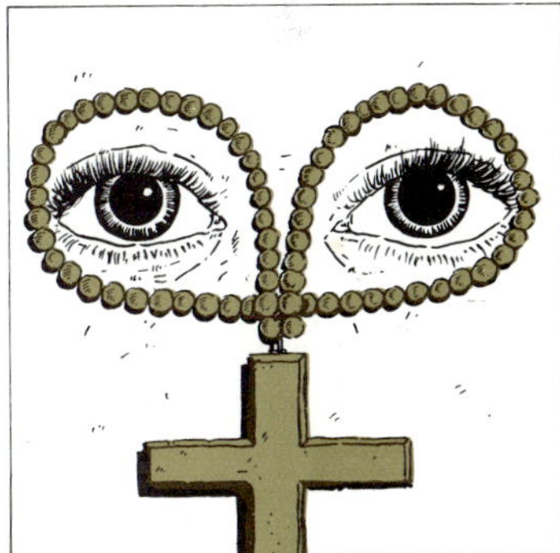

Scoring

†1 yes scores 1, no scores −1
2 yes +, no −
3 yes +, no −
4 yes scores A, no scores Z
5 yes A, no Z
6 yes +, no −
7 yes A, no Z

8 yes +, no –

†**9** yes –, no +

10 yes +, no –

11 yes + and A, no – and Z

***12** yes +, no –

***13** yes + and Z, no – and A

14 yes – and Z, no + and A

15 yes –, no +

16 yes +, no –

17 yes A, no Z

18 yes Z, no A

†**19** yes +, no –

20 yes A, no Z

***21** (a) +, (b) –

22 yes +, no –

23 (a) +, (b) –

24 yes Z, no = no score

25 (a) A, (b) Z

26 no –, yes = no score

27 yes +, no –

28 yes –, no +

29 yes +, no –

30 yes +, no –

If you have answered 'yes' to all three asterisked questions, add a bonus of 10 to your score. If you have scored – on the three questions marked†, deduct another 10 marks.

Interpretations

The religious sense is intangible and in some respects irrational; and it is therefore difficult to draw conclusions from the result of any test. If, however, you have scored between +10 and +31 in the above test, it can safely be said that you are something of a right-wing fundamentalist in religion: you tend to accept the authority of whatever church you were brought up in; and to question any statement made either in its dogma or by its officials will be more difficult for you the higher you score. You tend to separate religion and everyday life, to the extent that you believe that your church should be 'above' politics, should confine itself to laying down moral lines of action and should only occupy itself with the safest kind of charity work. You will regard the members of other churches, certainly those of other faiths, with a greater or lesser degree of suspicion. You will probably tend to score more *A*s than *Z*s; if so, this may indicate that you accept the dogma of your church without argument and even without much thought or consideration. This is a matter for your own conscience; it may be worth asking yourself whether unquestioning acceptance is a particularly dignified stance for a human being to take, though you may feel that human dignity has little to do with the revealed truth your church possesses.

If your score is on the minus side – especially between –10 and –31 – you will tend to be nonconformist in your beliefs, questioning not only your own faith but also its means of expression. You will at times be bemused or even worried at the thought that your church may own property, invest money, treasure valuable ancient relics; you may have argued about this with your priest or minister. The apparently irreconcilable statements of the scriptures and modern science will not have escaped you, though you may feel the religious elements of life are still of the greatest importance. But you will not accept any statement handed down by church tradition as necessarily a divine revelation. It may be that over the years you have grown away from the religion, or the religious practices, of your parents; you will not, in any event, have swallowed them whole and without thought. You cannot imagine anyone accepting any religious theory without perplexity and much soul-searching: you think that such searching is important and necessary. You will be far more likely to have scored a higher number of *Z*s than of *A*s; in fact, if you score more than two or three *A*s, you might wonder whether you are being completely honest with yourself.

20 How do you tick?

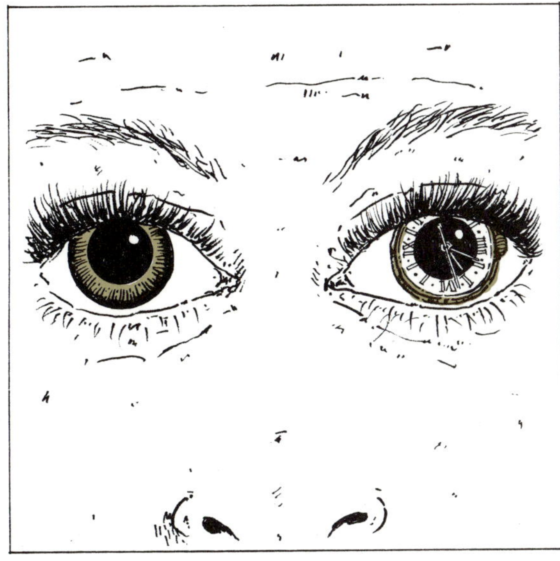

When you were born,

an internal clock started ticking,

which may govern how you feel

and act today, at this moment.

Synchronize your internal

watch with the calendar

and test the theory.

EVERY DAY THE sun rises and sets, the tide comes in and goes out, the planets seem to move round the earth at different speeds but with a regular motion, the most elementary elements of life react in time to the movement of the tides or the sun; there are earthquake cycles, meteorological cycles. And there are various cycles that seem to affect human beings.

The most familiar of these is the human female cycle – the discharge of blood every twenty-eight days from the uterus of a woman. Round the turn of the century a set of three cycles was discovered which influences the life of every human being, male or female. These cycles are called 'biorhythms'; and within the last ten years or so they have not only become fashionable with people who are responsive to new ideas, but have also been increasingly under examination by scientists.

Two men working independently – one in Vienna and one in Berlin – 'discovered' biorhythms. Dr Hermann Swoboda, a Professor of Psychology at the University of Vienna, noticed over the years, as he treated his patients, that inflammations of certain tissues seemed to recur at regular intervals, that fevers and some other illnesses seemed to behave as though regulated by some invisible clock.

He came to the conclusion that two cycles, of 23 and 28 days, seemed to affect the physical and emotional lives of all his patients; he developed the idea in a book entitled *The Periods of Human Life*, published in 1904. Five years later, he devised a slide-rule with which people could work out the 'critical days' on which they might be vulnerable to various illnesses or tensions.

Wilhelm Fliess was originally an otolaryngologist – a nose and throat specialist – at the University of Berlin, who became in 1910 President of the German Academy of Sciences. He became interested in biorhythms when he began to notice the puzzling phenomenon which has preoccupied so many doctors: the way in which at different times people – children in particular – seem to have a different degree of resistance to disease. In the course of sixteen years he published four books on the subject.

Fliess worked on the earliest theory to attempt to explain, as well as to prove, the existence of 'biorhythms', as he called the cycles. He believed that – as life evolved – an original single bisexual cell had developed into male and female cells and that the human male and the human female in modern life still retain some cells and perhaps tissues of the opposite sex. (This fitted in well with his theories of bisexuality, a subject in which he and his most famous patient, Freud, were extremely interested.) The female cells, he believed, were regulated by a 28-day 'emotional rhythm' and the male cells by a 23-day 'physical rhythm'.

Another researcher was, in the meantime, studying what seemed to be a third 'bio-rhythm' influencing the intellectual life of man. A doctor of engineering at Innsbruck, Alfred Teltscher, believed that the variation in the intellectual performances of his students could be related to the same sort of cycle as apparently related to their physical and emotional lives. He made a careful study of the days on which individual students seemed particularly bright or particularly dim, got good results or bad results in examinations, and related these to their dates of birth – coming up with a 33-day 'intellectual cycle' which Fliess and Swoboda later interpreted as originating in secretions of glands affecting the brain: probably the pineal and thyroid glands.

The theory of biorhythms is essentially simple. On the day of birth, each of the three cycles starts at a neutral base-line from which it begins to rise in a regular curve during which the qualities associated with each of the rhythms (physical wellbeing in one case, emotional wellbeing in another, intellectual wellbeing in the third) are at their most active. After a while, the curves reach their height and begin to decline, halfway through their period ($11\frac{1}{2}$ days in the case of the physical cycle, 14 days in the emotional cycle and $16\frac{1}{2}$ days in the intellectual cycle) crossing the base-line and going into a 'negative' phase during which the energies associated with them are re-charged. After similar periods each rhythm reaches a nadir, climbs again to cross the base-line and goes into positive.

Because each rhythm has its own length, the three curves move against each other and only occasionally do two (or more rarely three) of them cross the base-line on the same day. On days when this happens, there seems to be a vulnerability to all sorts of ills – a critical time in an illness or emotional upset, a susceptibility to carelessness or accident. But the days on which any of the curves cross the base-line also seem to be 'critical' to one degree or another and it does not seem to matter much whether they are crossing from positive into negative or the other way about. On those days, a certain instability is likely.

Any of you can try out this theory. It is usually true that the physical or emotional cycles seem to have the strongest effect: on 'physical critical' days you may feel more tired and exhausted than usual, or perhaps you are hyperactive, but in any event it is easier to misjudge your physical state – to pull a muscle at exercise, for instance, or in some other way to overstrain yourself. Some people find they get drunk on much smaller amounts of alcohol; others have difficulty in sleeping well on 'physical critical' days. On 'emotional critical' days it is easier to lose your temper, to carp and criticize; but easier also to be moved to tears by a piece of music or a foolish soap opera. The intellectual cycle seems to affect the judgment, so that it is easier to make mistakes in business, in working out the electricity bill or the number of shopping days to Christmas, to dash into some silly error or misjudge someone's character.

The potency of biorhythms has been tested now in a number of impressive ways. Hans Schwing, for instance, working in Zurich in 1939, found that of 700 accidents to individuals which he studied, 401 had occurred on single, double or triple critical days. Of 300 natural deaths, 197 occurred on days when the emotional or physical rhythms were crossing the base-line. The percentages, respectively, were 57 and 65.7. On his calcula-

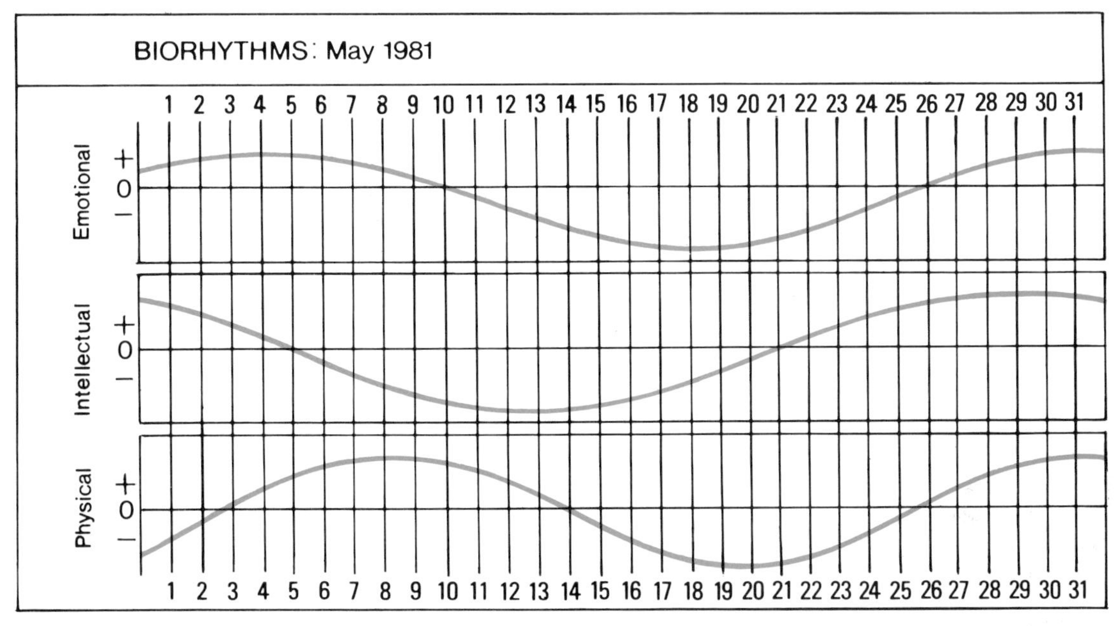

YOUR BIORHYTHMS

There are a great many gadgets on sale by which you can discover how your biorhythms work: these vary from slide-rules and circular revolving discs on which you dial your birth-date, to computer print-outs or books of tables which detail the moving biorhythms much as an ephemeris details the movements of the planets. But it is not necessary to be a mathematical genius to work out the days nearest and preceding your next birthday on which the three rhythms will cross the base-line on their way upwards.

Simply take your age at your next birthday and multiply it by 365 (the number of days in a year). Then add the number of leap years you have lived through – that is, the number of times you have lived through a 29 February: do not count any leap year when that date occurred before your birth or will occur after the birthday you are working to. Divide the resulting total by the number of days in the cycle you are working out. The number of days you have over will be the number of days previous to your birthday on which the cycle crosses into positive.

Example

Take someone born on 27 May 1932. On 27 May 1981, he will be $49.49 \times 365 = 17{,}885$. Add 13 for leap years: 17,898. Divide by 23 (the number of days in the physical cycle). The answer is 778 with two left over (round the figure upwards if the next figure after the decimal point is more than 5). So the physical curve will pass the base-line, going upward on 25 May 1981, for that subject. Make a similar calculation for the 28- and 33-day cycles.

Once you have the three dates, nearest your birthday, on which the cycles go into positive, it is easy enough with the help of a diary to plot the critical days for the rest of the year, counting backwards and forwards for *half* of each cycle. Taking the example above, for instance, the 'physical critical' days will occur $11\frac{1}{2}$ days forward or backward from 25 May. (In theory, the 'half day' should be counted from the time of your birth, but the effect of the cycle seems general enough for you to be able to ignore this.)

There is a simple check. Since the emotional cycle is a monthly cycle, its critical days will always fall on the day of the week on which you were born: in the example above, on a Friday.

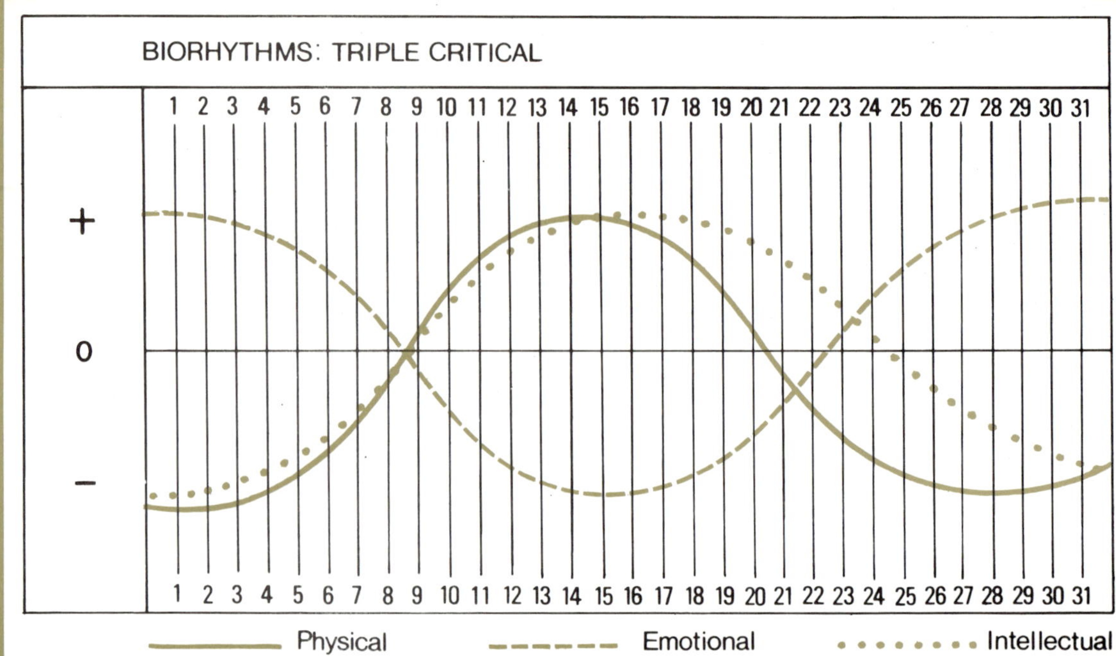

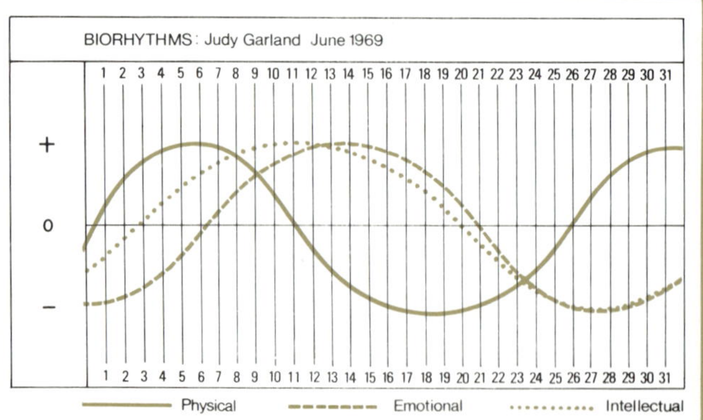

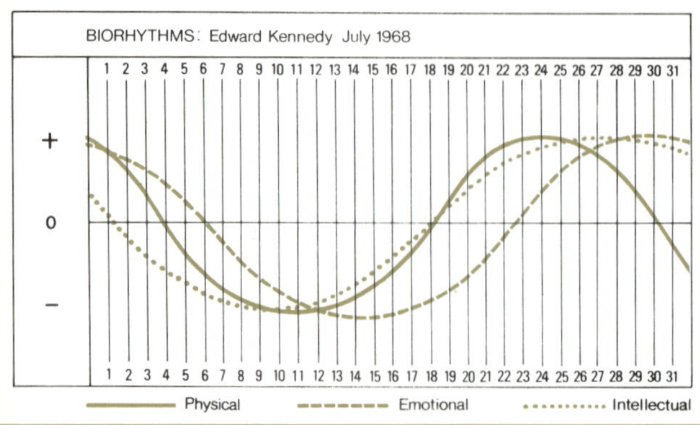

'Triple critical' days occur when all three curves cross the base-line on the same day (in the example, top, on the 9th of the month). In Judy Garland's June 1969 chart the emotional cycle crossed the base-line on the 21st, at a time when the physical and intellectual curves were in negative; she died of a drug overdose on that night. Edward Kennedy's July 1968 chart indicated a physical and intellectual critical on the night of the 18th – the time of the Chappaquiddick incident.

tions, accidents were five times more likely to happen on critical days and natural deaths almost eleven times more likely.

This was one of the earliest serious attempts to confirm the theory by statistics. There have been many others: Dr Friedrich Pirchner found that, of 204 Swiss civil aviation accidents he examined, almost 70 per cent occurred when the pilot was experiencing a critical day; Colonel Wolfgang Karnbach, of the Swiss Cadet Training Centre, found that a similar percentage of accidents experienced by student flyers occurred on critical days. More spectacularly, Professor Reinhold Bochow of Humboldt University, studying accidents involving agricultural machinery, calculated that such accidents were 171 times more likely to occur on critical days than on non-critical days.

Of course there are positive ways in which to use this knowledge. Swissair, for instance, has been studying the critical days of its pilots for over a decade; two pilots are not allowed to fly together if both are experiencing critical days and there have so far been no accidents caused by human error when this rule has been applied. The Zurich Municipal Transit Company has applied biorhythms to its drivers and conductors and the accident rate per 10,000 kilometers has been cut by fifty per cent.

One of the most impressive sets of statistics so far produced comes from the Ohmi Railway Company, which runs a fleet of buses and taxis in Kyoto and Osaka. Looking at accidents to its drivers between 1963 and 1968, Ohmi found that 59 per cent had happened on a critical day or on the days immediately before or after. For the most accident-prone drivers, the figures rose to 61 per cent. In 1969, the company issued cards to all its drivers showing their critical days. Within the first year the accident rate dropped by almost 50 per cent and it continued to decline in each following year, despite a severely rising general accident rate; by 1973 Ohmi's bus division had set up a record for the whole of Japan of four million kilometers travelled without one reported accident.

There now seems to be far too much statistical evidence to allow anyone to ignore the probability that the biorhythm theory is a viable one. Personal experience generally confirms it even on the simple level of slight accidents or miscalculations at home or at work. And fortunately, it is extremely simple to work the theory out and apply it to yourself.

A cyclic system that does not need to be worked out – that imposes itself on women with monotonous regularity – is the menstrual system. Much has been written about the psychological effects of this during the past few years, mostly in the form of generalizations: you are likely to make serious mistakes, be more accident-prone, more irritable, more anxious or depressed, during a time of pre-menstrual tension.

There is no lack of theories; what is usually lacking is observation by the woman herself. It takes time and patience before a woman can reliably 'know' how her own menstrual cycle affects her. The most dependable way of discovering this is to keep a 'menstrual diary' – a record of the days during which you suffer from depression, irritability, headaches, or even apparently irrational minor quirks such as putting off a necessary phone call, feeling unreasonably optimistic, feeling particularly sensual.

Once the pattern becomes clear, it can be enormously helpful. It may not help you to fight irrational depression – but at least if you know on what days of your cycle you seem to be most vulnerable, you can make sure you are not out of whatever pill you find most effective in dealing with it. You can also avoid social commitments of one kind and another.

There are certain discoveries to be made about the best way of combating irritability or depression. Some women find it far less irksome than usual to do the dullest housework during the day or two before the period.

During the years when 'the curse' was unmentionable, not discussed even among women, there was perhaps an excuse for not thinking about it. Today, however, it is obviously important to yourself and to those around you that you should understand the way your own menstrual cycle works.

21 You in the Zodiac

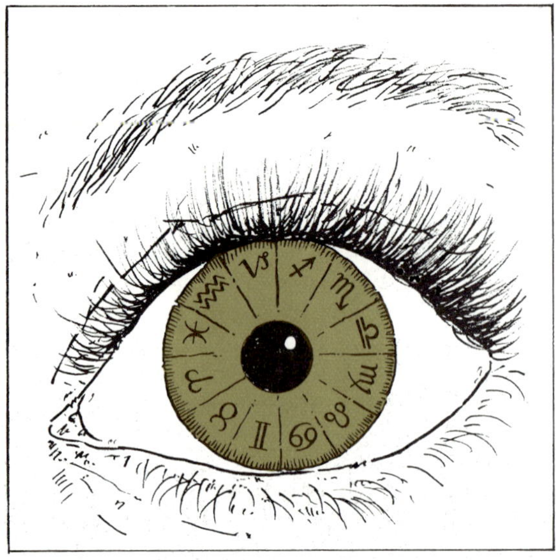

The Sun, Moon and Planets,

say astrologers, affect

human character and behaviour;

nothing occult or magical

– all empirical observation.

True or false?

ASTROLOGY HAS FASCINATED man, and to some extent ruled his life, for at least five thousand years and probably for considerably longer. Apparently starting in the Middle East, the theory spread throughout Europe and in a slightly different form originated at roughly the same time in the Far East; elaborated by the Egyptians and especially the Greeks, it was prominent in Imperial Rome and, as our own civilization took hold of the rest of Europe, its influence was felt there from medieval times until the seventeenth and eighteenth centuries. Only then was there a temporary eclipse, due partly perhaps to great upsurges of quackery at the time of the English Civil War, the French Revolution and other disturbances, and partly to the discovery – or rather the confirmation of the fact – that the earth moves round the sun rather than the other way around.

Just before the turn of the last century, there was a renewal of interest (led by Carl Gustav Jung). Although science has officially been suspicious of astrologers, there has been a fast-growing interest in the 'cosmic clocks' and the theories of cycles which are at the heart of the theory.

Astrology at the moment is in a somewhat curious position. While the majority of people read the newspaper astrology columns for amusement (and it would be extremely foolish to suppose that they could aim at anything else), there is also awareness of the use of astrology in medicine, weather forecasting and psychology. Prediction is no longer emphasized (no serious astrologer will now claim to be able to predict an event) and astrologers have become counsellors who see their work as enabling their consulting clients the better to understand themselves, their natures and their actions.

Astrology and medicine were allied for centuries: in a 15th-century woodcut the Zodiacal signs and planets are given control over various parts of the anatomy.

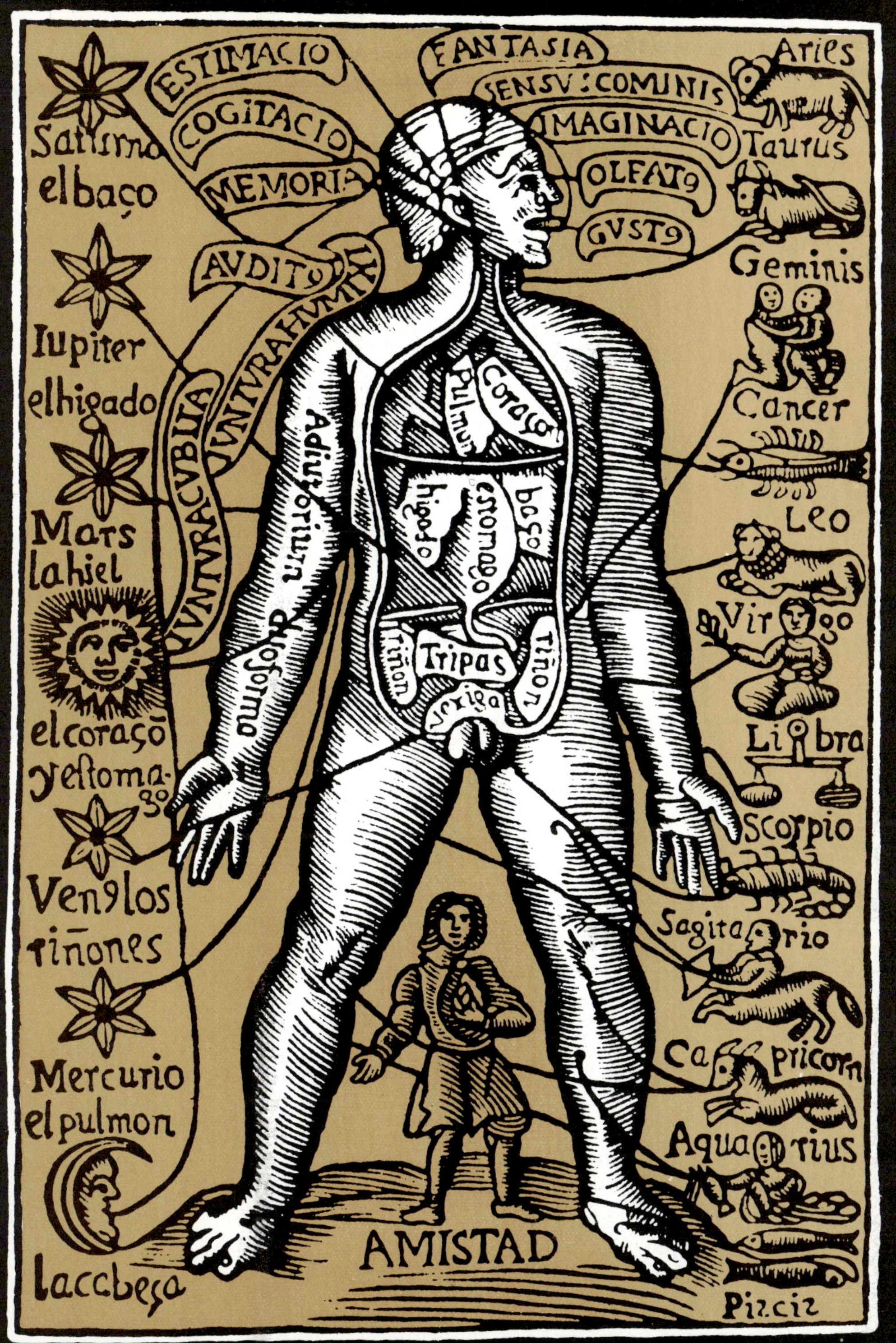
ESTIMACIO
FANTASIA
Aries
SENSV: COMVNIS
COGITACIO
IMAGINACIO
Taurus
el baço
MEMORIA
OLFAT9
GVST9
Geminis
AVDIT9
Iupiter
elhigado
Cancer
Coraçõ
Pulmon
Mars
lahiel
higado
estomago
baço
Leo
Virgo
riñon
Tripas
riñon
elcoraçõ
yestomago
Libra
Scorpio
Ven9los
riñones
Sagitario
Mercurio
elpulmon
Capricorn
Aquarius
AMISTAD
laccbeça
Pizciz

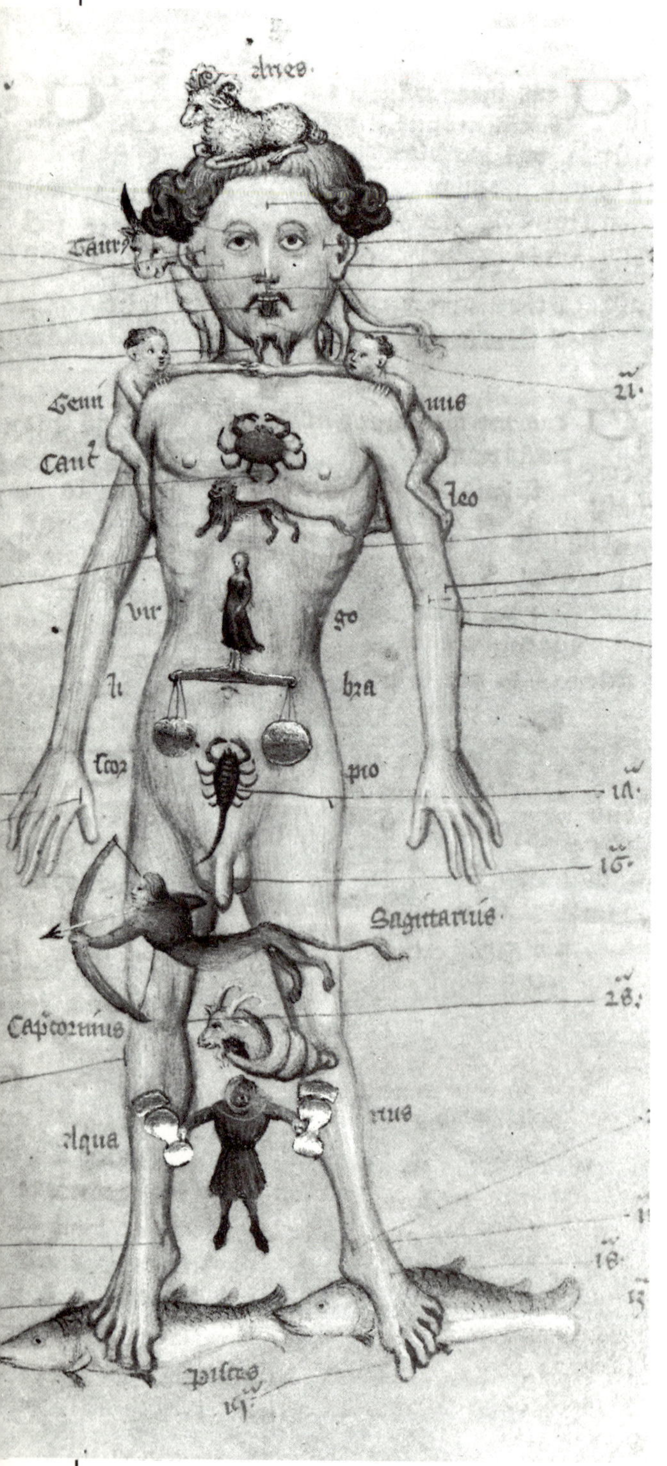

SUN SIGN AND RISING SIGN

'What Sign are you?' is a very popular conversational opening gambit these days. The only correct answer is, 'I'm all twelve.'

Unfortunately, due to the popularity of the Sun Sign columns in newspapers and magazines (which only started about fifty years ago), there has been an over-emphasis on the Zodiacal Sign in which the Sun was placed at the time of your birth. This is because everyone knows their Sun Sign simply by knowing their birthday. Your full 'horoscope' or Birth Chart is a map of the sky for the precise date, time and place of your birth, showing the twelve Signs of the Zodiac and how they were seen from Earth, and, most importantly, the positions of the planets in relation to each other, also as seen from Earth.

There is much popular talk of 'the stars'. Astrology is nothing to do with the stars. The only star used in astrology is the Sun. Astrologers use this and the planets as a basis for their theories. The Zodiacal names of the constellations, household words to all of us, refer to areas of the ecliptic (the apparent path of the Sun around the Earth) which once coincided with those constellations. Now, due to precession of the equinoxes (a kind of wobble which occurs as the earth turns on its axis, rather like the wobble of a slowing spinning top), the two no longer coincide, so the names of the constellations refer only to areas of the ecliptic and *not* to the constellations themselves.

While the position of the Sun in the Birth Chart is not unimportant, there are several other factors of great importance. The most vital is the Sign which was rising over the

Astrology has been astonishingly long-lasting in its influence: the 'Zodiacal Man' from Foxton's *Liber Cosmographiae* was created nearly 600 years ago. Opposite: Finding your Ascendant – the hour disc (see p. 148).

eastern horizon at the precise time and place of your birth. To discover this involves astronomical calculations – which must also be done to find the exact positions of the other planets in their 'Signs' (or, more accurately, areas of the ecliptic). Your Sun Sign – the bit you know – may be Aries or Gemini or Cancer, but the Moon occupies a Sign too – and so do Mercury, Venus, Mars, Jupiter and all the other members of the Sun's family.

So to whet your appetite for astrology, look at the following pages and discover what your all-important Rising Sign or Ascendant is. Next time you are asked, 'What's your Sign?', you will be able to say, perhaps, 'Aries with Scorpio rising', or 'My Ascendant is Gemini and I have the Sun in Pisces.'

Having discovered what your Rising Sign is, read the Sun Sign characteristics for that Sign – but remember that they work in rather a different way. While the Sun Sign generally gives you your image, your public face as it were, it seems that the Rising Sign reveals the real you – the you known to your closest circle. For instance, you are likely to wear the kind of clothes, and make the kind of environment, attributed to the Sun Sign; but when reading about your Rising Sign you are most likely to recognize your innermost aspirations and behaviour patterns. 'Well, yes, I suppose I *am* like that', is likely to be your reaction.

Remember, too, when reading the characteristics attributed to your Sun Sign – here or anywhere – that if there is a list of about twenty, you can expect only to recognize perhaps eight. Neither the Sun nor the Rising Sign alone can give anything like a complete picture of yourself; the other characteristics may be traced in the other planets and the way they relate to each other, in your full Birth Chart. (If you were born at

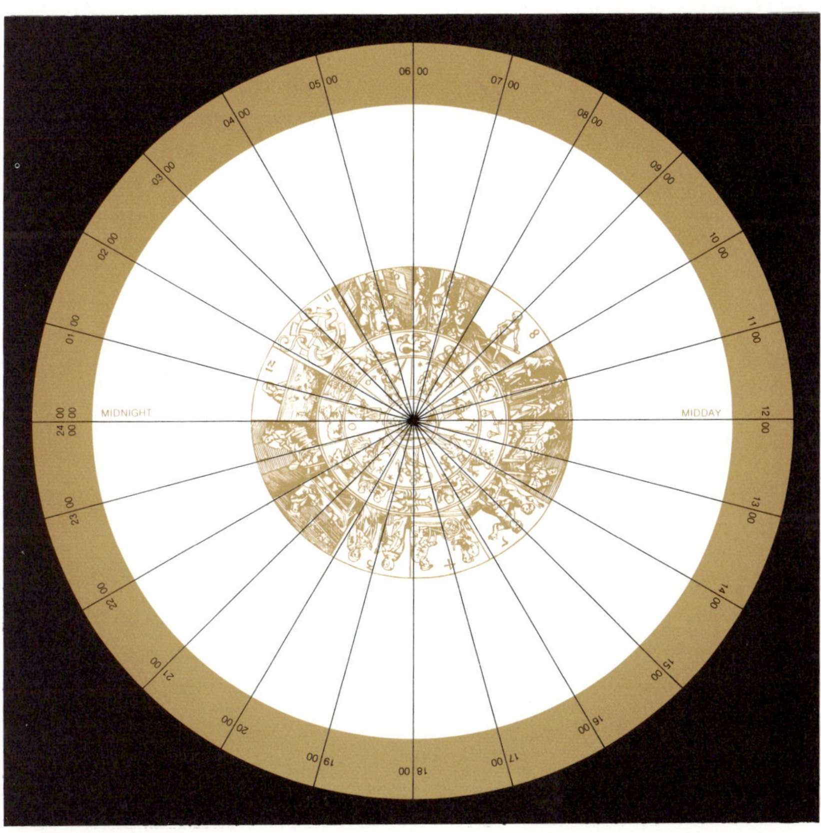

HOW TO FIND YOUR ASCENDANT

If you were born in a place on approximately the same latitude as one of the cities on pp. 148–51, you will probably be able to find your Ascendant sign. The discs work equally well for northern or southern latitudes.

1 Find out the time of sunrise on the day on which you were born. An ordinary diary will usually give you this – but check whether Daylight Saving Time (also called Summer Time) was in operation. If Daylight Saving Time was in operation, you must deduct an hour from the time of birth given on your birth certificate. In some countries during the war Double Summer Time was observed, and – if this affects you – you should then deduct *two* hours. In other words, you must make sure that all the times, whether of sunrise or of your birth, are in 'true' time, which is GMT in England and Eastern Standard Time in America.
Example: *born 26 September at 13.30 hours, New York. As Daylight Saving Time was in operation, deduct one hour, making birth time 12.30 hours. Sunrise was at 5 a.m., or 4 a.m. Eastern Standard Time: i.e., 04.00 hours.*

2 Either trace out the hour disc, and then write on the tracing paper, or mark direct onto the printed hour disc opposite, the time of sunrise. (Don't forget to subtract for Daylight Saving Time if applicable.)
Example: *On the hour disc, put a cross against 04.00 hours.*

3 Choose the Ascendant disc for the latitude nearest to your place of birth, and copy or trace it.

4 Each Sun Sign of the Ascendant disc is divided into three segments, marked 0° – 10°, 10° – 20°, 20° – 30°, in a counterclockwise direction. If your birthday falls in the first ten days of the Sun Sign period, draw the symbol (glyph) for the sun – ☉ – in the first segment; if in the second ten days, in the second segment; likewise the third. Remember to move counterclockwise around the disc.
Example: *26 September: the Sun Sign is Libra, which begins on 23 September in most years, so place ☉ in the first segment of Libra ♎.*

5 Place the Ascendant disc concentrically over the hour disc, so that the sun symbol is next to your hour of birth on the hour disc. Your Ascendant or Rising Sign is the one shown on the Ascendant disc next to the time of sunrise which you previously marked on the hour disc.

This is a rough means of determining the Rising Sign or Ascendant, which normally should be accurately calculated. If the characteristics of the Sign seem to be out of tune with your own personality, read the ones for the Sign before or the Sign after; it may be that one of these is your true Ascendant.
Example: *Put the two discs together with the hour disc underneath, so that you can see all the hours round the outside of the Ascendant disc. Then put the ☉ marked on the (inner) Ascendant disc against the hour of birth (12.30: remember to deduct Daylight Saving Time if necessary) on the outer disc. Read off the Ascendant or Rising Sign – in this case Capricorn.*
If the Capricornian traits seem foreign to your personality, read those of Sagittarius and Aquarius.

Ascendant disc for Bombay.
Lat 19° 0′N
Also applies to:
Bangkok 13° 45′N
Dakar 14° 34′N
Guatemala City 14° 40′N
Haiphong 20° 55′N
Mecca 21° 30′N
Mexico City 19° 26′N
Brasilia 15° 55′S
Bulawayo 20° 7′S
Rio de Janeiro 22° 5′S

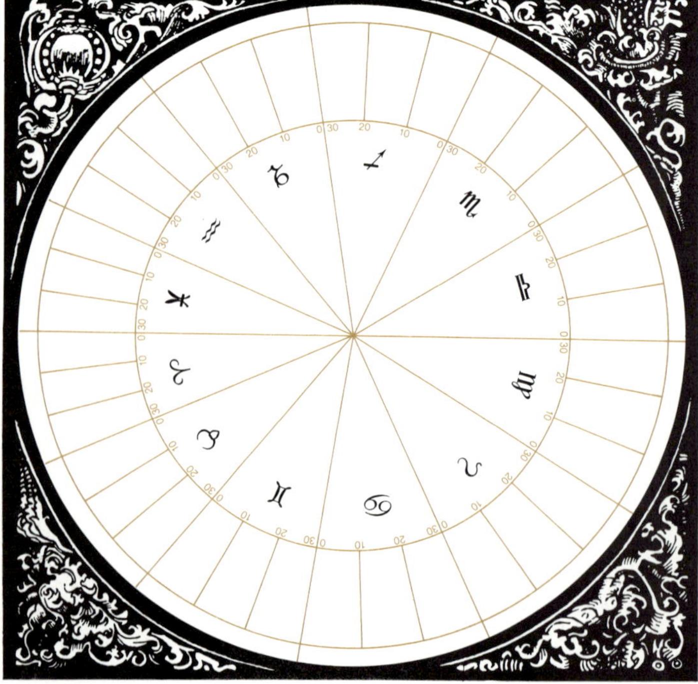

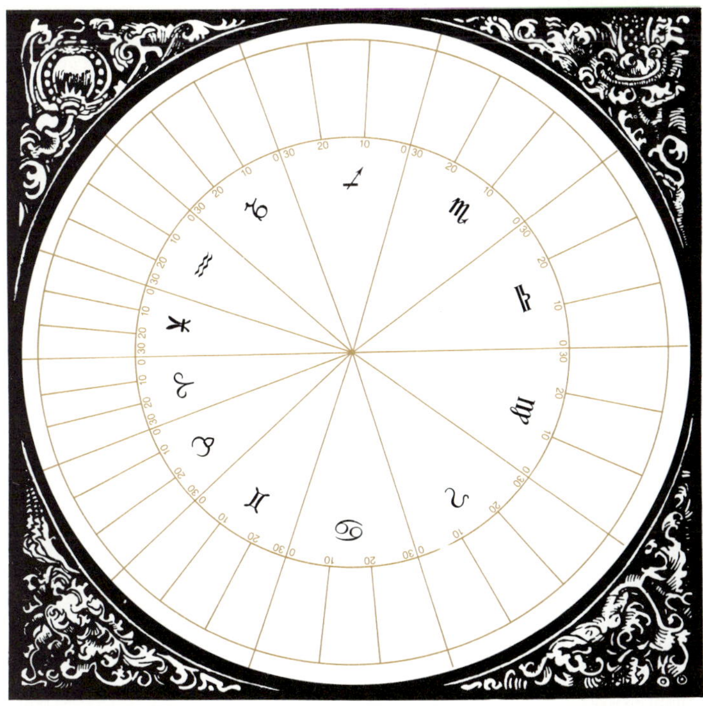

Ascendant disc for Cairo.
Lat. 30° 2′N
Also applies to:
Delhi 28° 42′N
Houston 29° 45′N
Jacksonville 30° 15′N
Marrakesh 31° 40′N
Shanghai 31° 15′N
Brisbane 27° 30′S
Durban 29° 57′S
Perth 32° 0′S
Porto Alegre 30° 7′S

Ascendant disc for Tokyo.
Lat. 35° 39′N
Also applies to:
Albuquerque 35° 5′N
Chattanooga 35° 2′N
Kyoto 35° 0′N
Los Angeles 34° 0′N
Memphis 35° 7′N
Oklahoma City 35° 25′N
Pasadena 34° 5′N
Tangier 35° 50′N
Teheran 35° 44′N
Adelaide 34° 55′S
Auckland 36° 52′S
Buenos Aires 34° 40′S
Canberra 35° 15′S
Cape Town 33° 59′S
Port Elizabeth 33° 58′S
Sydney 33° 52′S

Ascendant disc for New York.
Lat. 40° 43′N
Also applies to:
Ankara 39° 58′N
Chicago 41° 50′N
Denver 39° 50′N
Lisbon 38° 43′N
Madrid 40° 27′N
Peking 39° 49′N
Pittsburgh 40° 30′N
Reno 39° 32′N
Rome 41° 54′N
Salt Lake City 40° 45′N
Tashkent 41° 7′N
Valencia 39° 27′N
Washington, D.C. 38° 58′N
Bahia Blanca 38° 35′S
Wellington, N.Z. 41° 18′S

Ascendant disc for Montreal.
Lat. 45° 30′N
Also applies to:
Belgrade 44° 50′N
Bilbao 43° 16′N
Boise 43° 38′N
Bordeaux 44° 50′N
Bucharest 44° 27′N
Halifax, Canada 44° 45′N
Milan 45° 28′N
Minneapolis 45° 0′N
Turin 45° 2′N
Dunedin 45° 51′S

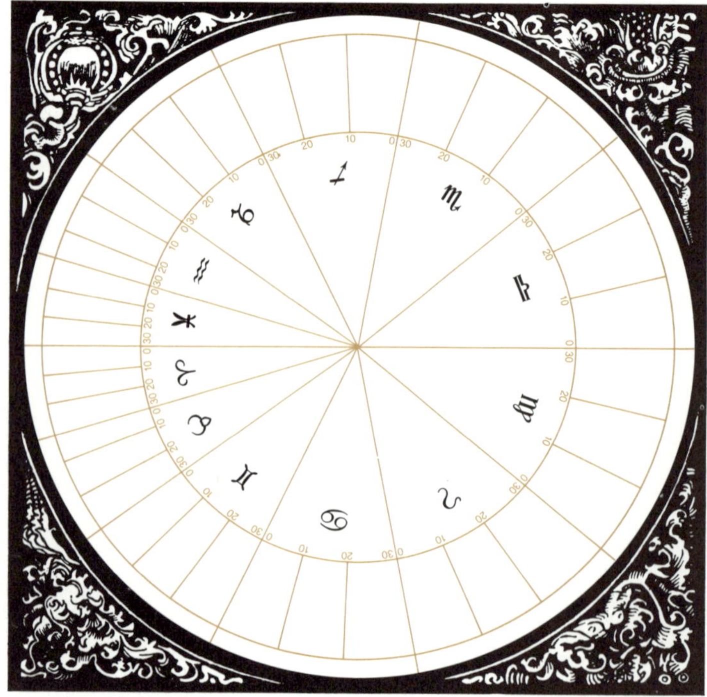

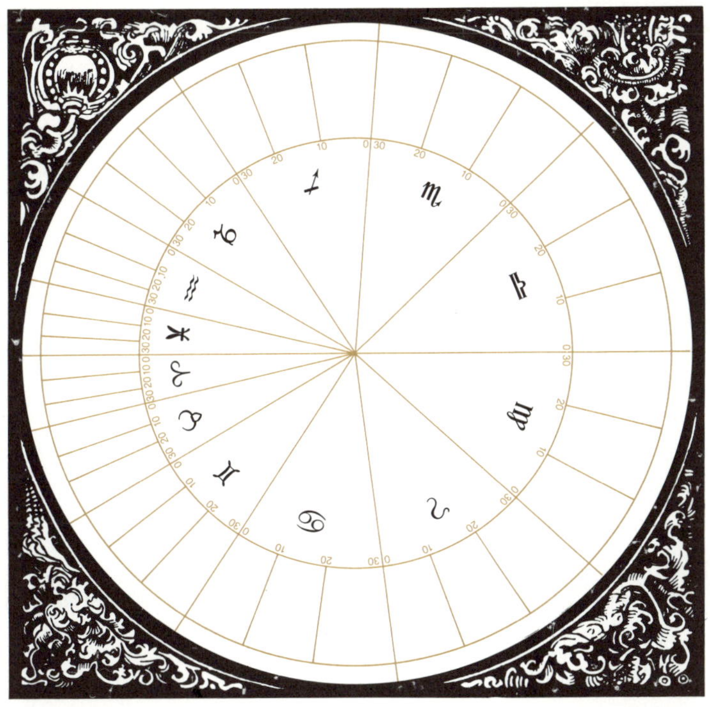

Ascendant disc for London.
Lat. 51° 32′N
Also applies to:
Amsterdam 52° 23′N
Antwerp 51° 13′N
Berlin 52° 32′N
Birmingham, England 52° 30′N
Calgary 51° 2′N
Cardiff 51° 28′N
Dortmund 51° 31′N
Leipzig 51° 20′N
Saskatoon 52° 10′N
Warsaw 52° 13′N

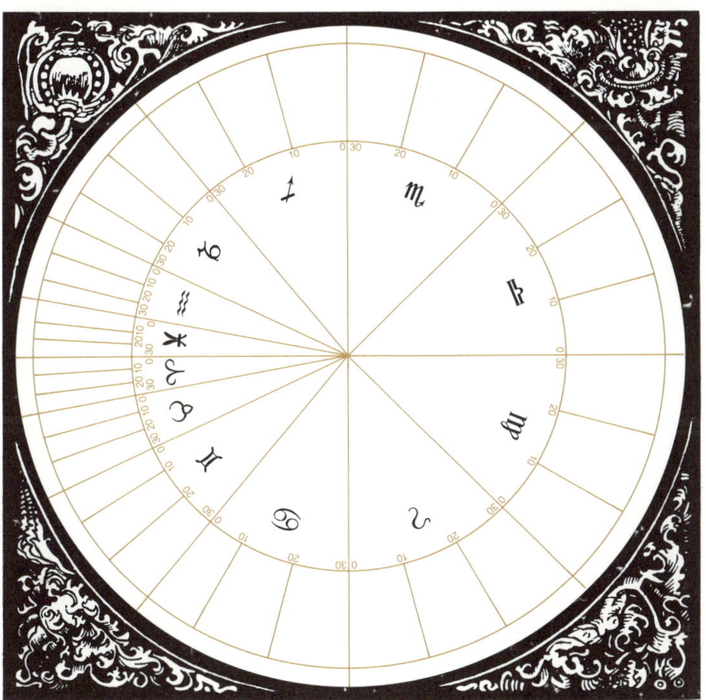

Ascendant disc for Glasgow.
Lat. 55° 53′N
Also applies to:
Copenhagen 55° 40′N
Edinburgh 55° 57′N
Malmö 55° 38′N
Moscow 55° 50′N
Novosibivsk 55° 10′N
Omsk 55° 0′N
Prince Rupert, B.C. 54° 20′N

sunrise, both your Sun and Rising Sign will be the same, so the proportion of accuracy is considerably increased; and if you were born within a day or two of the new Moon, both the Sun and Moon were then in the same Sign, and you will respond and react to situations as described by the characteristics of the Sun Sign.)

Astrology is surely one of the most fascinating and revealing of all systems of classification that man has devised. Sun Sign astrology is a rather boring area of it; the more you know about real astrology, the more exciting it becomes – and it is claimed that it can give you a much greater understanding of yourself, your psychological motivations, reactions and potential. Whether this is so or not, only someone who has studied the system can judge; and certainly anyone studying it seriously need never be bored again!

Astrological groups

Centuries ago the Zodiac Signs were grouped in various ways. The characteristics attributed to the groups are general and rather vague, but are worth considering – especially if your Rising Sign and Sun Sign both fall into one group.

Masculine/Feminine or Positive/Negative
Masculine Signs tend to show extrovert qualities and feminine Signs introvert (note how you score in the extrovert/introvert tests on p. 106).

Masculine Signs	*Feminine Signs*
Aries	Taurus
Gemini	Cancer
Leo	Virgo
Libra	Scorpio
Sagittarius	Capricorn
Aquarius	Pisces

The Triplicities or Elements
This grouping refers to the four elements – Fire, Earth, Air and Water.

There is an added element of enthusiasm and positive emotion in Fire Signs; a practical approach to life and a certain stability notable in Earth Signs, which need more security than others; the accent in Air Signs is on a lively intellectualism added to a basic desire to communicate; while Water Signs add an intuitive dimension and a deep, instinctive emotion.

Fire Signs	*Earth Signs*	*Air Signs*	*Water Signs*
Aries	Taurus	Gemini	Cancer
Leo	Virgo	Libra	Scorpio
Sagittarius	Capricorn	Aquarius	Pisces

The emotion of Fire and the emotion of Water are quite different. Someone with a Fire Sign Sun and a Water Sign Ascendant will undoubtedly have both kinds present in their personality. The emotion of Fire is the kind that moves you into *action*, into doing something about what has moved you. The emotion of the Water Signs is deep, moving and more sensitive – the sort that on one level makes tears flow freely at a 1940s tearjerker film and on another is very much moved by sad news stories or pictures of suffering.

The Quadriplicities or Qualities
This is the final traditional grouping of the Signs.

Cardinal Signs contribute an outgoing quality, a tendency to move forward and outward, both psychologically and in more practical ways. Fixed Signs have a tendency to get too set in ideas and life-style. Mutable Signs give the ability to adapt more easily than others to change; sometimes restlessness can be present.

Cardinal	*Fixed*	*Mutable*
Aries	Taurus	Gemini
Cancer	Leo	Virgo
Libra	Scorpio	Sagittarius
Capricorn	Aquarius	Pisces

ARIES

Sun Sign period: 21 March–20 April
Ruling planet, Mars. Colour, red. Stone, diamond. Metal, iron.

There is somewhere in every Arien an element of the pioneer. Aries likes to be first – to win. Ariens are straightforward, uncomplicated people who can achieve a logical and positive perspective on life and on their problems. They like to come to grips with a problem and can be verbally quite aggressive. It is important for them to realize that patience is not, generally speaking, one of their strong qualities and isn't easily learned. The enthusiasm of Fire, the element of their Sign, is definitely present; but in becoming involved in a project it is necessary for them to make a conscious effort to maintain that enthusiasm – the Arien fire burns very brightly, but can fade.

Of their faults, selfishness is the worst; and it often emerges because of their basic thrusting psychological motivation. Ariens can be extremely brave and, less positively, have a liking for taking risks, which prompts vulnerability to minor accidents – with cuts and burns dominating (Ariens should look to their score in Part Four of the tests in chapter 6, p. 60). There may well be a strong liking for driving fast, but they may also like to develop their driving skills and techniques at an advanced level. The Ariens' body area is the head – Aries can either suffer a well above average number of headaches, or swear they never have any at all!

Arien occupations need an element of adventure: Ariens like working in a noisy, busy atmosphere, with plenty of scope for initiative. The pioneering spirit can be expressed in the career – in scientific research, in exploring (in all senses of the word, from mapping little-known areas of the earth to probing the depths of the mind through psychoanalysis). Physical energy must be burned up, expressed through sport perhaps, or some demanding form of exercise; and in all spheres of life monotony and a totally disciplined existence with no excitement must be avoided. Many Ariens, however, flourish in the modern army.

Work must be competitive; engineering of all kinds is excellent, as is the fire department, metal-working and hairdressing. Odd? – but it involves the head, the Arien body area, and also heat, the Arien element! To sum up: avoid predictable, dull, desk-bound jobs – or even jobs that seem too secure.

Ariens are passionate and highly sexed. They will go through hell and high water to achieve the partner of their choice; and generally speaking their enthusiasm for their love-life and their partners makes them lively and spirited company in bed and out. The tendency to put themselves first should be consciously controlled, but their zest for life and love is very much to their advantage in their emotional relationships.

TAURUS

Sun Sign period: 21 April–21 May
Ruling planet, Venus. Colour, pink. Stone, emerald. Metal, copper.

Taureans are extremely reliable and steady; they have a well above average need to feel secure in all spheres of life. They like routine and can get quite distressed if that routine – which has probably been carefully built up and well tried – is disrupted in any way. Taureans in fact are creatures of habit. This is fine: in many ways Taureans, because of their reliability and common sense, are the salt of the earth. However, it is very important that they are not stick-in-the-mud and they must make a conscious effort to consider, for instance, present-day opinions and new ideas and developments. The Sign falls into the 'Fixed' quality and, while this is indicative of strength, there is always the possibility that the fixity can take over. Taureans learn slowly but thoroughly; their minds work well, but cannot be rushed. Taureans are by no means lacking in patience and are slow to get angry, though once they are angered a bull-like temper can be expressed.

There is in every Taurean an element of possessiveness. It can be expressed through pride of possession – having beautiful things round the home, buying always (if possible) what is most expensive and beautiful. All this, of course, gives an additional feeling of security. But possessiveness can extend quite seriously to the partner or the children, since Taurus can think of partners as 'Mine' – something that must be controlled; not easy for Taureans.

A sense of security must be embodied in Taureans' careers. It is all important to Taureans that the regular pay cheque will turn up on time, so that they can budget, save, plan their financial affairs . . . money makes the world go round for them (they should note their scores in the money section of the ambition test on p. **114** – it will probably be high).

Banking, all forms of 'big business' and insurance, and stockbroking are all excellent professions. Beauty care, sculpture and architecture can also be rewarding. Taureans are often very muscial; the Taurean body area is the neck and throat and quite a high proportion of successful singers have Taurus as their Sun or Rising Sign.

The throat is a vulnerable part of the body and because Taureans like good, rich, sweet food (chocolate cake, for instance!) there can all too easily be a weight problem (how did Taureans score in the tests on p. 60?) Regular exercise is important to them (as to everyone), but it may well be more of an effort for Taureans. That effort must be made!

Taureans have the tradition of being the best-looking of all the Signs. Who would want to spoil that by becoming over-weight and flabby, especially when you are passionate and make an excellent lover? Perhaps slightly slow to arouse, Taureans are considerate and loving as well as sensuously sexy. But watch that possessiveness. . . .

GEMINI

Sun Sign period: 22 May–22 June
Ruling planet, Mercury. Colour, varied; but bright yellow is a favourite. Stone, agate. Metal, mercury.

Geminians are excellent representatives of their element – air. They are always lively, always on the go and very, very talkative. They *need* communication in one way or another and this need is well expressed by the free movement and flow of air; but if we look at the legends related to Mercury, the messenger of the gods, the characteristics of Gemini make even more sense.

Geminians will talk to any old tramp, write to (or for) the newspapers, give lectures, or work in the media in general. Certainly they are great fun to be with and lesser mortals are unlikely to be bored when with a member of this Sign. Perhaps what they themselves dread more than anything else is boredom, or feeling that they might be boring to other people. When visiting a Gemini, you will have a book thrust under your nose, only to have it whisked away almost immediately and another substituted; one record will no sooner be on the turntable than it will have to make way for a second and a third; and conversation will flow throughout. However, Geminians tend to know rather a little about rather a lot of subjects and must be on their guard against superficiality, however amusing. This is their worst fault. Restlessness can be quite a serious problem, too. Basically highly-strung, the Geminian can very easily tax his nervous system and under stress there is a tendency to nervous breakdown, so care is needed. There is a lot of talk about the Geminian duality and it is usually present. 'One thing at a time' is *not* the right rule for Geminians; but they do need to ensure that in changing occupations, hobbies, interests, they do not leave behind them a trail of once-used ice skates, half-finished models, half-written novels.

The Geminian profession must be in communication; journalism and work for the media in general is right for them. They usually have a great natural ability to 'sell', too. Working for the Post Office or in telecommunications is fine, work in department stores (leading perhaps to a position as buyer) is also good, providing the individual Geminian can convince himself that life is interesting and not boring. As the Geminian body area is the hands and arms, Geminians make good masseurs and manicurists.

Geminians are the sort to 'live on their nerves' and usually are not bothered by weight problems. For them, tough and demanding exercise can be a great unwinder – very important. So much of Gemini goes on in the mind that we wonder how they score in the IQ test (p. 124)?

In love, Gemini is flirtatious and (ideally) likes to have more than one relationship. Sexually, Geminians like to experiment, so need a willing and lively partner in bed. Of all the Signs, they are considered to hang on to a youthful appearance most tenaciously, often into old age. Again, we return to the mind: the Geminian attitude to life is lively, always wanting to learn about new ideas and attitudes; because of this they retain a flexible and inquiring mind, a good recipe for eternal youth.

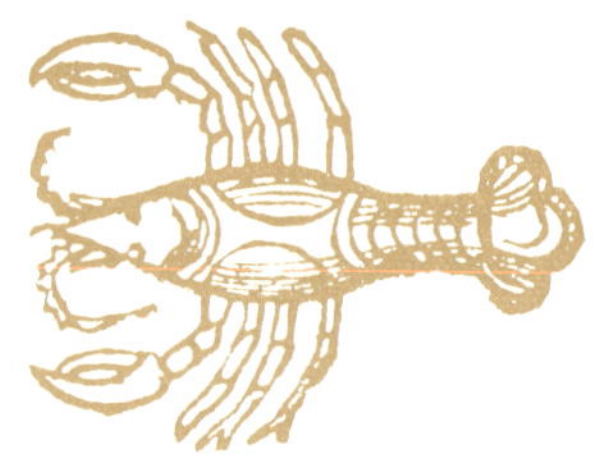

CANCER

Sun Sign period: 23 June–23 July
Ruling planet, the Moon. Colour, pale grey. Stone, pearl. Metal, silver.

While Cancerians are kind, helpful and considerate, they are not always easy to understand. On first meeting they do not usually show themselves to advantage, since they have a psychological defence-system which, very like the crab's hard shell, protects their soft inner selves; they tend to hide behind this and use it to defend their opinions and anything or anyone dear to them – including themselves. Under such constraints they can all too easily snap out a sharp and cutting answer or comment, for which they soon feel sorry.

Nevertheless, the real Cancerian is loving and sensitive and very, very nice. So do not be put off by a first impression of any Cancerian you happen to talk to – you do need to get to know them. The Cancerian sensitivity is well known and is certainly sometimes present; while Cancerians are guilty of causing some minor injuries due to the sharpness of their tongues, they don't take it too well if they are treated in a similar way. This, and possible moodiness, is something they need to be very aware of.

There is in every Cancerian an extremely strong protective instinct. When Cancerians are little, they 'take care of' younger brothers, sisters and friends, or even any small animal. This habit goes on through their lives and very often they are anxious to have their own homes and families – sometimes tending to rush into marriage for that very reason, in spite of a naturally cautious instinct and a shrewd streak. They also need to be careful that they do not object too strenuously to their 'birds' flying the nest when young, when the family wants to move on away from home. The family unit is important to them.

The Cancerian body area is the breast – nourishment, nurturing, parenthood are well symbolized, of course, by the woman's breasts. Cancerians are prone to worry; their way through their problems is to use their intuition – if they 'feel' that they should take a certain line of action, it will probably be right for them. Through worry, digestion can be a problem and Cancerians are vulnerable to such upsets – the two are inevitably linked (see chapter 6, How healthy are you?).

Professions for Cancerians are many and varied: because they love to collect and even to hoard things, they are naturals to learn about and work with antiques. The 'caring' professions are marvellous for them – nursery teaching, nursing in particular; and because they are often excellent cooks, any work in the field of catering is appropriate. In love, the Cancerian is very kind and forbearing – as one would expect – but also very sensuous, tender and often sentimental. Cancerians are faithful to their partners and take care of them – another form of expression of one of their most basic psychological motivations. However, it is advisable for them not to be too keen to set up home or ring the wedding bells, since this can be off-putting to some partners who might thereby be made to feel claustrophobic.

LEO

Sun Sign period: 24 July–23 August
Ruling planet, the Sun. Colour, all the 'Sun' colours from palest yellow to dark orange. Stone, ruby. Metal, gold.

If you know a Leo who isn't full of enthusiasm for life and enjoying every moment of it, then something is seriously wrong and that particular lion's Sun isn't shining as it should. However, when there are clouds, generally speaking they pass over the Sun quite quickly, as if in a balmy summer breeze.

Leos often also seem to have a basic motivation to get other people to enjoy life and get as much out of it as they themselves do; and if others don't respond they must take the consequences! Leos organize every moment of their own lives to the best possible advantage, usually persuading others to do the same. They need to be rather careful, nevertheless, because they can sometimes seem bossy, autocratic and 'pushy' – just big show-offs. Many Leos literally and metaphorically want to (and indeed *do*) take full centre-stage: and if the spotlight isn't on them, they are quite capable of climbing into the flies to make sure it is redirected to their advantage.

Leos have natural powers of leadership. If challenged about this they may at first be slightly surprised, but will then add – perhaps in self-defence – 'well, someone's got to do it'. Leos make it to the top very often, becoming chairmen or presidents – whether of their countries or of the local women's luncheon club; it doesn't much matter as long as they're the top in their own way.

Every Leo aims to have a 'kingdom', even if it's only in one room. 'They don't have hobbies, they only have careers', said one shrewd astrologer; and this is true, because whatever the Leo interest (and it's usually geared towards the arts, or at least creative in some way), they will take it to its highest possible level, not learning any skill superficially or cheaply, but expensively and expansively, often the hard way, and *very* thoroughly.

Leos' liking for life can be expensive, as they love to spend money on giving others a good time, organizing parties of all kinds with all the finest trimmings. This kind of atmosphere extends to their love-life: generous and passionate, they like to take the lead in relationships (and sometimes sexually, too), though making sure that love-making takes place in comfort and warmth – they hate the cold.

The Leo career potential is very good. They need prominence in some form. They can work well with children and make excellent teachers (Leos have a happy knack of not forgetting what it was like to be little). Youth work, acting, dancing, jewellery, painting, designing – and many Leos are astrologers. (How do you fare in the ambition tests on p. 114?) The Leo body area is the spine and heart and it's vital that they keep both in good working order. Probably their best exercise is dancing, but any exercise that keeps the heart active and makes it work well is right for them.

VIRGO

Sun Sign period: 24 August–23 September
Ruling planet, Mercury. Colours, dark brown and green. Stone, sardonyx. Metal, mercury.

There is no doubt about it, Virgo is *the* world's worker! Virgo is practical, with a craving for detail, usually in a hurry, always busy, but not always very well organized – though getting everything done eventually. There is in nearly all Virgos a genuinely modest trait, which is charming, sometimes disarming and always genuine. It can be the pleasant modesty of the young girl, but it can also be expressed in over-modesty – denigrating Virgo's own achievements, which are far greater than they themselves will often allow.

The worst Virgoan fault is to be over-critical; and perhaps to nag. Virgoans must be careful about this and, while at root they are willing slaves, they are not beyond carping if they feel they are being pushed too far. They have a precision and a neatness which is delightful: a typical Virgoan would be a neatly dressed girl in, say, a trim, small-patterned dress (of navy blue and white), being the perfect secretary to her boss; no ambition to be the boss herself – she needs direction – but in her own way keeping him 'in order'. The Virgoan critical streak and need for perfection can at times work very negatively for them. This is something important in their love-life, because in their quest for perfection in a partner they may well find it difficult to accept a partner's small mannerisms or habits. Petty annoyances may become disproportionately annoying, spoiling a lot of the fun of a relationship. To take the theme a little further, Virgoans bothered by such difficulties should perhaps ask themselves whether, in seizing on the small faults of others, they are not really making excuses for some kind of inhibition in themselves – which may well be the real problem, and could be sexual in origin. (Virgoans may have low scores in the libido test, p. 110.)

The Virgoan body area is the stomach and Virgos can all too easily fall victim to stomach upsets. With Cancer, they are the great worriers of the Zodiac; it is often the case that the Virgo stomach complains or is worried before the Virgo is consciously aware of a problem.

Virgo potential can be well expressed in many ways. Virgos are often craft-workers, good at weaving and sewing, for instance. They make analysts and researchers of all kinds – whether in the laboratory or the library. Many famous writers are Virgos and many work in the media (they share with Gemini the planet Mercury as their 'ruler' – and Mercury is the planet of communication). Often Virgoans are interested in health and may make a career in either conventional or unconventional medicine. Health food and vegetarianism are very much a part of the Virgoan scene. Virgos usually like the great outdoors, so exercise can be taken cycling or hiking round the countryside. Gardening too is rewarding and good for them. Worry and nervous tension remain the serious bugbears: Virgos must approach their problems by making use of their analytical and critical qualities (making lists of every aspect of a problem). And they really must *try* to relax, just sometimes!

LIBRA

Sun Sign period: 24 September–23 October
Ruling planet, Venus. Colour, pale blue. Stone, sapphire. Metal, copper.

Libra is romantic, loving, good company, and most certainly likes 'fair play'. The sign of Libra is the scales, representing balance and harmony – the two essential qualities of life for our Libran brothers and sisters. For Libra there is time for everything; while many Librans are quite hard working, they usually manage to give the impression that all is calm and serene. This is how they like to be seen – glamorous and unruffled – and even if an anxious partner is waiting for his lady to finish getting ready for the theatre, she will say: 'Don't worry, the curtain will ring up late' – and infuriatingly, it does, seemingly just to oblige Madame Libra!

Although there is a strong need for harmony in the Libran life, Libras can very often upset it by their own actions. It is as if there is a *need* for animosity – so that they can calm troubled waters later. Their worst fault is indecisiveness. Any phrases you have read about Librans 'sitting on the fence' are true; many will simply delay making a decision so long that one is never made – the projects don't ever get started. If this indecisiveness can be directed positively, it is useful, for Libra sees both sides of a problem: justice will finally reign as securely over any court of justice, the scales exactly level. This is marvellous.

Librans are very sociable and like to entertain. They usually give lavish dinner parties, since – like Taurus, the 'sister' sign (Taurus is 'ruled' by Venus) – they enjoy good food. The Libran body area is the kidneys and sometimes, due to slight malfunction, Librans tend to get headaches. However, they must not use this as an excuse at bedtime, for while they are romantic to a fault, they can be (as in Marlene Dietrich's song) 'the laziest girl in town' – sexually very languid. They need a permanent relationship and their tendency to be 'in love with love' must not be ignored. Because of this they tend to rush into marriage; should friends be marrying all round them, they too will want to jump on the bandwagon. This can be disastrous and they should be aware that it is more likely to happen to them than to many other Zodiac types.

They work very well in the luxury trades and make marvellous dress designers – often having an especial flair for fashion. The beauty business attracts them; all aspects of it. They make good businessmen and women, but definitely in partnership and not alone, since responsibility must be shared (and Libra can be very extravagant). Art dealing, acting as an agent, the record business, all are profitable areas for Libra.

Librans need gentle but regular exercise and should watch their weight very carefully (how do they fare in the test on p. 60?) Tennis and badminton are appropriate for them. Exercising alone is not so good – they soon feel lonely, cut out, and just lounge around; friends need to encourage them to keep moving!

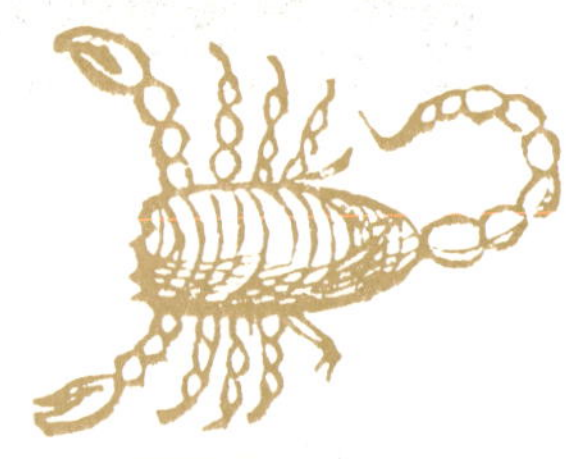

SCORPIO

Sun Sign period: 24 October–22 November
Ruling planet, Pluto (traditionally, Mars). Colour, dark red and maroon. Stone, opal. Metal, iron.

Scorpios have the greatest psychological strength of any Zodiac sign and the highest level of energy – an energy that is powerfully emotionally charged. Scorpios have to find a positive outlet for this energy, if they are not to feel unfulfilled; otherwise, they are restless and find life frustrating. They have a terrific intensity and sense of purpose, and can be very fixed in their opinions, very stubborn. They are of a 'water' sign and their 'water' is the water of the deep, dark pool – murky and mysterious. When all these qualities are positively expressed, they are marvellous people – people who get things done, work well and hard, and for whom life has a sense of direction. Sometimes, however, Scorpios use their potential negatively, directing it towards darker interests; there can be an obsession with sex or the occult, indeed an over-involvement with any one area of life. When all the energies 'flow', however, we have someone who is excellent company and gets a great deal of concentrated pleasure out of life.

Scorpios often have an almost hypnotic power over others. This can fascinate them – and can give satisfaction all round. But Scorpios will often work hard and long on some project, then for reasons best known to themselves will cut that interest – whatever it may be – out of their lives and even destroy what they have built up. It could be a flourishing business, it could be a relationship; the 'cutting out' could be expressed by selling all the contents of a house and the house itself, and starting again. To change completely life-styles, professions, partners is something that does happen to Scorpios. It may be necessary for them – a sort of deep-rooted psychological spring cleaning. But they can, in taking such a line of action, throw out much effort, which is a pity.

The Scorpio body area is the genitals and it may be that the Scorpio sex life is sometimes over-emphasized in summaries like this. Nevertheless, it is often of much greater importance to Scorpio than to other Zodiac types; if the sex life isn't as fulfilling and rewarding as it should be, the Scorpio could well suffer considerably more than many other types under similar stress or with parallel problems. Scorpios probably score highly in the sexual libido test (p. 110). The worst Scorpio fault is jealousy and naturally this is most likely to occur within an emotional relationship. It is difficult for Scorpios to avoid. They must try very hard not to keep a compulsive, even obsessional hold over partners.

The Scorpio career potential is geared to discovery: detective work or a career with the police; pathology, surgery, butchery, insurance, the Armed Forces all have a good Scorpionic ring for them. Indeed, there could be a tendency to a successful career in crime! Many Scorpios do very well in positions of power, which they enjoy. Heavy exercise is to be recommended – water sports, judo, karate and boxing.

SAGITTARIUS

Sun Sign period: 23 November–22 December
Ruling planet, Jupiter. Colour, dark blue and purple. Stone, topaz. Metal, tin.

Sagittarius is the hunter, the philosopher, the sage – and the untamed, unbridled stallion. Sagittarians can be all these even in this day and age and can develop steadily and positively from one to the other. In youth many Sagittarians are rather wild; they probably like driving round in fast cars. Many do not care too much about their grades, their eventual degrees or diplomas; yet conversely they are in many ways eternal students. There is an element of the student in the wisest and most philosophical, sage-like Sagittarian; and there is, too, always a delightful element of fun and enthusiasm for life. Young Sagittarians – more than most Zodiac types – learn from their mistakes. But there is always a youthful outlook on life, even if wisdom in the end dominates. (This is a tendency shared with the opposite sign across the Zodiac, Gemini.)

For most Sagittarians the grass is always and irresistibly greener over the hedge. Duality (again shared with Gemini) is present, but Sagittarians will be more likely to be versatile; while wanting to have a lot of projects under way and do a lot of things, they will not usually be inconsistent, or superficial. The modern Sagittarian expresses his hunting instincts through visiting charity shops and hunting for bargains, swopping furniture or clothes. The worst Sagittarian fault is restlessness: it will creep up on them if they feel that freedom of movement is restricted. They hate claustrophobia: a claustrophobic house, a room with no view, lack of fresh air, or (most importantly) a claustrophobic relationship. They cannot tolerate possessiveness and need to be given quite a large element of freedom within the confines of a relationship, or in marriage. They need *very* understanding and sympathetic partners.

The Sagittarian has an excellent mind which needs stimulation; all-round challenge is important and this is especially relevant in the choice of career. Sagittarians are good teachers at university level, good lawyers, attorneys, judges. They can be attracted to philosophy and religion, and are well suited to become librarians, publishers, writers and booksellers. Many Sagittarians are professional sportsmen, though the connection with horses and racing is sometimes overstressed. Freedom of expression is as necessary as good food for them. Good food *is* necessary – Sagittarians usually have healthy appetites, and healthy bodies too, since they positively enjoy exercise (mental and physical). We think they should do rather well in the intelligence test (p. 120) and will certainly give Geminis a run for their money – that is, unless their liver is giving them problems, for the liver is the Sagittarian organ, and the hips and thighs the body areas. Sagittarian women tend to put on weight round their hips and thighs and should exercise with this in mind.

CAPRICORN

Sun Sign period: 23 December–19 January
Ruling planet, Saturn. Colour, dark grey and black. Stone, turquoise. Metal, lead.

Capricorn climbs the heights, and Capricorn stays in the valleys. Capricorn is the top, and the wet fish. So, generally speaking, there are two types of Capricorn: the giddy mountain goat that climbs neatly and expertly from one rocky crag to another – and always upward – and the downtrodden domestic animal who in all ways remains tethered. We are not saying that one type cannot ever *become* the other and it is surprising how the transformation can take place – sometimes, of course, in the wrong direction! Friends of Capricorns will know which type of goat they are dealing with, for even the giddiest of them, and the most successful, will make free with their problems, their burdens in life, their difficulties, emphasizing how unsuccessful they have been even while going on to recount their latest success or *coup* or promotion. There is nevertheless an element of the 'loner' in most Capricorns and this is no less present in the most ambitious and power seeking of them; when Capricorn reaches the very top, after all, he is alone on the pinnacle.

The truly ambitious Capricorn cannot 'pass the buck'; he has to make the final decision, take the praise or blame. Perhaps one of the most endearing qualities of our Capricornian friends is their off-beat sense of humour. This takes quite a bit of getting used to, but is generally present; and the odd throwaway comment can be extremely rewarding and worth waiting for. They hate showy things, usually; quality, with a capital Q, is all-important. They like the most expensive and the best, but it must be in quiet good taste. Plain, quality china, cut glass, elegant silver, handsome paintings will all come into the scheme of things, and we wonder how Capricorns score in the 'power' and 'social advancement' sections of the 'ambition' tests on pp. 114–19. Probably high – which is wonderful for them!

The successful Capricorn is often a self-made man; Capricorns do very well in building up their own businesses, but also in local and central government – they make able politicians. Geology and mineralogy will attract them; so will osteopathy and dentistry; they would make good master-builders or architects and any form of administration will suit them. A large number of professional musicians are Capricorns. But the Capricorn way is not to take short cuts or try to get rich quick: ask them – they will tell you it is through careful planning and steady progress. Capricorn needs financial security and a stable background to life (the 'earth' element of the sign making itself felt).

Capricorns in love are very cautious, but make faithful partners. However, they are not, generally speaking, noted for an excess of feeling and emotion, so those attracted to Capricorns need to make their intentions clear – with the greatest discretion of course. The Capricorn body area is the legs and knees; skin and bones are also important. Capricorns tend to get rheumatism; their exercise should be steady with a stress on keeping moving. Jogging would be particularly good, also hiking, or rock-climbing. The worst Capricorn fault is pessimism and (sometimes) meanness.

AQUARIUS

Sun Sign period: 20 January–19 February
Ruling planet, Uranus. Colour, turquoise. Stone, aquamarine. Metal, uranium.

Aquarius is unpredictable, friendly and humanitarian. Aquarius understands, and is forward-looking. Aquarians are the most complex people to write about, and to generalize about, because they are the individualists of the Zodiac and will always disagree about their possible shared characteristics. We have had more discussions about their characteristics with Aquarians than with any other Zodiac types. However, we think that (individuality aside for the moment) some traits do emerge that they all share, whether they like to admit them or not. Usually there is something individual about the life-style, for instance; it will probably be in some way 'different'. There is a sort of distant glamour about them: magnetic, but at the same time somewhat cool – a Snow King or Queen quality. Most Aquarians are more stubborn than they care to admit. Their most fascinating feature is that, while they are usually the trendsetters of a generation and can be very 'way out', they may become 'frozen' in that generation, failing to move with the times. A generation gap may open up between them and their children which is wider and more unbridgable than with other types.

The Aquarian is a marvellous friend – perhaps the very best of friends, who will move heaven and hell for you – but it is possible that unpredictability in behaviour patterns can be an obstacle to perfect confidence; or, at best, you will find yourself saying, 'Well, we must make allowances for old ——.'

Their life-style is often so dear and so important to Aquarians that they delay settling into a permanent relationship, or even reject it altogether. Their sex life can be somewhat enigmatic, though they certainly have a romantic streak. They are faithful once committed and can be sexually rather adventurous; but these things are only discovered by those who have a close relationship with an Aquarian – which makes them all the more fascinating, distant, glamorous. . . .

Aquarians have very lively minds and can cope with many varied professions: the number of people in show business and the theatre with Aquarius as their Sun or Rising Sign is above average. Astronomy, astrology, being in the technical side of television, radio and space projects are also strong possibilities. Working for the United Nations or in large charity organizations would also appeal and the latest scientific developments would benefit from the presence of an Aquarian or two.

The Aquarius body area is the ankles. Circulation too is considered under Aquarius and this must be kept in good order; while one thinks of the Aquarian as a 'winter' person, the cold could be adverse. Winter sports and, perhaps, athletics and gymnastics, or working in gymnasiums, would be pleasant, positive exercise for this sign.

PISCES

Sun Sign period: 20 February–20 March
Ruling planet, Neptune. Colour, sea green. Stone, moonstone, Metal, tin.

Pisces swims against the tide and sometimes against itself. Pisces is kindness and confusion, intuition and sensitivity. While Pisceans are often vague and sometimes lacking in confidence, they are equally or more often very talented and creative. However, they need support; they need strong, enthusiastic (but not gushing) friends and partners constantly to encourage them to produce more results, to go on writing those marvellous poems, painting those splendid pictures, or to work on that fantastic evening gown so that it will be ready for them actually to wear to the Prince's ball! And it is the Pisces Cinderella that can hit the high spots on such occasions, although all too often Ms Pisces will swear she looks *awful*, or 'a mess', when she is *the* one in the Zodiac who can look as attractive in a length of fabric she's pinned or draped around herself as in the latest de Givenchy model. Pisceans are capable of doing a great deal, though they nearly always underestimate themselves and will tell everyone they have no potential. Here we have self-deception running wild, and it isn't easy for friends to make them realize it.

Pisces emotion is never very far away – indeed, one way to tell a Pisces is by the look in his or her eyes; even when they are smiling there is an element of the tearful about Pisceans (no, they are not miseries, but they could well change moods as the tide flows and ebbs). It is not easy for Pisces to be disciplined and compromises must be made in partnerships. The Piscean is very loving, affectionate and sensuous – sometimes getting a little unstuck in relationships and being led blindly into them, which is a pity, since people can all too easily take advantage of them.

So to Pisces potential, which as you will have gathered, emphasizes creativity. It is a good Sun Sign if you are a dancer or actor, since there is the ability to 'take impressions' and reproduce them. This, in a different way, applies to photographers – an ideal career for Pisces, who (if interested) will love the whole photographic process. Working in films calls for the same kind of enthusiasm, whether behind or in front of the cameras. Pisces cares very deeply, so the nursing profession is also appropriate. Many like to go to sea, on liners or in the navy. However, if you have a Pisces friend, remember always to encourage any creativity and help to get him or her organized – especially if selling is concerned. Pisces would be pretty hopeless at that.

The Pisces body area is the feet; usually they either wear and love extravagantly smart shoes, or foot exercise sandals – or no shoes at all, if they can get away with it. For exercise, dancing, ice-skating and swimming are naturals. We think that many Pisces will score low in the ambition tests (pp. 114–19), especially where money is concerned.

22 You in your handwriting

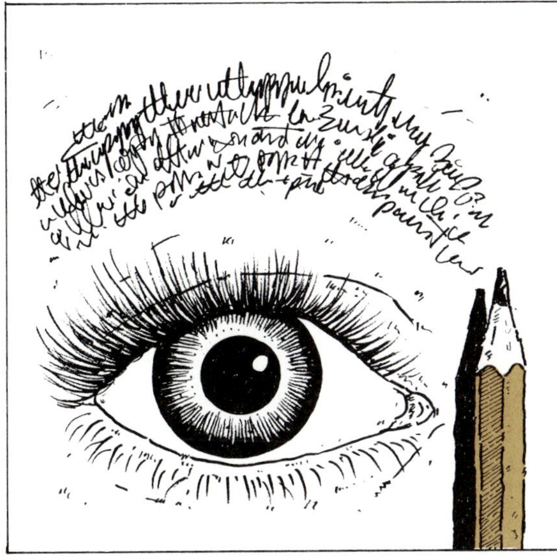

Caesar's handwriting was studied, and a textbook of graphology was printed in 1622. Does large handwriting show restlessness? Or underlining, a romantic personality? Might it be that coarse, irregular letters indicate sexual indulgence?

THE THEORY THAT you reveal a great deal about your character and motivation in the style of your handwriting is of some antiquity. Suetonius left a detailed description of Augustus Caesar's writing and the eleventh-century Chinese philosopher Kuo Jo-hsu thought he could discover from a man's script whether he was noble or plebeian.

In 1622 Camillo Baldi, a professor at Bologna University, published *The Means of Knowing the Habits and Qualities of a Writer from his Letters*, while Johann Kaspar Lavater included a chapter on handwriting in his *Physiognomical Fragments* (1758). The idea occurred to numbers of distinguished men. Goethe wrote, in 1820, that 'there can be no doubt that the handwriting of a person has some relation to his mind and character; from it one may conceive at least some idea of his manner of being and acting, just as one must recognize not only appearance and features, but also bearing, voice, even bodily movements as being significant and congruent with the total individuality.'

But it was in France during the first half of the nineteenth century that the subject was first thoroughly studied, by a number of clergymen including Cardinal Regnier, Archbishop of Cambrai, Bishop Soudinet of Amiens and the Abbé Flandrin – one of whose pupils, Jean Hippolyte Michon, was the first true expert on the subject and coined the term *graphology*.

The Abbé Michon made a large collection of samples of handwriting, catalogued the various deviations from what he considered the norm and by 1872 had begun to publish his findings. These were based on empirical observation: if the handwriting of twenty 'dishonest' people contained one common factor, then this was held to indicate dishonesty. The samples were, of course, statistically tiny and the indications seemed somewhat simplistic – as they still do: it is not surprising, for instance, to find that very small writing is regarded as indicative of introspection, or very large writing of extroversion.

The Mysteries of Handwriting and *A System of Graphology* none the less created a sensation in the 1870s. A number of interested students continued the Abbé's work – notably J. Crépieux-Jamin, who classified handwriting in seven categories and pointed out seventy-five 'elements' still used by modern graphologists.

At the turn of the century Germany became the centre of graphological studies. Dr George Preyer and Dr George Meyer began to look at handwriting as an expression of the whole personality of the writer rather than as a mere reflection either of his physique or his psyche. Dr Ludwig Klages went further, asserting that every emotion a human being feels can be shown reflected in his handwriting; that a change of character will show; and that writing displays the constant conflict between the writer's natural self and and outside influences.

Klages founded the first German graphological society (in 1886), while elsewhere in Europe the study grew – Robert Saudek was working in Czechoslovakia, Max Pulver in Switzerland, Schwiedland and Langenbruch in Austria. Pulver worked particularly on graphology and criminology, claiming that the science could be of particular help in police detective work.

There was little interest in the subject in Britain – but it was taken up enthusiastically in America in the 1920s, when Louise Rice formed the first American Graphological Society. In the thirties there were experiments at Harvard designed to show a connection between character and styles of writing. Gordon W. Allport and Philip Vernon, in *Studies of Expressive Movements* (1933), concluded that 'no-one who has considered carefully the experimental and theoretical work on handwriting seems to deny the *a priori* case for graphology. Graphic movement apparently is not activity that is dissociated from the complexities of personality; on the contrary, it seems to be intricately woven with deep-lying determinants of conduct.'

Today the American-based International Grapho-analysts' Society presides over an enormous number of working graphologists, while in Western Germany there may be as many as three thousand analysts. In Britain the trend seems to be for individuals to work away quietly in their own corners.

Few people would deny that one person's handwriting almost always differs radically from another's (the banks, for instance, would be in deep trouble if this were not so). Experts can clearly discover whether Mr A or Mr B wrote a particular letter, or even whether Mr A had imitated Mr B writing it. Whether it is possible to say much about Mr A's psychological or physical make-up by an examination of the handwriting remains at least in part an open question.

The rules laid down for the examination of a piece of handwriting are fairly simple. It is

THE WHITE HOUSE
WASHINGTON

SECRETARY OF STATE
DEC 6 - 1941
NOTED

740.0011 Pacific War/1856

Dear Cordell
Shoot this to Grew —
I think can go in
gray code — saves time —
I don't mind if it gets
picked up

FDR

President Roosevelt's note to his Secretary of State prescribed the code to be used in dispatching a last-minute appeal for peace to the Emperor of Japan before Pearl Harbor. His own handwriting, like that of all of us, may provide its own private code – a key to personality.

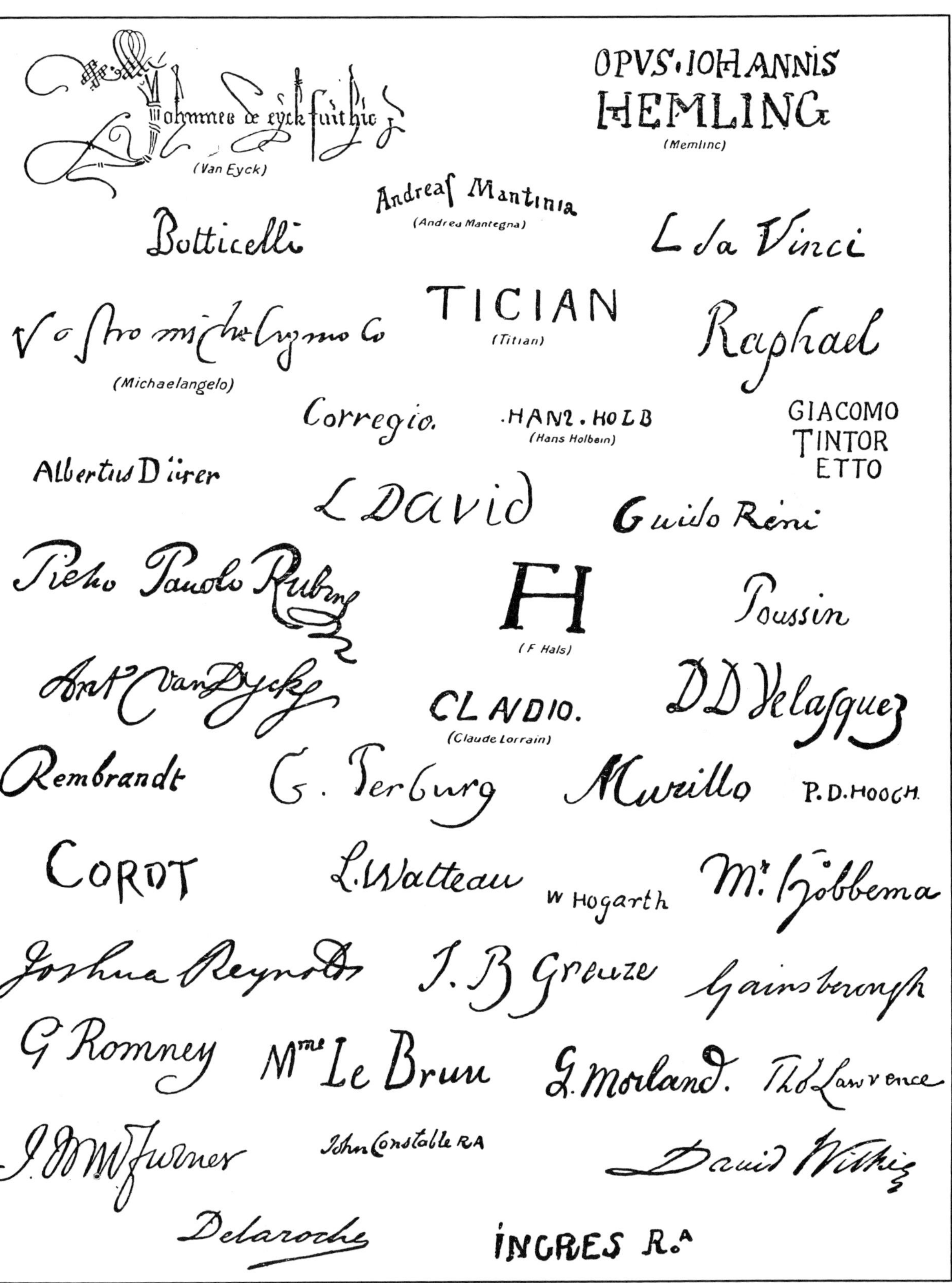
(Van Eyck)
OPVS·IOHANNIS HEMLING
(Memlinc)
Andreas Mantinia
(Andrea Mantegna)
Botticelli
L da Vinci
TICIAN
(Titian)
Raphael
(Michaelangelo)
Corregio.
.HANS.HOLB
(Hans Holbein)
GIACOMO TINTORETTO
Albertus Dürer
L David
Guido Reni
FH
(F Hals)
Poussin
CLADIO.
(Claude Lorrain)
DD Velasquez
Rembrandt
G. Terburg
Murillo
P.D.HOOGH.
COROT
A.Watteau
W Hogarth
Mr Hobbema
Joshua Reynolds
J. B Greuze
Gainsborough
G Romney
Mme Le Brun
G.Morland.
Thos Lawrence
John Constable RA
David Wilkie
Delaroche
INGRES R.A

best to look at several different examples of the handwriting in question. For preference, these should be written in ink (the ubiquitous ball-point pen has been of no help to graphology) and they should *not* have been written especially for analysis. They should be lengthy enough to include, if possible, all the letters of the alphabet.

The analyst then looks at the various aspects of the formation of the letters, the connections between them, the pressure of the pen, the spacing of the words and their arrangement on the page. Some of the conclusions seem straightforward: *Positive People Write Large, Negative People Write Small*, one textbook forthrightly declares. Legible writing, it is argued, shows that the writer has come to terms with his personality;

Left: Three signatures of Napoleon: at the height of his power, in the hour of his defeat, and in imprisonment. Below: Dr Ludwig Klages, pioneer of graphology in Germany.

illegible handwriting suggests the opposite.

Certain aspects of the handwriting show certain aspects of the personality. The connections between the letters show how the writer deals with life, the affections and emotions; the small letters show something of his way of life, his subconscious; the capital letters his originality, talent, mental capacity.

The theory is complex. What follows suggests some of the simpler assumptions of graphology, which you can test out on your own handwriting.

The slope of the letters

Letters which slope from the vertical at over 45 degrees either to left or right are considered to have 'extreme slant'. Within 45 degrees, the slant is 'moderate'; within 5 degrees of the vertical, it is 'upright'.

The writer whose handwriting is 'upright' is realistic and independent, may tend to be too sure of his opinions; is restrained and unemotional, even to the point of coldness. He may tend to be pessimistic and egoistic, and will probably remain calm in most circumstances.

A slant to the right indicates an extrovert personality, sociable and active, talkative and enthusiastic, friendly and affectionate; being emotional he may be easily influenced and blunder into situations without sufficient thought. If the slant is extreme, the temperament will be highly excitable, even to the point of violence.

A slant to the left is relatively rare (more women than men seem to show it); it seems to indicate repression and detachment, but also ambition and caution; the writer may be somewhat arrogant and an extreme leftward slant may show cynicism, cruelty, envy and jealousy.

The size of the writing

Very small handwriting indicates a very introspective person. *Small* writing shows a scientific mind with a degree of conscientiousness and power to assimilate facts. *Medium-sized* writing indicates a moderate man or woman, middle of the road, a conformist, practical and materialistic. *Large* writing can show self-importance, extroversion, restlessness, boldness – often very small men have large writing. *Abnormally large* writing shows vast enthusiasm, immaturity, thoughtlessness.

Punctuation

Lack of punctuation – with *t*'s left uncrossed, *i*'s undotted – shows absentmindedness, indecision, impetuousness. *Careful* punctuation shows a meticulous mind, an orderly nature, someone who considers all aspects of a situation before acting. *Many dashes* in a piece of writing show a practical writer, somewhat aggressive. *Circles* used as periods or *i*-dots show a calm, unruffled disposition. A plethora of *explanation marks* and *underlinings* shows a romantic personality, with enthusiasm and a tendency to exaggerate.

Connections

The ways in which the letters of words are connected are divided by graphologists into the *garland* (a series of rounded underhand loops), the *arcade* (similar loops, but overhand), the *angle* (a jagged line) and the *thread* (a straight meandering line). These take much practice to discriminate between with accuracy. Roughly, the *garland* indicates ease, confidence, sympathy, tolerance, though also laziness and superficiality; it is the most common of all types of connection. The *arcade* shows trustworthiness, shyness, caution, but also perhaps a certain deviousness. The *angle* can indicate aggression, a strong will, discipline and thoroughness, if also intolerance and irritation. The *thread* shows flexibility, versatility, a wide intelligence, perhaps insincerity, and feminine nature in men.

Easier for the amateur to discern is the way in which the letters of words are sometimes *not* connected (in looking for this, you must ignore the places at which a line may be broken specifically to cross a *t* or dot an *i*). If all the letters of words are *connected*, the writer will be a strongly logical person with high powers of reasoning and a strong sense of purpose. If the letters are *occasionally broken*, the writer will be always interested in new ideas, flexible in his approach to life and

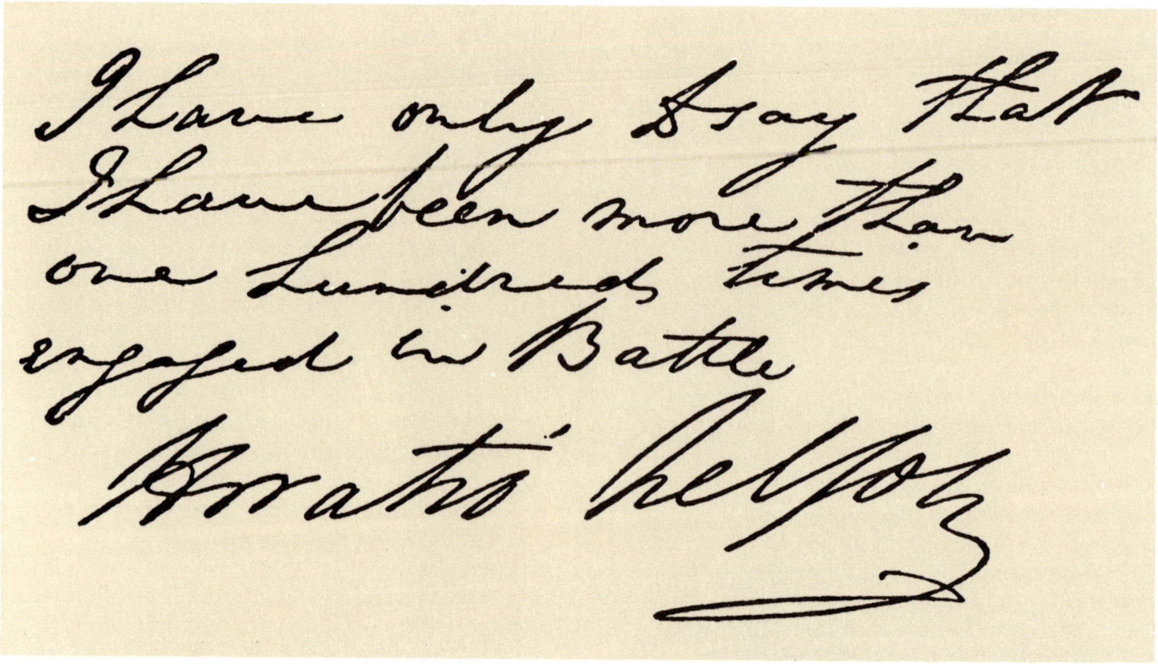
I have only to say that
I have been more than
one hundred times
engaged in Battle
Horatio Nelson

The handwriting of Admiral Lord Nelson: above, with his right hand; opposite, with his left hand, after an arm had been lost in action.

very versatile. *Entirely disconnected* letters may show intuition, but can also show loneliness and uncertainty, inner tensions and restlessness, though sometimes also self-reliance and quickness of understanding. The connection not only of letters but of *words* can show high executive ability.

Dots and crosses

Undotted i's show carelessness, laziness, forgetfulness. A dot placed *close* to the *i* shows caution, reserve, a good memory. A dot *high to the right* of the *i* shows an enquiring mind, impulsiveness, enthusiasm. A dot *high to the left* shows inquisitiveness, deliberation. A dot *high above* the *i* indicates a person who is certainly inquisitive, but also rather cautious, an excellent planner. A dot formed like a tiny *dash* denotes energy.
The crosses of *t*'s usually show a degree of leadership and your relationship to others. Crosses to the *left* of the *t* can show inner inferiority feelings, lack of drive, hesitation to use what powers of leadership are present. Crosses which are *through* the bar of the *t* (in the conventional position) vary from a *low* position on the letter (caution but a drive to ignore it) to *high* (a desire for the unattainable, overweening ambition). Bars to the *right* of the *t low* on the letter show timidity, and at the *top* of the letter care and consideration for others, adaptability and an open mind.

The letters

Each letter in the alphabet is considered with care by the practised graphologist and it is not possible here to do anything but sketch some of the more forthright examples of how the expert views some of them.
a and o When left open at the top, these letters indicate a talkative person; closed in every case, caution is shown; some open, some closed, and the writer is changeable; open at the bottom – dishonest.
m and n If the *m* and *n* in a piece of writing commonly look more like *w* and *u*, the writer is adaptable, a good mixer, perceptive, rounded and clear-minded – sometimes

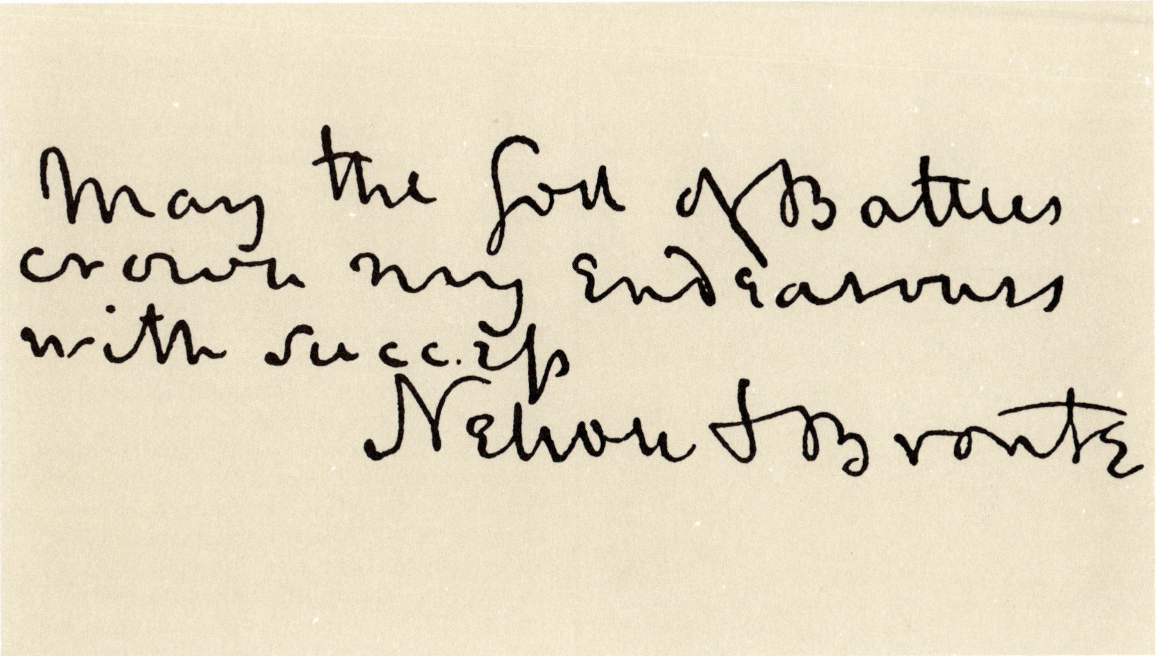

perhaps a mite simple.

p The *p* formed with a long loop at the bottom indicates a love of the outdoors, a very 'physical' nature. A sharp *p* with a high spike above it shows aggression and a *p* which is short above the line and long below shows physical strength. A *p* with the lower loop very rounded displays a love of peace.

Capital letters

Large capital letters – and it is fair to look especially at the capital *I* – can show abnormal self-esteem, pride, ambition, vanity, affectation, a desire to dominate, arrogance: in fact most of the qualities associated with too much concentration on self. *Small* capitals can show modesty, tolerance, a love of detail, but perhaps also a lack of confidence, an inferiority complex, fussiness or depression.

There is much more that the graphologist will look at: the spacing of lines and words, the margins left on the page, the slanting of the lines on the paper, the apparent speed of the writing, the degree of pressure, the shading of the writing, the width and narrowness of the letters. . . . The study is complex enough to be fascinating; an overall scheme enables the analyst to come to rough conclusions about the character of the writer at a glance. Here are just a few indications of how certain character traits show themselves:

Sincerity The writing lies straight on the page, with small letters of an equal size.

Insincerity The letters slope to the left and may decrease in size as the writing progresses.

Friendliness The letters sprawl on the paper.

Emotional coldness The writing slopes to the left, the letters being medium or large in size and set down with a very light pressure.

Meanness Crowded writing fills the paper, all the letters pushed together and small; the *t*'s are largely uncrossed.

Sexual indulgence Heavy writing with coarse and irregularly formed letters.

Frustration Cramped, small writing, perhaps sloping to the left, with the small *a*'s and *o*'s tightly closed and even 'knotted' with a little loop on top.

Fear An extreme variation in the size of the letters, an untidiness in the writing and unsteadiness in the formation of the letters.

23 You in your palm

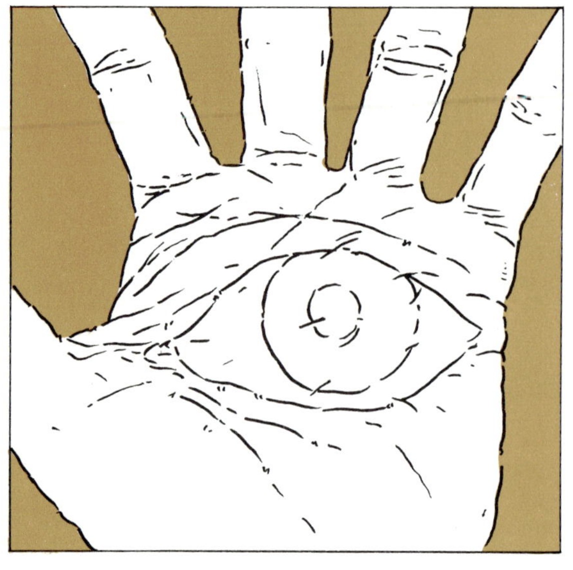

Palmistry was practised five centuries BC. Later, Cheiro became palmist to the Hollywood stars. Does your square hand show punctuality? . . . do your supple fingers betray inquisitiveness? . . . your Mount of Venus a violently sensual nature?

PALMISTRY IS ONE of the few aspects of physiognomy which is still relatively popular. Its early history is obscure. 'Cheiro', the best-known modern palmist (Count Louis Hamon, an Irishman whose great personal charm helped him to an enormously successful career in the salons of Victorian England and later in the US), argued that it had been practised in ancient China, Tibet, Persia and Egypt, but it seems to have been in Greece that the foundations of modern cheirognomy and cheiromancy were laid.

Anaxagoras is believed to have practised palmistry in the fifth century BC, and there are references to it in Aristotle (d. 322 BC), Pliny (d. AD 79), Albertus Magnus (d. 1280), Paracelsus (d. 1541) and others. During the Middle Ages the church took a dim view of it and the text, 'He sealeth up the hand of every man; that all men may know his work' (Job XXXVII, 7), was taken as a condemnation of the art. More modern translators argue that the text was distorted and it is perhaps significant that in the most modern versions (*The Good News Bible*, for example) there are no references at all to palmistry.

Towards the beginning of our own century palmistry had survived mainly in the traditions of gypsies and travelling fortune-tellers. It was during the 1890s that Hamon came to London from Dublin and attained a reputation for being able to interpret the character from the hands, as well as to see into the future. He is said to have read Oscar Wilde's hands and to have forecast his downfall. In 1900 he read Mata Hari's palm and saw signs of a tendency to deceive, as well as predicting her death in 1917. He read Edward VII's hands in 1902, when he was ill, and predicted that the king would survive for another seven years – as indeed he did.

Perhaps his most famous coup was in 1894, when he read the hands of Lord Kitchener; apart from apparent success in reading his character, he predicted that Kitchener would die at sea at the age of 66. Twenty-two years later, in 1916, he was proved right.

Cheiro wrote many textbooks on the subject and ended his life in Hollywood, running a school of metaphysics. There is little doubt that he was, almost single-handed, responsible for the modern revival of the art – though no doubt he would have been the first to denigrate the end-of-the-pier quacks who multiplied with alarming rapidity during the first twenty years of the century.

Modern palmists divide palmistry into three separate parts – cheirognomy, cheiromancy and dermatoglyphics. Dermatoglyphics concerns the patterns made by tiny ridges of skin on the hands and feet; it is especially useful because the patterns on the fingertips are entirely individual and are used by the police for identification of criminals.

The dermatoglyphic patterns are the only ones which never change, from infancy through to old age. The pattern forms as the skin itself forms: once fixed it never alters; even a heavy scar will only interrupt the pattern, distorting but not destroying it. So far no way has been found of altering it artificially; nor have two sets of fingerprints ever been found which match precisely. This is invaluable as far as identification is concerned, though palmists, of course, interpret the shapes in different ways than the police.

Cheiromancy is the best-known 'fortune-telling' aspect of palmistry, concerning itself with the study of the lines on the palms of the hands. These do change, and change very rapidly; the palm-print of a person before and after a severe emotional crisis will show marked differences, for instance. The lines are said to show the normal course of thought-patterns in the mind of the subject: the most recent theory of palmists seems to be that thought-patterns in the brain are in some way correlated with the patterns electrical brain-impulses seem to make on the palms of the hands. It follows that, while you can see the present state of a person's personality in the hand, it is impossible to 'read the future'; prediction in palmistry is regarded with suspicion by most palmists, as by most astrologers.

The third category in palmistry, cheirognomy, is concerned with the shape of the hands; the thickness and shape of the palm, the length of the fingers and thumb, and the way they are formed, the colour and texture of the skin and nails, the manner in which the subject uses his hands to gesture. The shape of the hands alters with age, but very slowly; occupation has its effect (as Sherlock Holmes was quick to see), but there are general themes in cheirognomy which are believed to hold good (the square palm being associated with practical people and the long, thin hand with emotional, artistic people, for example).

Most scientists attack palmistry on the grounds that it is not a science. Professional palmists, on the other hand, argue (as astrologers argue) that since palmistry may be learned from a textbook, and textbooks are

Count Louis Hamon, or 'Cheiro'.

prepared from a well of original knowledge gathered through the centuries by empirical observation, it is precisely a science.

There is some scientific support for palmistry, though so far it is slender. It appears, for instance, that there are links between palm-prints and specific diseases. New York paediatricians discovered in 1966 that half of the babies affected by their mothers' infection with German measles had abnormal hand-prints; the mothers almost without exception bore the same abnormal prints. There are one or two similar, scientifically observed phenomena.

No serious scientific investigation seems yet to have been directed at correlating the shape of the hand, or the patterns on it, with general character or behaviour; the palmist is open to the same criticism as the astrologer – that character may be intuitively observed, or may be detected from various clues of behaviour, or from such obvious pointers as hard muscular hands, bitten finger-nails and so on. There are, however, cases of very accurate character readings by palmists; the most startling of them seem to have been capable of 'seeing' and dating major events in the subject's past life.

Palmistry is a complex art or science and in cheiromancy especially the most minute observation of the lines on the palm is necessary. Palmists also have their own theories, developed after years of work; and there are new developments from time to time. The following hints are derived from Cheiro, whose *Language of the Hand* is now many years old, but remains a classic textbook.

The Types of Hand

Cheiro proposed seven basic types of hand:

I The Elementary
II The Square
III The Spatulate
IV The Knotty
V The Conic
VI The Psychic
VII The Mixed

Each of these types has subdivisions, according perhaps to the shape of the fingers. A square hand could have long, short, knotty or spatulate fingers, for instance, and its basic indications would be accordingly modified. Here are Cheiro's observations about the general basic types:

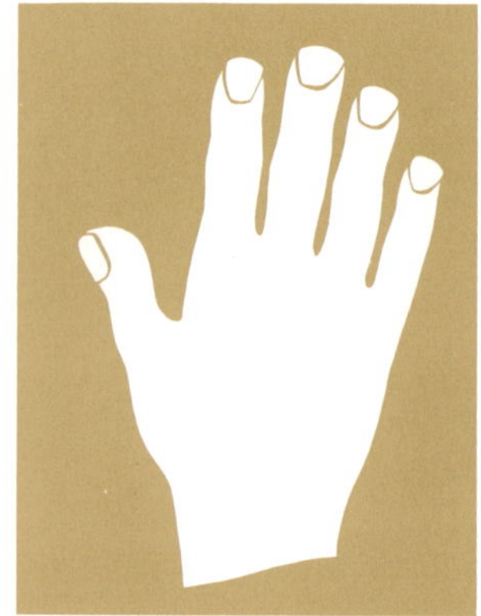

I The Elementary Hand

By the 'elementary' or 'lowest type' of hand, Cheiro seems to have meant that of a caveman, somewhat clumsy, with a thick, heavy palm, short fingers, short nails. The longer the fingers on this type of hand the more intelligent the subject is, but always within fairly tight limits. The subject will be passionate and with a lack of control over his passions; love of 'intellectual' pleasures will be almost entirely absent, and there will be a tendency to violence – though at the same time the subject will be cowardly. 'These are people', Cheiro says, 'without aspirations; they but eat, drink, sleep and die.'

II The Square Hand

The palm of this hand will be square at the wrist, and the line across the base of the fingers will also be square; the fingers, too, will tend to be square rather than tapering. These subjects will be conformists – punctual and precise, for instance, but not out of politeness; just because it is 'the thing to

'Fortune-tellers' have always found a ready clientele: here, a fashionable 17th-century Frenchwoman consults a palmist.

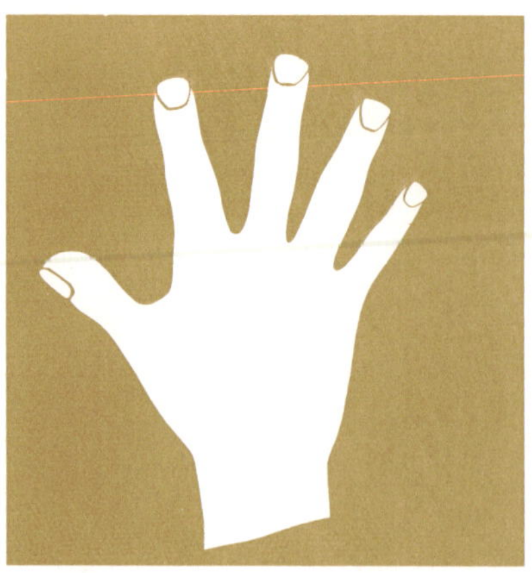

do'. They will live happily under an authoritarian regime, for they thrive on law and order, discipline and hierarchy. They generally think before they act and will very rarely follow their instincts. They are materialists, love their homes and families – though they will not be demonstrative. Good, staunch friends, they are honest and forthright, dogmatic and perseverant. They believe nothing until it is proved to be true.

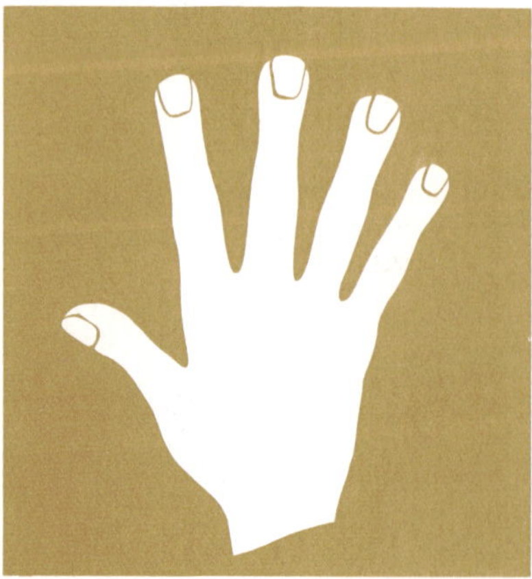

III The Spatulate Hand

This hand will be unusually broad at the wrist or the base of the fingers and the tips of the fingers will tend to broaden out into a spade-shape. The spatulate hand broadest at the wrist will taper towards the fingers, and vice versa. A firm spatulate hand shows an energetic, positive, enthusiastic person; a flabby, soft spatulate hand shows restlessness and irritation – the kind of person that flies quickly from job to job, rarely finishing anything. All possessors of spatulate hands are lovers of action rather than thought, very independent and inventive, individual to the point of setting themselves apart from their fellows. Their individuality sometimes defeats them: ahead of their time, they will choose the wrong way in which to present their ideas and often be denigrated for them. The possessor of the spatulate hand with the broad base to the fingers will be more practical than the one with the broad base at the wrist, in whom ideas will predominate.

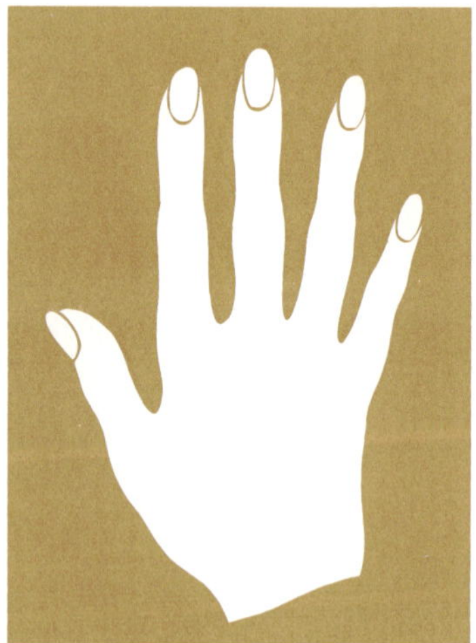

IV The Knotty Hand

Cheiro calls this hand – long and angular with bony fingers and prominent joints – 'the philosophic hand', the hand of the student, individual again but by no means seeking after power or (much less) money. These subjects are lovers of mystery, it appears; aesthetic, they favour the abstract in the arts. Knotty hands are particularly prominent among Eastern mystics, but Cheiro found them also in the mystics and poets of Victorian England – in Cardinal Manning and Cardinal Newman, and Alfred Tennyson. Jesuits, he believed, very often possessed them – but not the more independent-minded Protestants. Those with knotty hands tend to be silent and secretive, meticulous, patient, never forgetting an injury, and in general egotistical. They could become fanatics. If the fingers are pointed, they will tend to follow their instincts; knotty finger-joints denote the reasoner, the analyst.

V The Conic Hand

In the conic hand the palm tapers somewhat and so do the fingers (this is rather easily confused with the 'psychic hand' with its long, tapering fingers; the conic hand is generally rather smaller). *Impulse* and *instinct* are the words Cheiro most strongly associates with this type; the subjects are very clever and quick, but often almost totally lack patience. With strangers, they make a good first impression with their quick-witted and amusing conversation; but they are superficial, changeable in affection, quick tempered and extreme in their likes and dislikes. They are in and out of love in a flash. Generous and sympathetic, though selfish about their own comforts, they are impetuous enough to give offence over-easily. They are very quickly moved to laughter or to tears and tend to display their emotions.

VI The Psychic Hand

The 'psychic' seemed to Cheiro the most beautiful but also the most unfortunate of hands. Long, narrow and fragile-looking, with slender, tapering fingers and long, almond-shaped nails, it indicates want of energy and strength as well as a visionary and idealistic

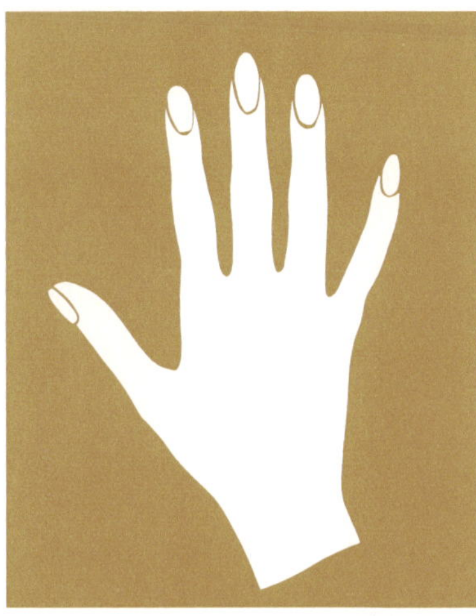

nature. These subjects are besotted by the beautiful to the extent of altogether neglecting the practical; consciously or not, they are 'religious' in the sense of constantly seeking after their notion of the Truth, whatever that may be. They can be fine mediums, clairvoyants, sensitives, often extremely introspective and too inclined to see themselves as useless in a materialistic world. For this reason Cheiro believed them to be inordinately inclined to emotional or mental breakdowns and even to suicide. They are, he wrote, 'lilies thrown by some ruthless hand upon the tempest-tossed river of life'!

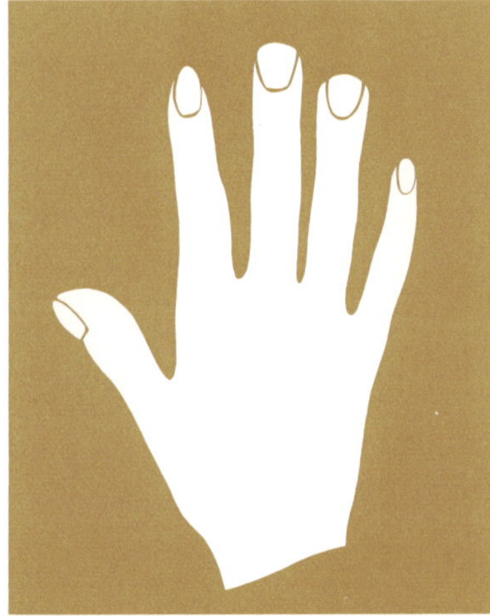

VII The Mixed Hand

Cheiro's final category is one which he could

not classify under I–VI – the hand of versatility, changeability; a brilliant conversationalist on any subject, artistic in some way but never at the top of an artistic profession; restless, fond of new ideas, a dabbler and amateur. But the hand seemed rarely to have been found by Cheiro, perhaps because to fit into his seventh type it would have had to have no recognizable characteristics at all.

Shapes of Fingers and Thumb

The higher set on the palm and the better proportioned, the more intellectual the subject. A short, clumsy thumb indicates a coarse, brutish subject; a long, well-shaped thumb, intellectuality and refinement. A thumb standing at right-angles to the hand indicates unmanageability and aggression; a thumb lying in towards the palm, nervousness, caution. A thumb with especially supple joint denotes extravagance, 'a natural spendthrift'.

Short fingers show speed and impulsiveness, quickness of thought, unconventionality. Thick, clumsy fingers show cruelty and selfishness. Supple fingers which bend backwards show a charming nature, cleverness, but caution and inquisitiveness. Crooked, distorted fingers show a crooked, distorted nature. Fingers thick at the base indicate gluttony, fingers slim at the base, unselfishness and fastidiousness. A wide space between the first and second fingers, when the hand is splayed, shows great independence of thought; a wide space between the third and fourth indicates independence of action.

The Palm

A thin palm indicates timidity and nervousness; a thick palm, sensuality; a soft, flabby palm, indolence and love of luxury; a hollow palm, disappointment in life.

Right and Left Hands

There is some confusion about the use in palmistry of right and left hands. Cheiro held to 'an old saying' that 'the left is the hand we are born with, and the right the hand we make', so looked upon the left hand as indicating the natural character and the right the character imposed by environment, education, observation of life.

The Mounts

In general, a well-developed mount indicates emphasis on the qualities mentioned; less prominence weakens the emphasis.

Venus An abnormally large mount of Venus indicates a violently sensual nature; a well-developed mount, good health; a small one, less robust health and a low sexual libido.

Jupiter Ambition, pride, enthusiasm, desire for power.

Saturn Love of quietness and solitude, appreciation of classical music.

Sun or Apollo Appreciation of the beautiful, love of painting, poetry, literature, 'grace of mind and thought'.

Mercury Love of change, travel; wit, quickness of thought and expression.

Mars There are two mounts of Mars. The first, beneath Jupiter, shows courage, a fighting spirit, a tendency to quarrel. The second, between Mercury and Luna, shows passive courage, self-control, resignation.

Luna Refinement and imagination, romance.

The Lines of the Hand

We have only space to concentrate on the five most important lines (according to Cheiro); these are complex and difficult to 'read' and the following is only the lightest gloss on them. They should be clear and well marked. If pale, this indicates indifferent health or lack of energy; if red, this shows an active, robust temperament and a hopeful disposition; if yellow, liver trouble or biliousness, a self-controlled nature, reserved and proud. Very dark lines show 'a melancholy, grave temperament', and a haughty nature, revengeful and unforgiving.

The Life-line

This should be long, narrow and deep, thus indicating a long life and good health. Ill

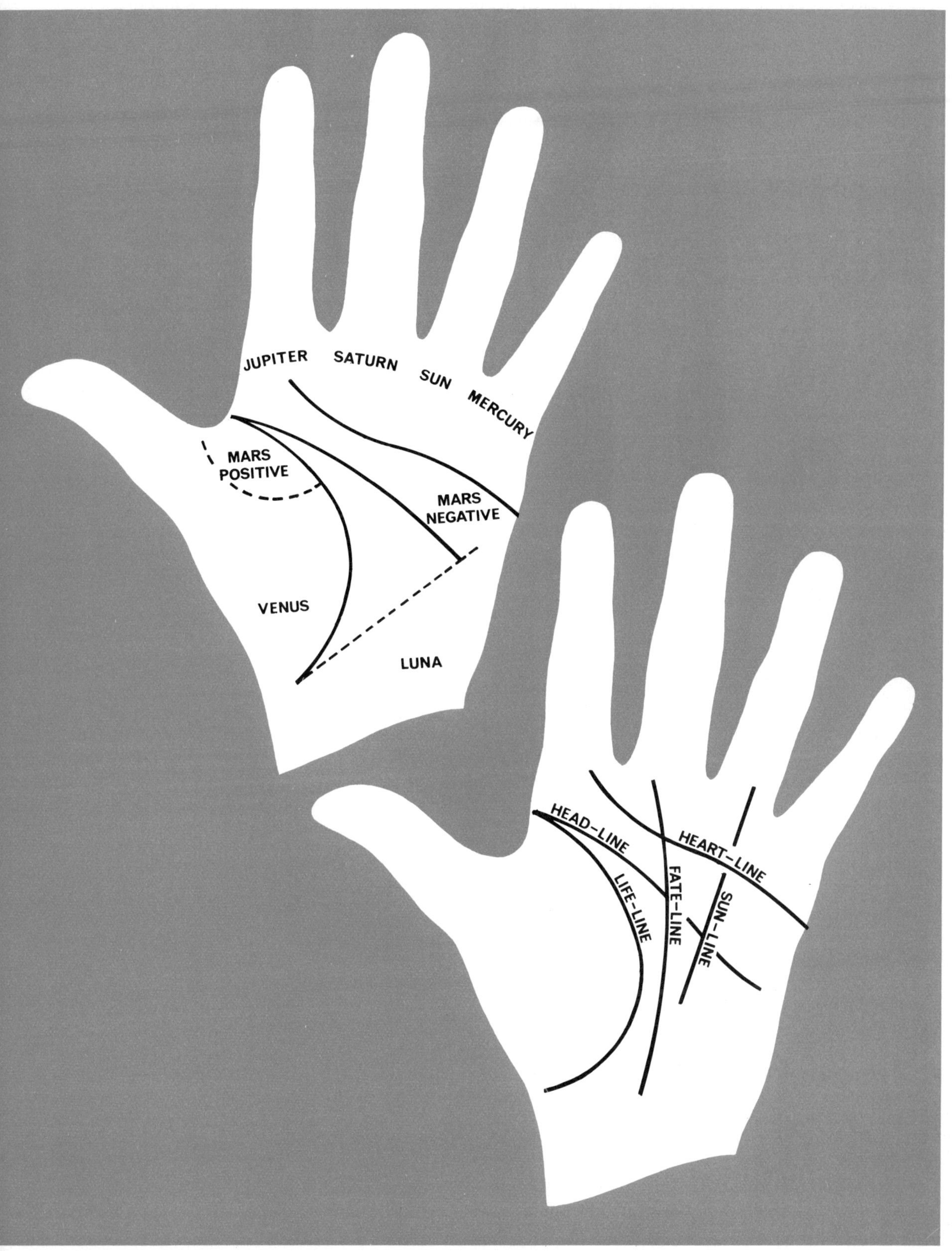
JUPITER
SATURN
SUN
MERCURY
MARS
POSITIVE
MARS
NEGATIVE
VENUS
LUNA
HEAD-LINE
HEART-LINE
LIFE-LINE
FATE-LINE
SUN-LINE

health is indicated by fractured, broken lines. If this line joins that of the head, the subject will be ruled by reason and intelligence, but very sensitive to criticism. A medium space between the Life- and Head-lines shows energy and a go-ahead spirit; a wide space shows too much self-confidence and impulsiveness. If the Life-, Head- and Heart-lines are joined at the beginning this shows a tendency to rush into danger or trouble. Lines leaving the Life-line show successes in life, depending on the direction in which they run – a line running to the Mount of Jupiter, for instance, will show promotion, additional power; one to the Mount of Mercury, success in business. On the whole, lines running parallel to the Life-line, in its vicinity, show favourable influences; lines which cut it show worries and obstacles. Cheiro did not in general believe that death could be foretold from the palm.

The Head-line

A long Head-line touching the Life-line indicates talent, energy, determination and boundless ambition – but combined with reason. Slight separation from the Life-line shows slight lack of control or diplomacy, a certain impetuosity. If the Head-line is actually joined to the Life-line at its beginning, this shows a sensitive, nervous temperament, generally at odds with friends, highly strung and irritable. A straight, even Head-line shows practical common sense and love of material things. If straight, but gradually sloping, a balance between the imaginative and practical is shown; if the entire line is sloping, it shows imagination, romance, idealism. Lying straight across the hand and finally curving up towards Mars, the line shows unusual success in business and a keen sense of the value of money. A short Head-line shows a thoroughly material nature. Made up of little pieces, like a chain, it shows indecision. A double Head-line shows great intellectual power.

The Heart-line

This should be deep, clear and well coloured. If it crosses the whole palm from side to side, it shows an excess of passion and possibly extreme jealousy. A lot of small interruptions to it, in the shape of a crowd of little lines, emphasizes inconstancy and flirtation. Breaks in the line show disappointment in love. If the line forks, with one branch resting on the Mount of Jupiter and the other between the first and second fingers, a contented, tranquil nature and great happiness in love is shown. Cheiro paid great attention to where the Heart-line started: if on the Mount of Jupiter, this showed 'the highest type of love', with great ambitions for the partner; if from the Jupiter finger itself, an excess of ambition. The line rising between the first and second fingers shows a calm, deep nature in love; rising from Saturn, great passion, but lack of demonstrativeness.

The Fate-line

'The line of destiny' relates to worldly affairs, success or failure. If it rises from the Life-line it shows the winning of success and riches through personal merit. If from the wrist it goes right up to the Mount of Saturn, it shows extreme good fortune. If it runs to any mount other than Saturn, it shows success in that particular direction; if it is stopped by the Heart-line, success will be gratified through love. A break in the line shows misfortune or loss. A double Fate-line is excellent. People without a Fate-line can be very successful, but lack depth of feeling.

The Sun-line

If it rises from the Life-line, 'the line of Apollo' shows that the subject will worship beauty and be successful in artistic pursuits; from the line of Fate, it increases any success arising from that and shows an improvement in the fortunes. Rising from the Mount of Luna it shows success based on other people's help; on the plain of Mars, success after difficulty. Rising from the Head-line, the talents of the subject will bring success, but in the second half of life; from the Heart-line, it shows a taste for art and, again, distinction late in life. Well marked, it shows sensitivity; with a straight Head-line to help it, it shows a love of attaining riches and social position.

24 Basic types?

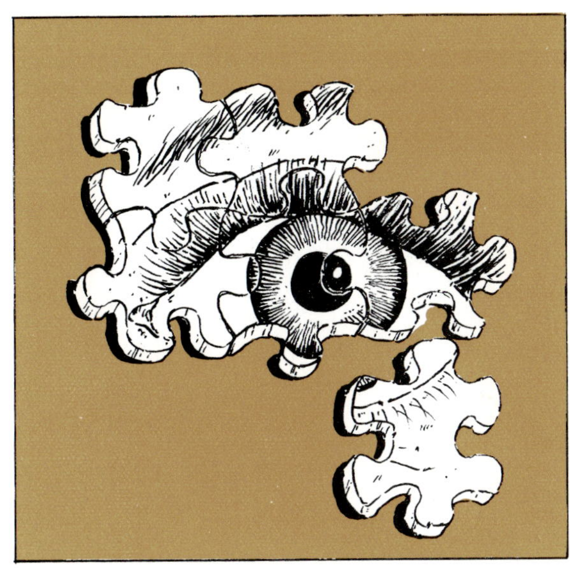

Photo-Fit, devised for the police,

can build ten billion

faces from 204 foreheads,

96 pairs of eyes, 101 mouths. . . .

How does your face shape up?

How individual can it be?

How do you know who you are?

AND SO, FOR all these attempts – rough or sophisticated – to classify men and women according to their behaviour or appearance, does it remain a scientific fact that each individual is in some respects unique? The fingerprint has been recognized as one indication of individuality; more recently, it has been confirmed that certain voice-patterns, when recorded and analysed, can be shown to be unique to an individual speaker, whatever the language spoken or the attempt made to disguise the voice. It seems, too, that the arrangement of genes on the chromosomes in the nucleus of every cell in the human body is unique to the individual person.

Some of these facts have great advantages in law, for they mean that in criminal investigations or disputes about property the identity of an individual can be established without question. Where cruder identification is attempted, there are many opportunities for confusion, and some classic cases of mistaken identity are on record: a quick glimpse of a criminal making an assault or committing a robbery can all too easily leave a false impression of identity, for many people are bad even at evaluating height and build, let

Pugilist twins: Jim and Henry Cooper.

alone recalling a face, despite the fact that the face is the part of a man or woman most frequently looked at – the part which, in most civilizations, generally remains uncovered, and seemingly the easiest available evidence of an individual's identity.

All faces, of course, have much in common, and it is not difficult to categorize them – round, long, pale, flushed, bearded, smooth.

'Frizzle-haired, rowdy and 100 per cent boy', the O'Leary triplets (left) are not just alike in physical appearance. The Cholmondeley sisters (below), painted c. 1600, provide an early record of identical twins. But appearances may be wholly misleading – see (opposite) Eleanor Bron, contemporary actress, and Lady Agnew, fashionable hostess of ninety years ago.

Looking more closely, we see that – except very rarely, with some identical twins – faces are as individual as fingerprints. Most people must study a face closely if they are to remember it accurately, though an observant person can quickly establish certain landmarks: the shape of the hair, for instance, the height of the forehead, whether the eyebrows are shaggy or narrow. (Bushy eyebrows, incidentally, were long regarded as marks of virility in man, while in women narrow brows contributed much to the beauty of the eye – and many odes were written to a lady's eyebrow.)

It is difficult to remember that eyes are eye-*balls*, for the surrounding skin gives them a very different appearance in different people. When we speak of 'large' or 'small' eyes, for instance, we really refer to the window of flesh through which they look – and the creasing of the skin on the eyelids or at the side of the eyes can radically affect the appearance.

The cheeks – full or sunken, smooth or wrinkled, hairy or shaven – not only vary in shape, but are very mobile, and even colourful: they contribute to a show of pleasure or anger, humour or embarrassment, and the muscles which govern their movement contribute characteristic wrinkling, as they do to the forehead. The nose can take many shapes, snub or beaked, Roman or turned-up, and the mouth may be thin- or thick-lipped, the lips themselves pale or red, their characteristic appearance humorous or sober. The mouth, where character is concerned, is as much a tell-tale as the eyes.

And finally, the ears may be the most individual of facial characteristics, for their shape differs widely from person to person, not only in the gentle curve or more pointed aspect of their upper part, but in the shape of the lobe – if there is a lobe at all – and the whorl, sometimes extremely distinctive and certainly difficult to recall (some artists have found this so elusive that they have gone to some lengths to see that the ears of their sitters are concealed!)

Various attempts have been made to rationalize the shapes of the human face in order to help witnesses of a crime to recall and to record for the police just what the criminal looked like. Perhaps the best so far is the Photo-Fit system, used by British police since 1970, and adopted to date by over thirty other world police services.

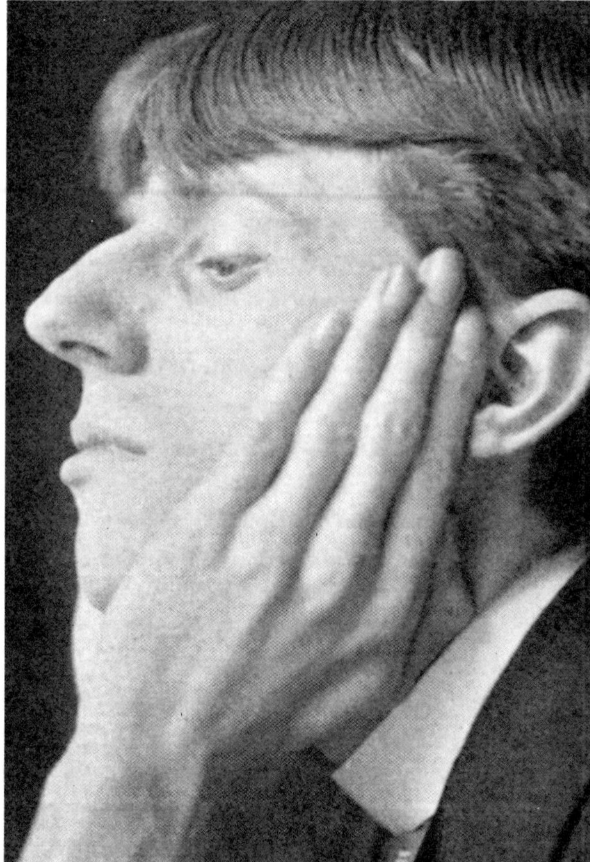

Photo-Fit was devised by the 'facial topographer' Jacques Penry, whose first book on the subject had been published as early as 1938. In the 1960s, Mr Penry received the cooperation of the British police and, from their massive identification files, built up a 'kit' containing sets of different Caucasian facial elements – 204 foreheads, 96 pairs of eyes, 101 mouths, 74 chins. . . . These can be combined to make over ten billion different faces. Later, an Afro-Asian kit was also developed, containing, for example, 57 foreheads and 67 pairs of eyes; from this smaller

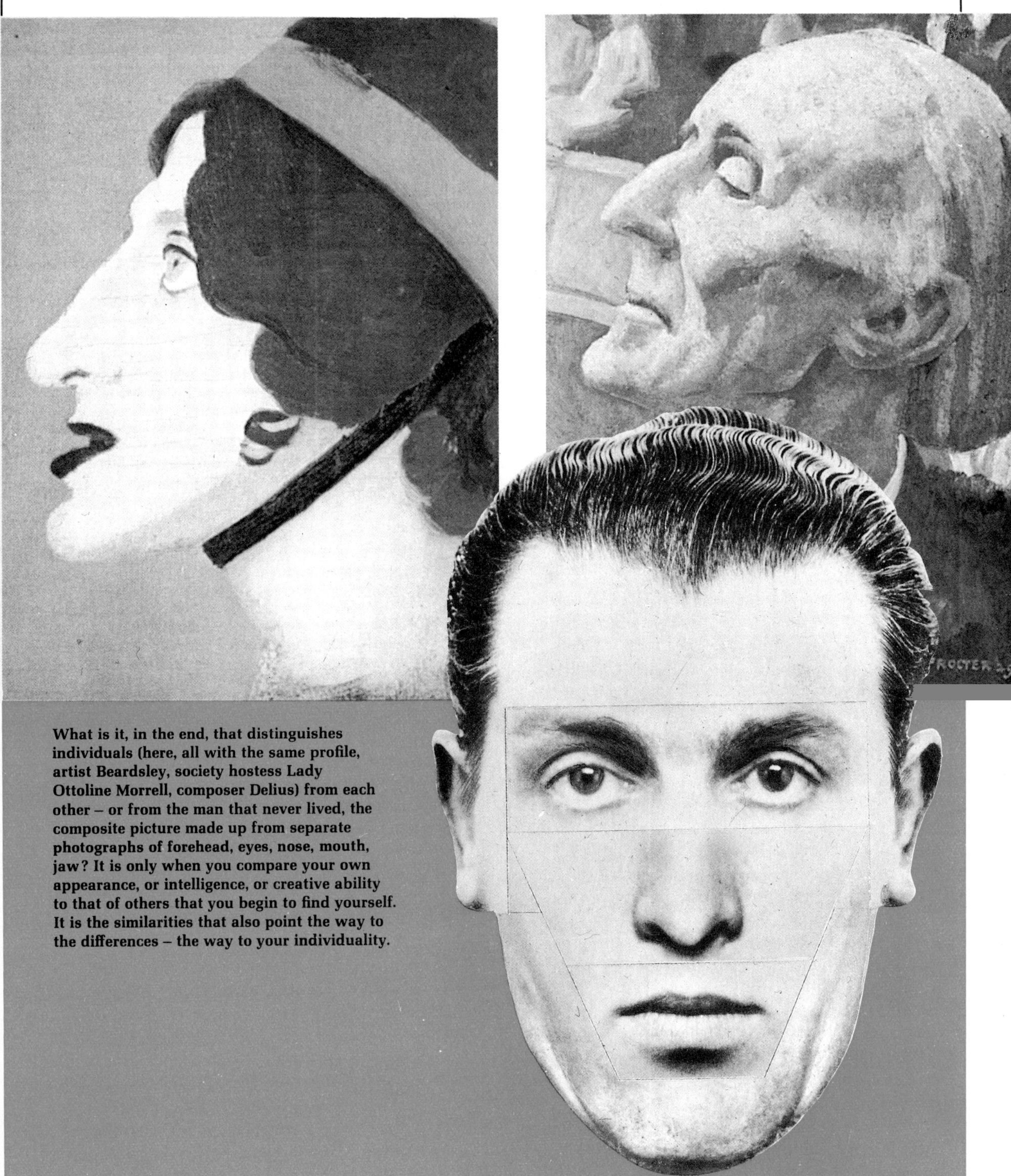

What is it, in the end, that distinguishes individuals (here, all with the same profile, artist Beardsley, society hostess Lady Ottoline Morrell, composer Delius) from each other – or from the man that never lived, the composite picture made up from separate photographs of forehead, eyes, nose, mouth, jaw? It is only when you compare your own appearance, or intelligence, or creative ability to that of others that you begin to find yourself. It is the similarities that also point the way to the differences – the way to your individuality.

selection, five hundred million separate faces can be contrived. And Mr Penry has now added North American Indian, Arabic and various female supplements to the system.

Mr Penry argues that it seems to be the case that no single person can claim to have totally unique facial features – nose, ear or eye (unless one of these features has been scarred or marked by accident or design). A similar feature will be found in perhaps hundreds of other human faces. It is only when the *combination* of features closely resembles that of another face that we notice how 'alike' two people seem to be: they will have similar hair-lines, eyes, noses; their colouring will be similar, so will the general shape of their faces.

Your facial appearance is, like the shape of the rest of your body, the result of the functioning of the glands (Mr Penry believes); the adult face which evolves as the result of endocrine influence 'advertises' the personality behind it – a theory obviously allied to those of Lavater, Kretschmer and Sheldon (see chapter 7).

Ideally, the witness to a crime will have seen the suspect from both full- and side-face; the Photo-Fit system is so elastic that it is quite possible to start with the feature the witness remembers most clearly – the eyes, the mouth, the facial shape; the separate components are then matched to those available in the Photo-Fit kit and mounted in a frame until, combined, the result is a picture as like that of the suspect as the witness can recall (and needless to say, the result can only be as good as the witness's recollection).

A quick and observant person will also note certain characteristics of movement, which relate to personality and psychology as well as to physique; the general shape and posture of the body, for example. A rough caricature of the suspect will be the result, except where witnesses are uncommonly observant. Once again, a man or woman will have been broadly categorized, broadly classified; but only broadly, for any attempt to classify an individual comes closer to disaster the closer it comes to those elements which are singular in us; and a marked singularity, as in any secret code, for instance, is the combination of a large number of factors in a particular way: the whole individual is more personal than the sum of parts.

We must guard this individuality especially carefully in an age when individuality is increasingly under attack from several directions – most notably from central government and all large organizations, for which it is convenient to regard the human race as readily divisible into a few clearly recognizable categories ('workers', 'managers', 'the middle class', 'dissidents'). As the American jurist and teacher Felix Frankfurter put it, 'anybody who is any good is different from anybody else', and the difference is inestimably valuable.

Why, then, a book apparently designed to show how *similar* you are to everyone else? Human resemblances can be revealing not only by showing to what degree we behave like a large group of other people (extroverts mimicking extroverts, introverts miming introverts), but to what extent we do *not*. Looking at a baby and recognizing 'his father's eyes' or 'his mother's mouth', friends and neighbours soon identify the baby's individuality – by first noticing, then disregarding, the points of similarity to the parents. It is at the point where you begin to explore the perimeter of your own 'grouping' that individuality begins to emerge; and if you have found yourself 'placed' here as having a high or low sexual libido, as being of medium intelligence, or of a particular 'class', the most valuable result of that exercise may be to prompt you to pace out the walls of the prison of personality, gauge where they may be breached and escape to explore the surrounding countryside.

How do you know who you are? Many psychiatrists would answer that no one *can* truly know; and some people decline to inquire. ('If I knew myself,' said Goethe, 'I'd run away.') And yet . . . you are, in the end, all you have; and in seeking to define yourself you cannot help but flex the muscles of the self, and thereby settle more comfortably into your personality.

Bibliography

For further reading about some of the subjects treated in this book, we suggest the following:

Dress and social behaviour

Quentin Bell *On Human Finery* (1976)
C. G. Bradley *Western World Costume* (1954)
A. Gernsheim *Fashion and Reality* (1963)
James Laver *A Concise History of Costume* (1969)
Bernard Rudofsky *The Unfashionable Human Body* (1972)
Geoffrey W. Squire *Dress, Art and Society, 1560–1970* (1974)
Ruth T. Wilcox *The Dictionary of Costume* (1970)
Doreen Yarwood *European Costume* (1975)

Acting and reality

A. D. Adeev *Acting and the Art of the Stage* (1959)
Rose E. Bruford *Teaching Mime* (1972)
Mary E. N. Burns *Theatricality—convention in the theatre and social life* (1972)
T. Cole *A Handbook of the Stanislavsky Method* (1960)
R. Lewis *Method or Madness?* (1960)
K. S. Stanislavsky *Building a Character* (1950)
—— *On the Art of the Stage* (1950)
Lee Strasberg *Stanislavsky at the Actors' Studio* (1966)

Gesture and its meaning

John M. Argyle *Bodily Communication* (1975)
Charles Darwin *Queries about Expression* (1972)
Desmond Morris *Manwatching* (1977)
—— *Gestures* (with P. Collett, 1979)
Gerard I. Nierenberg and Henry H. Calero *How to Read a Person Like a Book* (1973)
C. Wolff *Psychology of Gesture* (1945)

Physical fitness

Fred M. Alexander *The Alexander Technique* (1974)
John Arlott *The Oxford Companion to Sports and Games* (1975)
Sir Francis Chichester *How to Keep Fit* (1969)
Doris M. L. Grant *Your Daily Food* (1973)
D. G. Johnson and O. Heidenstam *Modern Body Building* (1960)
V. H. Mottram *Fitness and the Family* (1925)
Magnus Pyke *Fitness and Society* (1968)
—— *Technological Eating* (1972)
William D. Smith *Stretching their Bodies* (1974)

Physiognomy

J. Brophy *The Face in Western Art* (1963)
Sir Ernst Gombrich *The Mask and the Face* (1972)
W. K. Gregory *Our Face from Fish to Man* (1929)
J. K. Lavater *Essays on Physiognomy* (1810)
J. Metham *Physiognomy* (1916)
M. Montessari *Pedagogical Anthropology* (1913)
R. Penrose *The Wonder and Horror of the Human Head* (1953)

Human sexuality

N. J. Berrill *Sex and the Nature of Things* (1954)
Alex Comfort *The Anxiety Makers* (1967)
—— *Sexual Behaviour in Society* (1963)
M. Delcourt *Hermaphrodite* (1961)
Carolyn G. Heilbrun *Towards Androgyny* (1973)
Arno Karlen *Sexuality and Homosexuality* (1971)
Ronald D. Laing *The Facts of Life* (1976)
Katherine M. Millett *Sexual Politics* (1971)
Ann R. Oakley *Sex, Gender and Society* (1972)
Vance O. Packard *The Sexual Wilderness* (1968)
Wilhelm Reich *The Sexual Revolution* (1961)
Paul A. Robinson *The Sexual Radicals* (1970)

Ageing

Simone de Beauvoir *Old Age* (1972)
Ronald Blythe *The View in Winter* (1979)
Alex Comfort *Ageing* (1964)
—— *The Process of Ageing* (1965)

A. E. Davies *Our Ageing Population* (1938)
Eric J. Trimmer *Rejuvenation* (1970)
R. N. Tronchin-James *Arbitrary Retirement* (1962)
Adolf L. Vischer *On Growing Old* (1966)
J. H. Wallis *The Challenge of Middle Age* (1964)
A. T. Welford *Ageing and Human Skill* (1958)

Psychology

G. S. Brett *The History of Psychology* (1962)
J. A. C. Brown *Freud and the Post-Freudians* (1963)
James P. Chaplin and T. S. Krawiec *Systems and Theories of Psychology* (1974)
Reuben Fine *A History of Psychoanalysis* (1979)
P. Mullahy *Oedipus: myth and complex* (1948)
R. L. Munroe *Schools of Psychoanalytical Thought* (1957)
Paul Roazen *Freud and his Followers* (1976)
Abraham A. Roback and T. Kiernan *A Pictorial History of Psychology and Psychiatry*
C. M. Thompson *Psychoanalysis: evolution and development* (1952)
Robert Thomson *The Pelican History of Psychology* (1968)
Ved Varma (ed.) *Psychotherapy Today* (1974)
L. L. Whyte *The Unconscious Before Freud* (1962)
Dieter Wyss *Depth Psychology* (1968)

The human brain and intelligence

E. D. A. Adrian *Factors in Mental Evolution* (1960)
—— *Responsibilities of the Brain* (1951)
Colin B. Blakemore *Mechanics of the Mind* (1977)
Nigel Calder *The Mind of Man* (1970)
Edwin S. Clarke and K. Dewhurst *An Illustrated History of Brain Function* (1972)

Graphology

Robert Holder *You Can Analyse Handwriting* (1958)
Irene Marcuse *Guide to Personality Through Your Handwriting* (1974)

Palmistry

Cheiro *Language of the Hand* (1967)
H. Frith *Chiromancy* (1888)
E. Heron-Allen *A Manual of Cheiroscopy* (1885)
C. Wolff *The Human Hand* (1942)

Astrology

Geoffrey Dean and Arthur Mather *Recent Advances in Natal Astrology* (1979)
Jeff Mayo *Teach Yourself Astrology* (1970)
Derek and Julia Parker *The Compleat Astrologer* (1971)
Derek Parker *The Question of Astrology* (1970)

Biorhythms

Bernard Gittelson *Biorhythm* (1978)

Intelligence

Alice W. Heim *The Appraisal of Intelligence* (1970)
F. N. L. Poynter *History and Philosophy of the Knowledge of the Brain* (1958)
Gordon R. Taylor *The Natural History of the Mind* (1979)
J. Z. Young *The Memory System of the Brain* (1966)
—— *Model of the Brain* (1964)

Human physiology

Robert Ardrey *The Social Contract* (1970)
Jacob Bronowski *The Identity of Man* (1966)
A. Carroll *Man and the Unknown* (1942)
John S. B. Carroll *Living with a Stranger* (1978)
Steven Goldberg *The Inevitability of Patriarchy* (1977)
Sir Julian Huxley *Man in the Modern World* (1947)
Sir Peter Medawar *The Life Science* (1977)
I. P. Pavlov *Selected Works* (1955)
K. M. Walker *Human Physiology* (1962)
James D. Watson *The Double Helix* (1968)
W. P. D. Wightman *Emergence of General Physiology* (1956)

Comparative Religion

John M. Allegro *Lost Gods* (1977)
A. C. Bouquet *Sacred Books of the World* (1962)
Joseph Campbell *The Masks of God* (1968)
J. Chiari *Religion and Modern Society* (1964)
Albert K. Cragg *Christianity in World Perspective* (1968)
Mircea Eliade *A History of Religious Ideas* (1979)
—— *The Quest* (1971)
—— *The Sacred and the Profane* (1961)
Ann Gage *The One Work* (1961)
Margaret Isherwood *Searching for Meaning* (1970)
Joseph M. Kitagawa *The History of Religions* (1974)
Stephen C. Neill *Christian Faith and Other Faiths* (1970)
Edward G. S. Parrinder *Mysticism in the World's Religions* (1976)
John A. T. Robinson *Honest to God* (1963)

Acknowledgments

Authors' acknowledgments

Many friends and acquaintances have consciously or unconsciously (and chiefly, the latter) helped us in the compilation of this book. One of the conscious helpers has been Jonathan Clogstoun-Willmott, who was of special help with the section on astrology. We are also grateful to Jacques Penry, the inventor of the Photo-Fit system, for kindly allowing us to reproduce the illustration on page 185. The Health Education Council of Britain is an admirable body which collates and distributes advice on healthy living. British MENSA kindly allowed us to reproduce the IQ test on pages 124–6, from material available to the public from 13 George Street, Wolverhampton, Staffordshire.
We are grateful to the Hutchinson Publishing Group Ltd for permission to quote from Cheiro's *Language of the Hand*. Finally, thanks as usual to the staff of The London Library.

Illustration acknowledgments

t = top; b = bottom; l = left; r = right

Archivio Storico Ricordi, Milan 83 tr; Associated Press, London 42 br, 45, 122, 129; Barnaby's Picture Library 33; BBC Copyright 20 tl, 34, 183 tl; BBC Hulton Picture Library 21 tr, 121 t, 167; Cecil Beaton, Camera Press 83; Tom Blau, Camera Press 14; Mike Busselle 26; Cambridge, Trinity College 146; Camera Press 22 br, 42 bl; Denis Cameron, Camera Press 182 t; Cumberland County Historical Society and Hamilton Library Association, Carlisle, Pennsylvania 131; Dale Martin Promotions Ltd. 79 r; Colin Davey, Camera Press 135 bl; Francis Dias, Camera Press 79 tl; Edinburgh, National Gallery of Scotland 183; Evening Standard 56, 123; Gerald Friedlander, Camera Press 134; Gay News 93; Giraudon 43 t; Oliver Goldsmith Ltd. 23; Goya International Ltd. 25; Health Education Council 59; Heraklion Museum 16 l; Leon Herschtritt, Camera Press 16 r, 135 tl; Internationale Bilderagentur, Zurich 72, 103 tl, 168 b; Karsh of Ottawa, Camera Press 135 tr; Keystone Press Agency 20 b; Alex Levac, Camera Press 13; London: Apsley House 37 r; National Film Archive 31, 46, 78 r; National Gallery 121 b; National Portrait Gallery 30, 184, 185 tl, 185 tr; Tate Gallery 182 b; Victoria and Albert Museum 47, 113; R. S. Martin, Camera Press 181; Mansell Collection 21 l, 73, 133 b, 173; Milwaukee Art Center, Gift of the Women's Exchange 94; New York: Frick Collection 17; Metropolitan Museum of Art, Harris Brisbane Dick Fund, 1946 39; Public Library 91; Novosti Press Agency 35; Open University 29, 42 t; Bill Owen 50; Paris, Louvre 90; Jacques Penry 185; Petersburg Press, © David Hockney 1975 128; J. Powell 16 l; Mary Quant Cosmetics Ltd. 22; Rex Features 58; Mick Rock 92; Saul Hair Clinic 82; *Science et Vie* 103 br; *Slimming Magazine* 55; Edwin Smith 77; David Steen, Camera Press 78 l; Tokyo, Ministry of Foreign Affairs 136; Roger Viollet 66, 67, 68–9, 175; Gifford Wallace Inc. 43 b; Washington, National Gallery, Samuel H. Kress Collection 20 tr.

The drawings illustrating the theme of each chapter and the tests were prepared by Ivan Hissey.

Index

Numerals in italics refer to illustrations; in some cases, text references may also be found on the same page.